Portraits of Integrity

ALSO AVAILABLE FROM BLOOMSBURY

Dying for Ideas, by Costica Bradatan
Epistemology: The Key Thinkers, edited by Stephen Hetherington
Intellectual Humility, by Ian M. Church and Peter L. Samuelson
Skepticism: From Antiquity to the Present, edited by Diego Machuca and Baron Reed
The Philosophy of Knowledge: A History, edited by Stephen Hetherington, Nicholas D. Smith, Henrik Lagerlund, Stephen Gaukroger and Markos Valaris

Portraits of Integrity

26 Case Studies from History, Literature and Philosophy

Edited by
Charlotte Alston,
Amber D. Carpenter and
Rachael Wiseman

BLOOMSBURY ACADEMIC
LONDON • NEW YORK • OXFORD • NEW DELHI • SYDNEY

BLOOMSBURY ACADEMIC
Bloomsbury Publishing Plc
50 Bedford Square, London, WC1B 3DP, UK
1385 Broadway, New York, NY 10018, USA

BLOOMSBURY, BLOOMSBURY ACADEMIC and the Diana logo
are trademarks of Bloomsbury Publishing Plc

First published in Great Britain 2020

Copyright © Charlotte Alston, Amber D. Carpenter, Rachael Wiseman
and Contributors, 2020

Charlotte Alston, Amber D. Carpenter and Rachael Wiseman have
asserted their right under the Copyright, Designs and Patents Act, 1988,
to be identified as Editors of this work.

Cover design: Louise Dugdale
Cover image top to bottom: Ellea Baker (1903-1986), Granger Historical
Picture Archive/Alamy. Statue of Socrates, 1969 Indian stamp illustration
of Mahatma Gandhi, Virginia Woolf, Stamp with portait of Leo Tolstoy,
Statue of the Chinese philosopher Confucius, Hannah Arendt, German
philosopher © iStock, Simone Weil (1909-1943) © Granger Historical
Picture Archive, Alamy. Leo Tolstoy (1828-1910) © Shutterstock

All rights reserved. No part of this publication may be reproduced or
transmitted in any form or by any means, electronic or mechanical,
including photocopying, recording, or any information storage or retrieval
system, without prior permission in writing from the publishers.

Bloomsbury Publishing Plc does not have any control over, or responsibility for,
any third-party websites referred to or in this book. All internet addresses given
in this book were correct at the time of going to press. The author and publisher
regret any inconvenience caused if addresses have changed or sites have
ceased to exist, but can accept no responsibility for any such changes.

A catalogue record for this book is available from the British Library.

A catalog record for this book is available from the Library of Congress.

ISBN: HB: 978-1-3500-4037-3
PB: 978-1-3500-4038-0
ePDF: 978-1-3500-4040-3
eBook: 978-1-3500-4039-7

Typeset by Deanta Global Publishing Services, Chennai, India

To find out more about our authors and books visit www.bloomsbury.com
and sign up for our newsletters.

CONTENTS

List of figures viii
Notes on contributors ix

Introduction 1

1 Plato's Socrates: The oddness of the integrated soul *Amber D. Carpenter* 15

2 Boethius: Integrity as attunement to reality *Matthew Maguire* 27

3 Rāma: The imperfections of the perfect man in the Vālmīki *Rāmāyaṇa* *Emily T. Hudson* 35

4 Antigone: Staging integrity through sorority *Valentina Moro* 45

5 Job: 'And still he holdeth fast his integrity' *Katharine J. Dell* 53

6 Ella Baker: Leading with integrity in the service of a cause *Robin Zheng* 63

7 'Albert': Transformational agency and integrity in the workplace *Lisa Herzog* 73

8 Huang Zongxi: Making it safe not to be servile *Sandra Leonie Field* 83

9 Lambert Strether: 'What plays you least false' in a life with others *Danielle Petherbridge* 93

10 Confucius' village worthies: Hypocrites as thieves of virtue *Winnie Sung* 101

11 G. E. M. Anscombe: The false hypocrisy of the ideal standard *Rachael Wiseman* 111

12 Mohandas Gandhi: 'My life is its own message' *Stefan Rossbach* 121

13 Tolstoy and the Tolstoyans: Facing life as a whole *Charlotte Alston* 131

14 Simone Weil: Against being true to yourself *D. K. Levy* 141

15 Guan Yu: 'Righteousness that is not righteousness' in the *Romance of The Three Kingdoms* *Bryan W. Van Norden* 151

16 Gerrard Winstanley: Radicalism and the struggle for integrity during the English Revolution *David Loewenstein* 163

17 Amadou Bamba: Integrity and the struggle for spiritual cultivation *Alexus McLeod* 173

18 Abai Kunanbayev: Integrity and the law in nineteenth-century Kazakh society *Tenlik Dalayeva* 183

19 Amrita Sher-Gil: Identity and integrity as a mixed-race woman artist in colonial India *Nalini Bhushan* 195

20 Friedrich Christoph Dahlmann and Georg Waitz: Two models of scholarly integrity *Herman Paul* 207

21 Hannah Arendt: Integrity, truth and the political realm *Alexander Beaumont* 217

22 Anansi the Spider: Individual trickery and communal integrity *Stephen L. Bishop* 227

23 The Cookes and the Kayes: Assertions of virtue among the 'middling sort' in post-Reformation England *Robert Tittler* 235

24 Titus Pomponius Atticus: Writing the life of an uncommonly honourable Roman *Linda McGuire* 249

25 Henryk Sienkiewicz's *Letters from America*: Creating a speaker with integrity *Anja Burghardt* 259

26 Virginia Woolf: 'Writing without hate, without bitterness, without fear, without protest, without preaching': Integrity and the woman writer in *A Room of One's Own* *Lorraine Sim* 271

Afterword 281
Index 286

FIGURES

19.1 Amrita Sher-Gil, *Self-Portrait as Tahitian* (1934) 198
19.2 Amrita Sher-Gil, *Two Girls* (1939) 200
23.1 John and Joan Cooke, oil on panel, 813 x 755 mm. © Gloucester City Museum and Art Gallery 238
23.2 Anon., John Kaye of Woodsome, c. 1567. Oil on panel, 110 x 92 cm. Tolson Museum, Huddersfield, ref. KLMUS 1990/399 (recto). © Kirklees Museums and Galleries 241
23.3 Anon., Coats of Arms of Kayes' Friends and Kin, c. 1567. Oil on panel, 110 x 92 cm. Tolson Museum, Huddersfield, ref. KLMUS 1990/399A (verso). © Kirklees Museums and Galleries 242
23.4 Anon., Dorothy Kaye, c. 1567. Oil on panel, 110 x 92 cm. Tolson Museum, Huddersfield, ref. KLMUS 1990/398 (Recto). © Kirklees Museums and Galleries 243
23.5 Anon., Kaye Family Tree, c. 1567. Oil on panel, 110 x 92 cm. Tolson Museum, Huddersfield, ref. KLMUS 1990/398A (verso). © Kirklees Museums and Galleries 244

CONTRIBUTORS

Charlotte Alston is Professor in history at Northumbria University. She is the author of books and articles on the Russian Revolution and civil war, the post–First World War peace settlements and the international influence of Tolstoy's Christian anarchist thought.

Alexander Beaumont is Senior Lecturer in literature and politics at York St John University. He is the author of *Contemporary British Fiction and the Cultural Politics of Disenfranchisement* (2015), as well as essays on a wide range of contemporary British novelists. He has co-edited special issues on 'Ballard's Island' for *Literary Geographies* (2016), 'Melancholy Islands' for *C21 Literature* (2017) and 'Freedom After Neoliberalism' for the *Open Library of Humanities* (2018).

Nalini Bhushan is the Andrew W. Mellon Professor in the Humanities and Professor of Philosophy at Smith College and a member of the faculty in South Asian Studies. Her recently co-authored book, *Minds Without Fear: Philosophy in the Indian Renaissance* (Oxford University Press, 2017), explores the intellectual dimensions of the Indian Renaissance (1850–1947) during British rule, in areas such as art, philosophy, politics and religion. She is currently working on a new project in the philosophy of subjectivity tentatively entitled *Autistic Selfhood*.

Stephen L. Bishop (PhD University of Michigan; J. D. University of Michigan) is the director of the International Studies Institute and an associate professor of French and Africana studies at the University of New Mexico. Professor Bishop's interests encompass literature and culture of sub-Saharan Africa, law and literature, shame and guilt, feminism, FGM, cultural studies and child soldier narratives. Professor Bishop has published a number of articles on African literature and law, as well as his book *Legal Oppositional Narrative: A Case Study in Cameroon* (Lexington Books, 2008), which examines opposition to government-supported, dominant social orders through legal writing, including fiction that deals with legal themes, settings and language, as well as non-traditional narratives such as legal decisions and textbooks. He has a forthcoming book *Scripting Humiliation: Shame in the African Novel* (Liverpool University Press), on representations of shame in African literature. He teaches courses on African literature and culture, theories of law and literature, and European and African legal and moral traditions in literature and film.

Anja Burghardt (Munich) studied at Hamburg and London, and is now Assistant Professor at the Institute of Slavonic Studies (LMU Munich), with a background in Russian literature, focusing on Marina Tsvetaeva. Her current research focuses on Polish nineteenth-century travel literature, poetry, narratology and photography/photo documentaries.

Amber D. Carpenter is Associate Professor of philosophy at Yale-NUS College (Singapore). She publishes in ancient Greek philosophy, especially the ethics, epistemology and metaphysics of Plato. Her book on *Indian Buddhist Philosophy* appeared in 2014. She has held research fellowships and visiting appointments at the Einstein Forum (Potsdam), University of Melbourne, Yale University and with the Beacon Project (Templeton Religious Trust).

Tenlik Dalayeva is Associate Professor in the Department of History of Kazakhstan, at Abai Kazakh National Pedagogical University (Almaty, Kazakhstan). Her work focuses on the history of Kazakhstan from the eighteenth to the early twentieth century, particularly the history of social and political changes in the Kazakh Steppe under the influence of the Russian Empire, and Kazakh officials in the Russian imperial administration. Tenlik is a participant in the 'Transformation of the social organization of the Kazakh steppe: stratification and status dynamics (second half of the eighteenth – twentieth years of the twentieth centuries)' research project (2019–2020), led by Professor Sultangalieva G. S. (Al-Farabi Kazakh National University).

Katharine J. Dell is Reader in Old Testament Literature and Theology in the Faculty of Divinity at the University of Cambridge. She is fellow and director of Studies in Theology, Religion and Philosophy of Religion at St Catharine's College, Cambridge. She is a world expert on wisdom literature, has written four books on Job and edited a volume on Job and intertextuality.

Sandra Leonie Field is Assistant Professor of philosophy at Yale-NUS College. She is a political philosopher whose research topics include early-modern European political philosophy (especially Hobbes and Spinoza), democratic theory and concepts of power.

Lisa Herzog works at the intersection of political philosophy and economics. She focuses on the history of political and economic ideas, normative questions around markets (especially financial markets), ethics in organizations, economic democracy and political epistemology. Herzog studied philosophy, economics, political science and modern history at the universities of Munich (LMU) and Oxford. Between 2008 and 2011 she wrote her doctoral thesis entitled 'Inventing the Market: Smith, Hegel, and Political Theory' as a Rhodes Scholar at Oxford University. Since then, she has worked at the universities of Munich (TUM), St. Gallen, Leuven, Frankfurt and Stanford. In summer 2016 she took up the position of Professor of Political Philosophy and Theory at the Bavarian School of Public Policy and the Technical University Munich. In 2017–18 she was a fellow at the Wissenschaftskolleg zu Berlin.

Emily T. Hudson is an associate in the South Asian Studies Department of Harvard University. Her first monograph, *Disorienting Dharma: Ethics and Aesthetics of Suffering in the Mahābhārata*, won the Award for Excellence in Religion: Textual Studies from the American Academy of Religion. She is working on a second monograph entitled *The Book of the Beautiful: The Art of Being Good in the Vālmīki Rāmāyaṇa*.

D. K. Levy is a moral philosopher working in the Department of Philosophy at the University of Edinburgh. His research interests include political philosophy, the phenomenology of morality, the modalities of the good and the place of language in human life, especially as found in the work of Plato, Wittgenstein and Simone Weil.

David Loewenstein is Edwin Erle Sparks Professor of English and the Humanities at Penn State University Park, USA. He has published widely on politics and religion in early-modern English literature and culture and has edited, with Thomas Corns and Ann Hughes, the works of Gerrard Winstanley. His book *Treacherous Faith: The Specter of Heresy in Early Modern English Literature and Culture* (Oxford University Press, 2013) examines the construction of heresy and heretics from Thomas More to John Milton.

Matthew W. Maguire is an associate professor at DePaul University (Chicago, USA) and a European intellectual historian. He is the author of *The Conversion of Imagination and Carnal Spirit: The Revolutions of Charles Péguy*.

Linda McGuire teaches courses on gender, writing and biography at the École Nationale Supérieure d'Art in Dijon, France. Since 2011, her work has focused on the significant presence of women in Cicero's correspondence, especially *The Letters to Atticus*. Her current book project explores evidence for women in the Roman world penning, sending, reading and forwarding letters. She is one of the founding members of The Epistolary Research Network (TERN).

Alexus McLeod is Associate Professor of philosophy and Asian/Asian-American studies at the University of Connecticut. He works mainly in comparative philosophy, Chinese philosophy, Mesoamerican philosophy, metaphysics and philosophy of language. His most recent monograph is *The Philosophical Thought of Wang Chong* (Palgrave Macmillan, 2018), and he is the editor of the recently released *Bloomsbury Handbook of Early Chinese Ethics and Political Philosophy* (Bloomsbury, 2019).

Valentina Moro obtained her PhD in philosophy at the University of Padua (Italy) in 2018. In 2016 and 2017 she was a visiting research fellow at Brown University (USA). Her research intersects the fields of political theory, classics and gender studies. Currently, she is a research fellow at the Center for Advanced Studies in South East Europe in Rijeka (Croatia) and at the Hannah Arendt Center for Political Studies in Verona (Italy). She co-edited the book *Polis, Erōs, Parrēsia. Letture etico-politiche contemporanee della tragedia greca*, published in 2018.

Herman Paul is Professor of the history of the humanities at Leiden University, where he directs a large research project on 'Scholarly Vices: A Longue Durée History'. He is currently at work on a book-length study of virtues and vices in nineteenth-century historical studies and editing a volume entitled *Writing the History of the Humanities*.

Danielle Petherbridge is Assistant Professor in the School of Philosophy at University College Dublin and co-director of the UCD Centre for Ethics in Public Life. She is currently working on two book projects: firstly, a monograph entitled *When is One Recognizable?*; and secondly, a book project on inter-subjectivity entitled *Encountering the Other*. Her primary research interests include theories of vulnerability, empathy and recognition; the relation between perception, attention and affect; and theories of inter-subjectivity in phenomenology and social philosophy. She is also creator and co-founder of the Irish Young Philosopher Awards.

Stefan Rossbach teaches political theory in the School of Politics and International Relations at the University of Kent. His current research focuses on ascetic practices of political resistance.

Lorraine Sim is a senior lecturer in modern English literature at Western Sydney University. She is the author of *Virginia Woolf: the Patterns of Ordinary Experience* (Ashgate, 2010) and *Ordinary Matters: Modernist Women's Literature and Photography* (Bloomsbury Academic, 2016).

Winnie Sung's main research interests are in Xunzi's thought, pre-Qin Confucian ethics, moral psychology and self-knowledge. She holds a PhD from the University of New South Wales in Australia and is currently Assistant Professor at Nanyang Technological University in Singapore. Her recent publications are on Xunzi's ethical views and early Confucian conceptions of hypocrisy, loyalty, sympathy and resentment.

Robert Tittler is Distinguished Professor of History Emeritus at Montreal's Concordia University and a fellow of the Royal Society of Canada. His most recent books include *The Face of the City; Civic Portraiture and Civic Identity in Early Modern England* (2007); *Painters, Portraits, and Publics in Provincial England, 1500–1640* (2012); and (edited) *Two Weather Diaries from Northern England, c. 1779–1807: The Journals of John Chipchase and Elihu Robinson* (2019).

Bryan W. Van Norden is Kwan Im Thong Hood Cho Temple Professor at Yale-NUS College (Singapore), James Monroe Taylor Chair in Philosophy at Vassar College (USA) and Chair Professor in philosophy in the School of Philosophy at Wuhan University (China). He is the author, editor or translator of nine books on Chinese and comparative philosophy, including *Introduction to Classical Chinese Philosophy* (2011), *Readings in Classical Chinese Philosophy* (2nd ed., 2005, with P. J. Ivanhoe), *Readings in Later Chinese Philosophy: Han to the 20th Century* (2014, with Justin Tiwald), and most recently *Taking Back Philosophy: A Multicultural Manifesto* (2017). A recipient of Fulbright, National Endowment for the Humanities, and Mellon fellowships, Van Norden has also published a number of essays as a public intellectual, including 'The Ignorant Do Not Have a Right to an Audience' (*New York Times*) which earned him a place on *Professor Watchlist*.

Rachael Wiseman is Lecturer in philosophy at the University of Liverpool. She works at the intersection of philosophy of action, mind and ethics. She is the author of the *Routledge Philosophical Guidebook to Anscombe's Intention* (2016). Her next major publication will be a co-authored monograph (with Dr Clare Mac Cumhaill) on the Wartime Quartet (G. E. M. Anscombe, Philippa Foot, Mary Midgley and Iris Murdoch) for Chatto & Windus.

Robin Zheng is Assistant Professor of philosophy at Yale-NUS College. She specializes in ethics, moral psychology and feminist and social philosophy. Her recent publications include 'Why Yellow Fever Isn't Flattering: A Case Against Racial Fetish' in the *Journal of the American Philosophical Association*; 'Bias, Structure, and Injustice: A Reply to Haslanger' in *Feminist Philosophy Quarterly*; 'A Job for Philosophers: Causality, Responsibility, and Explaining Social Inequality' in *Dialogue: Canadian Philosophical Review*; and 'Precarity is a Feminist Issue: Gender and Contingent Labor in the Academy' in *Hypatia: A Journal of Feminist Philosophy*.

Introduction

Integrity is having a rather tough time of it. Gone are the days when 'a man of integrity' was a standard commendation on every other tombstone, or when the phrase itself might be applied without self-consciousness or sardonic undertones. Instead, the word tends to appear co-opted in a rather domesticated form, in such partial phrases as 'academic integrity' as a name for the absence of plagiarism and data falsification; or 'professional integrity' as a standard of behaviour set by the human resources department. Large volumes are written on integrity,[1] a sure symptom of scrambling to breathe fresh life into a dying concept. In place of a living language of integrity, we now speak the language of 'transparency', of 'accountability'.

But the imprint of our still vital concern with a rich and robust virtue of integrity is seen in our collective and personal preoccupation with its many absences, failures and challenges. Politicians are decried as corrupt or opportunist; leaders deplored for their spinelessness; decision-makers suspected of unprincipled self-servingness; sometime friends and lovers 'ghost' us; and the new social media so emphasizes the performance of self that young people suffer record levels of crippling anxiety connected to a loss of a sense of personal intactness independent of social confirmation.[2] In our workplaces and personal lives, we often feel compromised, and pulled in different directions; we apply different moral standards in different contexts, and check our morals at the door when we shop or work – some more reluctantly than others. The difficulty of acting with consistency, and staying true to our principles, in a dizzyingly complex and interconnected world is often demoralizing.[3] Where the presumption is always that professionals ought not to be entrusted to conduct themselves professionally, and must be ring-fenced with accountability procedures; where someone feels the futility of trying to do the right thing at work or in the supermarket; where the accusing cry of 'hypocrite!' invariably rises up to meet anyone who proposes that we need to do better – there we find an acute need for real integrity being felt and expressed, even if in a sometimes confused and counterproductive way.

The confusion and indirection in our thinking about integrity makes us vulnerable to exploitation. Not all those who cry 'hypocrite!' care deeply about integrity – but they know you do. And since you care, you will be increasingly discouraged at the ubiquity and inescapability of hypocrisy and compromise. If we lack a clear notion of the thing we value, then we become vulnerable to appearances. With something as complex as integrity, with so many forms of failure and facsimile, virtually anything might be made to appear as an unpardonable lack of integrity if it suits someone's purpose to make it appear so. False claims of successful integrity may be harder to generate, but they can be very destabilizing – as witnessed in the increasingly erratic and dissociated moral claims within American political and public discourse, where Donald Trump – whose name was made in wheeling and dealing – can be made out to be, of all things, an exemplar of integrity by virtue of appearing to say what he thinks, and appearing to be wealthy enough not to have his opinion 'bought'.

Although what is urgently needed is conceptual clarification, philosophers – whose stock-in-trade is conceptual clarification – have proven singularly unhelpful in this case. Typically a philosopher begins by choosing some definition or another of integrity – integrity as self-integration,[4] integrity as commitment to one's projects,[5] integrity as constancy of personal identity,[6] integrity as practising what you preach, or preaching what you truly think[7] – and defends or critiques it. Agreeing on the meaning of a term sounds like a reasonable starting point, and typically philosophical. Yet that approach in this case seems often to end up being partial and incomplete, leaving vital parts of what we might *value* about integrity out of the picture. No surprise, then, that precisely because of their abstractness and simplicity these conceptions of integrity frequently lead to the sort of silly implications for which philosophical thought is often derided and dismissed – for instance, that Heinrich Himmler might have had integrity, or that Huckleberry Finn lacked it.[8] Where we come to such conclusions, we have clearly come very far from the phenomenon we set out to understand in the first place. If Bernard Williams tries to console us, saying that while integrity is not a virtue, it is at least a precondition for virtue,[9] this is cold comfort. For this is very little help in recognizing when our hunger for integrity is apt or manipulated – or even for recognizing that it is the sort of thing that can be manipulated. It has not helped us in our consideration of whether integrity demands perfection; of whether a change of mind is a sign of hollowness or of integrity; whether an instance of steadfastness is an expression of integrity or of obtuseness or sheer bloody-mindedness; whether we are right to suspect that in politics there is no place for personal integrity.

'A main cause of philosophical disease – an unbalanced diet: one nourishes oneself with only one kind of example.'[10]

So it is vital to collect our divergent and disparate thoughts about integrity, and attempt to think it through in all its complexity. But we need a different approach. When confronted with elusive concepts which seem perpetually to evade our grasp, we might be moved to say with Justice Stewart that although definition seems impossible, 'I know it when I see it'. But do we know integrity when we see it? Some of us, through the direct experience of an exceptional person or a particular exceptional act might have found ourselves in the situation of trying to articulate our experience, and finding no fitter word than 'integrity'. But our contacts with integrity are often accompanied by more uncertainty than this – we look at the person or act in one light, and it resonates with integrity; we look in another light, and we wonder if perhaps the person is just mad or contrary. When John Brown, for instance, jeopardizes himself, his children and others in a quixotic attempt to change a slave-owning system of which he and his white family are beneficiaries, is he vainglorious and self-aggrandizing, or adhering to what is really right, insisting on holding us all to a higher standard, whatever the cost, in the face of all social and physical penalty? What about Michael Kohlhaas' cry of 'let justice be done, though the world perish' – adamantine integrity, or wild loss of all proportion?

Perhaps it is no wonder that our thinking about integrity might be confused. There are many facets of integrity; it is not at all clear that they cohere with each other, and each of them seems to defy reality in some way. In a world requiring compromise – and all worlds require compromise – sticking to principle goes against the grain. In a world that is badly out of joint – and the world has been badly out of joint since time began – doing what is right sometimes entails considerable, even unreasonable, cost to oneself and even one's loved ones. Where humanity demands responsiveness to plurality, the very unitariness of integrity is suspect. More than most other virtues, the very aspects that constitute the virtue can seem to be of dubious value.

Rather than avoiding these awkward cases by premature definitions and simplifying exclusions, this volume proposes that the way out of our confusion is to face these various dubious and challenging cases straight on. Focusing too much on too few examples distorts our thinking, particularly if the examples are thin or contrived. To collect our divergent and disparate thoughts about integrity, and think it through in all its complexity, what we need are *more* cases, considered in their full ambiguity. We do not claim that subjects of the portraits collected in this volume *have* integrity, on any of the several going definitions of that word; only that reflecting on them will illuminate and enrich our understanding of integrity.

This volume of portraits invites us, then, to explore the many different ways in which something that *might be* rightly called integrity has been manifested or depicted, in actual concrete cases that are as detailed and embedded as our actual lived experience of and thinking about integrity. Rather than beginning by simplifying our notion of integrity to some core, this volume invites us to begin our reflection by nourishing ourselves on a wide variety of candidates for integrity – or failures of integrity: a wide variety of really lived or richly imagined persons, actions or even works of art that may make us want to reach for the word 'integrity', whether in affirmation, or in order to identify what has been lost. Each case is an opportunity to test and explore the connections between the different aspects of integrity, and between integrity and other goods and virtues. The many cases together allow us to illuminate how the many components of integrity, its near kin and its facsimiles shift and change in their prominence and relations to each other. Studying the details of the many embedded ways in which integrity might be expressed, or compromised, challenged, maintained or lost, we can clarify for ourselves what value integrity has, what its preconditions and threats are, and what losing it costs.

We have deliberately collected a wide range of complex subjects: from literature, history, politics, art, philosophy and everyday life; some subjects are not even persons, for artworks and institutions and even modes of writing may have or lack integrity in a way that is relevant to understanding the integrity of persons. They are drawn from materials dating to centuries before the Common Era, from pre-modern, early-modern and contemporary times; from North America, Europe, and Africa; from Central Asia, East Asia and South Asia – for even linguistic cultures lacking any one word for integrity easily recognize the cluster of phenomena that arise under what we in English call 'integrity'. We make no claim to *completeness*, nor would we wish to. Martin Luther, who declared 'Here I stand; I can do no other', is for instance a conspicuous absence compensated for by the inclusion of less familiar, eminently fascinating subjects. If this volume inspires readers to vividly consider their own favoured figure who would have been equally at home here, then that is all to the good. The insights found in each of these portraits can be taken together as a guard against making any one form or facet of integrity absolute. They should help us to keep the conversation open, rather than closing it down prematurely.

The faces that we meet

We lead off with some displays of *conspicuous integrity* – perhaps even, pejoratively or not, *heroic* integrity. **Plato's Socrates** offers the European imagination its first philosophical martyr, and introduces us to the idea of integrity as grounded in an integrated soul whose unity is achieved by its overriding orientation to what is really good. Plato's depiction of Socrates' preternaturally integrated soul also foreshadows the queer interpersonal and social effects of such a singularly oriented soul. **Boethius** extends this idea of integrity as uncompromising and unconditional devotion to goodness by emphasizing that the good is to be *loved* – and that in a personal way. Although this love of real goodness is personal, it directs our attention away from everyday personal relations, to achieve a transcendently informed love, sustained by gratitude, rather than 'encased in one's own rectitude'. **Rāma** looks to be precisely so encased. The Vālmīki *Rāmāyaṇa* triumphantly celebrates Rāma's uprightness by claiming that he is the perfect man, while at the same time subtly undermining that claim by showing us that Rama's thoughtless adherence to a set of formalistic moral principles has turned his heart to stone. **Antigone**, by contrast, gives us a this-worldly example of non-encased integrity. Her performance of integrity is a socialpolitical and relational act, and not the act of individual isolation and defiance that it might appear. In the figure of **Job**, we see individual isolation tested, with ambiguous results. Does he still hold fast his integrity? *Ought* he? Ought *we*?

Integrity is not always heroic or conspicuous. There are everyday struggles for integrity that often highlight endeavours to live with integrity while maintaining a place in a shared, largely conventional, community. **Ella Baker** worked persistently and without fanfare to promote civil rights and welfare in twentieth-century America, eschewing the grandstanding of better-known figures for effective work with the real individuals whose rights and welfare were endangered. Her intense focus on the work prompted her to willingly sacrifice personal goods, but may have also caused her to overlook parts of the social system in need of fundamental change. With '**Albert**', a banker, we see starkly how situating integrity in a shared public world makes it vulnerable to corruptions, but is also potentially transformative. 'Albert' strives to bring into his professional life the ethical standards that govern his private life. He has a good understanding of what he wants his personal/professional life to look like, but operates within institutions that make this difficult to achieve. Is it possible, 'Albert' wonders, to retain integrity within an organization by shaping an institutional context? In a similar – though more bloody – vein, the seventeenth-century political theorist **Huang Zongxi** asks us to turn away from heroic models of integrity and, instead, to construct social and political conditions that will make it safe to live a life of integrity.

Lambert Strether struggles in a different way. The 'ambassador' in Henry James' novel of that name, the middle-aged Strether finds himself with a life that is not his own, in a world that is alien to him. His struggles against 'the Woollet view' – the unspoken established values and customs that feel so alien to him – speak to the dangers both of losing oneself in a life of conventionality and of finally finding one's voice. **Confucius' village worthies**, by contrast, have no voice to find. They fluidly adopt whatever the prevailing norms are – and with easy success, for unlike Lambert Strether, they have no view of their own with which any prevailing morality might conflict. They are 'thieves of virtue', robbing us of the possibility even of hypocrisy, to say nothing of integrity.

A similar corrosion of moral character and moral life can be traced back to what the philosopher **G. E. M. Anscombe** calls the *false hypocrisy of the ideal standard*. False hypocrites exploit the idea that integrity is beyond the reach of the ordinary person by posturing as reluctant hypocrites – 'I know that buying this supports sweatshops, and that's terrible; but it's just impossible to avoid betraying my principles, no matter what I do – so I might as well'. The false hypocrite uses the unrealistic demand for absolute purity to make inevitable failures of us all, feeding cynicism and actually generating the corruption it claims to decry.

Perhaps one reason persons of conspicuous integrity so often make us uncomfortable is that they make us aware of this creeping cynicism in ourselves. Certainly Socrates made his interlocutors ill at ease, eliciting from them accusations of disingenuousness. Similarly, **Mohandas Gandhi** – proposing through his own way of living that we may all hold ourselves to a higher standard – attracts accusations of charlatanism, as well as attributions of integrity and sainthood. For some he functions as a touchstone, encounters with him working as revelatory tests of their own integrity. **Leo Tolstoy** likewise inspired people to discover newer and truer ways of living, in recognition of the irremediably corrupted and corrupting social structures as they currently were. But his focus on following one's own conscience made it impossible for him to accept the movement of 'Tolstoyans' that took his name. Examining the difficulties **Tolstoyans** faced as they tried to live lives shaped by ideals that were at odds with wider society foregrounds the sometimes existential costs of maintaining integrity, and the difficulties of compromising it.

Simone Weil's thought and life similarly repudiates anything like a collective movement. Rejecting a popular and debased notion of integrity or 'authenticity' – one captured in Polonius' dictum, 'To thine own self be true' – Weil, like many of the figures in this volume, insists that it was only to an impersonal good, or God, that one must be true. Her attempts to do this in her own life attract the familiar mixed reactions to those who decisively undertake to live against the grain: Is she an inspiring model of one possible manifestation of real human goodness? Or is she just foolish, naïve or self-indulgent? (Does our doubt about her integrity perhaps, as Anscombe suggests, reveal more about ourselves?) A reading of the *Romance of The Three Kingdoms* focuses in on discerning virtue's lookalikes and approximations from the real thing. The characters of this widely read novel present a variety of forms of flawed integrity – the loyal, the courageous, the strategic. But the 'perfectly virtuous'

Lord Guan turns out to be the most serious failure masquerading as moral success: his blindness about himself does great harm to those around him, demonstrating most conspicuously that any one virtue separated from the others collapses into inflexibility, rashness, subservience or compromise.

Gerrard Winstanley, founder of the communist True Levellers (or 'the Diggers', as they were commonly known), had nothing against founding a social movement. His rejection of the world order came with the rallying cry to turn the world 'upside down'. Uniting iconoclasm in religion and in politics, Winstanley became increasingly radical as the effects of the English Civil War were visited upon the poorest of the people. The Sufi ascetic **Amadou Bamba** from Senegal similarly united in himself a deep devotion to knowing God directly with anti-colonial struggle, taking guidance in the latter from his commitment to the former. As with Gandhi, anti-colonialism is for Bamba a struggle against colonization of the mind; a life lived with integrity involves the overcoming of ego, which enables us to understand God and the cosmos.

But not all aspirants to a truer way of living set themselves in opposition to the corrupted social order. The Kazakh poet and politician **Abai** found himself with the task of constructing a coherent and fair political system out of the conflicting fragments of Kazakh culture and the legal systems imposed by the Russian Empire. His life shows us how an educated and respected leader might seek to reconcile conflicting moral and legal codes – using each to critique the other, without chauvinistic (or opportunistic) loyalty to either – while highlighting the risks to reputation and identity in doing so. The painter **Amrita Sher-Gill,** situated by birth and profession across cultural, national, class and even gender lines, enacts the integration of her multifaceted identity through her self-portraits, and in a different way through her portraits of other women, while at the same time taking a stand on what artistic integrity is, and can be, for an Indian painter of the early twentieth century.

The nineteenth-century historians **Friedrich Dahlmann and Georg Waitz** model opposing ideals of scholarly integrity, the ascetic and synthetic, with different understandings of the intellectual's role in creating political and national identities. In the conflict between those ideals we see where integrity might start to shade into fastidiousness or vanity, partiality or complicity. **Hannah Arendt,** meanwhile, counsels us to be cautious in our wish for more integrity in the political realm. Indeed, the integrity of the political realm, she argues, demands constant vigilance *against* forms of integration; for when things are too integrated, there is no space for contesting and challenging norms. Surprisingly, the integrity of the world demands that we set limits on the value of truthfulness within the political sphere. The trickster figure **Anansi**, common in the folklore of West Africa and its diaspora, similarly insists on the importance of the integrity of the community over the integrity of individuals. Playful deviousness and prudential duplicity are even *rewarded* in tales of Anansi – up to the point where such behaviour threatens the unity and stability of the community.

Integrity is not just something people or institutions may have (or lack); it is also something persons might be represented as having or lacking, often through a deliberate act of constructing a public image – sometimes, indeed, a literal image. The **Cookes' and the Kayes'** sixteenth-century family portraits demonstrate the use of convention and recognizable social cues in portraying unproblematic integrity – uprightness, honesty and propriety. The portraits the Cookes and the Kayes commissioned were an important part of their self-fashioning as respectable and aspirational families in post-Reformation England. But what happens when the subject of a portrait presents a less conventional form of integrity? **Titus Pomponius Atticus** makes for a curious subject of Roman biography. Already a poor candidate to be subject of a life due to his social status, Atticus' choices challenged prevailing notions of what might be considered honourable. Yet Cornelius Nepos' *Life of Atticus* purports to present its readers with a man possessing qualities usually associated with integrity. Did Romans accept Atticus' refusal to enter politics because it was so corrupt? Was his refusal seen as an expression of impeccable integrity or was Nepos' biography of Atticus instead just a portrait of sycophancy?

Sometimes, finding a voice that speaks with integrity is the most pressing task. The nineteenth-century Polish journalist Henryk Sienkiewicz must construct his portrait of integrity in words. His travel report, *Letters from America*, creates a narrative voice that can be trusted by the reader, while remaining entertaining. The *Letters* use literary devices to build a trust within the reader that the narrator is fundamentally sound – only playful at his own expense, and not frivolous in his ethics. Without projecting and sustaining such a voice of integrity, the *Letters* would fail to be informative, or to induce reflection, where it matters most. This portrait speaks to today's milieu and the problems that arise for those wishing to speak the truth in a world that has debased fact, expertise and truth. With **Virginia Woolf**, it is not so much the integrity of the character created that is the focus, but the integrity of the creator, which affects the integrity of the literary work. In particular, feelings of anger and bitterness – even when apparently warranted by real injustice – undermine the ability of the author to attain the universality necessary for great work, instead feeding the egotism that is anathema to genuine self-knowledge. Woolf writes particularly about women writing, knowing as she does the real injustices faced by women, making her essay itself a lesson in how to write with integrity.

In conclusion

Integrity matters to us. We want representatives who will speak truth to power, and not be bought by that power. We want friends who have the backbone to stand up to injustice even when it is not themselves who are primarily affected. We want our children to learn to be true to themselves, rather than pulled this way and that by the prevailing winds of social media. We want to be someone who, when there is a tough choice between what is right and what is easy, will do what is right. There is, indeed, a positive hunger for persons of substance, of the sort an earlier age would not have been too shy to designate 'integrity'. These portraits offer materials for exploring and reflecting upon the complexities and varieties of integrity, in its relation to other values, and embedded within social, political, religious and institutional contexts of human life.

The mode of exploration and examination in these portraits is not in the first instance conceptual, nor yet historical. The order of the chapters reflects thematic, rather than temporal associations – though the overlapping themes running throughout these portraits lend themselves to multiple thematic orderings; ours is just one of many possible illuminating orderings. These explorations offer material for unfolding the manifold meanings and manifestations of integrity. They present the stuff of life and literature, philosophy and politics and history that any thinking about integrity must be true to, if it is to speak to those whose moral lives are shaped, in part, by notions of integrity. We are interested in the borders between integrity and its kin; we want to illuminate its antitheses and its facsimiles. We hope that by becoming more attuned to the ways in which integrity can be lived and lost we might become better at teaching it, aiming for it and recognizing it when we see it.

The reader will look in vain for any *theory* of integrity defined and defended in these pages, or for an account of the use of this term in English over the centuries. However, you will find some of our reflections at the end of the volume, notes or reminders of connections and insights that have emerged for us as we curated this gallery of individuals struggling, whether successfully or not, to do the right thing in different circumstances, times and contexts, sometimes under terrible pressure and often in situations where it was difficult to see what truth and goodness required.

Recommended reading

The classic starting point for philosophical reflections on integrity and why it matters is Bernard Williams' influential 'Integrity' (in J. J. C. Smart and Bernard Williams, *Utilitarianism: For and Against* (New York: Cambridge, 1973), 108–117). Other important papers on the meaning and value of integrity are Lynne McFall, 'Integrity', *Ethics* 98 (1987): 5–20 and Gabriele Taylor, 'Integrity', *Proceedings of the Aristotelian Society (Supplementary Volume)*, 55 (1981): 143–59; Peter Winch's 'Moral Integrity', *Ethics and Action* (London and New York: Routledge & Kegan Paul, 1972) uses literary examples to illustrate forms of, and challenges to, integrity. Damian Cox, Marguerite La Caze and Michael P. Levine's *Integrity and the Fragile Self* is a compelling defence of integrity as a unifying virtue (Aldershot: Ashgate, 2003). Susan Wolf's 'Moral Saints', *The Journal of Philosophy* 79 (8) (August 1982): 419–39 challenges the idea that integrity – at least in its saintly guise – is desirable in a human life.

Cheshire Calhoun's 'Standing for Something', *Journal of Philosophy* XCII (1995): 235–60 is a study of a more political concept of integrity and Susan Mendus' *Politics and Morality* (Cambridge: Polity Press, 2009) asks whether integrity is possible or even valuable in the political realm.

Notes

1 Susan E. Babbitt, *Artless Integrity: On Moral Imagination, Agency and Stories* (Lanham, MD: Rowman & Littlefield, 2001); Martin Benjamin, *Splitting the Difference: Compromise and Integrity in Ethics and Politics* (Lawrence: University Press of Kansas, 1990); Stephen L. Carter, *Integrity* (New York: Basic Books, 1996); Cox, Damien, Marguerite La Caze and Michael P. Levine, *Integrity and the Fragile Self* (Aldershot: Ashgate, 2003); Mark S. Halfon, *Integrity: A Philosophical Inquiry* (Philadelphia: Temple University Press, 1989); Greg Scherkoske, *Integrity and the Virtues of Reason* (Cambridge: Cambridge University Press, 2013); Ian Shapiro and Robert Adams (eds), *Integrity & Conscience* [Collected essays from The American Society for Political and Legal Philosophy 1995]; and Hans Bernhard Schmid, *Moralische Integrität* (Berlin: Suhrkamp, 2011).

2 See for instance, L. D. Rosen, K. Whaling, S. Rab, L. M. Carrier and N. A. Cheever, 'Is Facebook Creating "iDisorders"?' *Computers in Human Behavior* 29/3 (2013): 1243–54, https://doi.org/10.1016/j.chb.2012.11.012; H. C. Woods and H. Scott, '#Sleepyteens', *Journal of Adolescence* 51 (2016): 41–9, https://doi.org/10.1016/j.adolescence.2016.05.008; and the much-discussed work of Jean Twenge (*The Narcissism Epidemic* with W. Keith Campbell, for instance, Atria Books, 2009). More recent and nuanced discussion is contained in Minna Lyons' *The Dark Triad* (London: Elsevier Academic Press, 2019).

3 This demoralization – in both senses, discouragement and making ourself un-moral – is even the theme of popular television (*The Good Place*, Season 3).

4 This view can be found in John Bigelow and Robert Pargetter, 'Integrity and Autonomy', *American Philosophical Quarterly* 44 (2007): 39–49; Harry Frankfurt, 'Identification and Wholeheartedness', in Ferdinand Schoeman (ed.), *Responsibility, Character, and the Emotions: New Essays in Moral Psychology* (New York: Cambridge University Press, 1987).

5 This view is in Elizabeth Ashford, 'Utilitarianism, Integrity and Partiality', *Journal of Philosophy* 97 (2000): 421–39; Mark Halfon, *Integrity: A Philosophical Inquiry* (Philadelphia: Temple University Press, 1989).

6 This view is associated primarily with Bernard Williams. See his 'Integrity', in J. J. C. Smart and Bernard Williams, *Utilitarianism: For and Against* (New York: Cambridge, 1973), 108–17; 'Utilitarianism

and Moral Self-Indulgence', in his *Moral Luck: Philosophical Papers 1973-1980* (Cambridge: Cambridge University Press), 40–53.
7 See Cheshire Calhoun, 'Standing for Something', *Journal of Philosophy* XCII (1995): 235–60.
8 For a comparative discussion of both, see Jonathan Bennett, 'The Conscience of Huckleberry Finn', *Philosophy* 49 (188) (April 1974): 123–34.
9 Bernard Williams, 'Integrity', ibid.
10 Ludwig Wittgenstein, *Philosophical Investigations* (New York: Macmillan Publishing Company, 1953), §593.

1

Plato's Socrates

The oddness of the integrated soul

Amber D. Carpenter

> *There are many other quite marvellous things one might applaud in Socrates. While some of his accomplishments may perhaps be said of others as well, still there is no one like him, not among the ancients nor among contemporaries – this is what is most amazing of all.*
>
> (SYMPOSIUM 221C)

In the *Gorgias*, Callicles accuses Socrates of lurking with boys in dark corners. Plato's Socrates has been lurking in the dark corners of the European imagination ever since. He is shoeless and rumpled, bug-eyed and snub-nosed, slightly shiftless – and yet, the hero of the story. What is it about him that haunts us – and at the same time attracts us?

Athenians of the fourth century BCE. were evidently equally bothered by Socrates (the man himself) – a jury of five hundred of your peers does not vote to have you executed for a non-capital offence unless you have really got under their skin. The comic poet Aristophanes mocks him in his comedy *The Clouds*; the historian-statesman Xenophon commits his admiring memories of Socrates to writing. Indeed, so many people wanted to have a say in drawing the definitive portrait of Socrates that a new genre of writing was born, 'the Socratic dialogue', in which Socrates generally appears as the unalloyed hero of civilized discourse. As Plato – one of these writers of 'Socratic dialogues' – tells it, these diverse reactions stem from the same source – and tell us as much about ourselves as about Socrates.

This common source lies, according to Plato, in what he has taught us to call Socrates' outstanding integrity. While there is no ancient Greek equivalent of 'integrity', the attribution is not merely a retrospective one. For Socrates as Plato describes him in his several dialogues is perhaps the figure more than any other that has shaped the complex resonances and tensions that virtue has in European moral thought generally.

This is not because Plato was simply the better writer – in most cases, it is impossible to judge (since rivals' works are lost), and about Xenophon, it is more seemly for the philosopher to acknowledge that literary style can be a matter of taste. The reason Plato's Socrates guides and grounds our moral thought in this area is that Plato married carefully chosen details of Socrates' life and behaviour, vivid depictions of 'the man himself' in conversation, to a searching diagnosis of what it is about human nature, our condition, and the good that enabled Socrates to have this extraordinary goodness, and affect those around him in the diverse ways he did.

In short, as Plato tells it, Socrates' unfailing consistency in word and deed, his steadfastness and incorruptibility, are all inevitable expressions of his unified soul. Our complex *psychē*s can be in conflict, and ordinarily are; but they can also be harmoniously unified, when governed by a commitment to truth about goodness. Note that this commitment is unifying only when it is a commitment to what is really and absolutely good – no adherence to mere partial or apparent 'values' will do the trick. Such inner unity of the person can only issue in harmonious fittingness between goals, words and action; there can be no deceit or prevarication, famously no weakness of will, in the person who has unified herself and her life around an overriding commitment to the truth about goodness. The notion of the properly integrated *psychē* as grounding consistent behaviour through a steadfast commitment to truth and goodness was born of Plato's attempt to create categories for articulating the uncanny exceptional goodness of Socrates.

What Plato captures particularly well is the way that Socrates is experienced by others as both maddening and charismatic. I use the present tense 'is' here because, as anyone who has taught Plato's dialogues knows, Socrates continues to be experienced as both maddening and charismatic. As Plato presents it, this is no accidental feature of a peculiar man. Socrates may strike us (all 'us's, at all times and cultures) as odd; but he is not a bundle of eccentricities. His behaviour, his words, are both infuriating and inspiring *for the same reason* – namely, because of Socrates' particular form of goodness, his whole self unified around love of the good and of wisdom. Our varied reactions to this reveal our own ambivalence and discomfort in the presence of this particular virtue. To come into contact with a person of outstanding integrity is demanding; as Plato shows us, it demands that one put oneself and one's life on the line. And that is uncomfortable.

Plato avails himself of all the tools of the dialogue form in order to convey a vivid, dynamic portrait of Socrates and the effect he had on those who came into contact with him. We are never given a full biography, which makes the carefully selected details we are given of Socrates' character and life more telling.

Plato's Socrates was a man of unimpeachable courage, seeing action at the battles of Potidaea and Delium, distinguished in the latter by dignity in retreating as ordered, even as others were running away around him (*Symposium* 219e–221c; *Laches* 181b). In the line of duty he also manifested outstanding fortitude, unaffected by cold or lack of shoes (*Symposium* 200b–c). This courage and fortitude were conspicuous in Socrates' civilian life. The oligarchy that seized control of Athens, trying to implicate others in their crimes, ordered Socrates to illegally arrest someone. Socrates refused, simply going home instead (*Apology* 32c–e); in another incident, Socrates alone refused to cooperate in an illegal mass trial (*Apology* 32b). Both of these refusals were made at significant personal risk.

Among his friends, Plato's Socrates is known for his indifference to drink in both senses: he neither cares whether he drinks, nor is he affected when he does drink. Nor is sex a temptation to him

(*Symposium* 217b–219a), though he is a well-known connoisseur of physical beauty (*Charmides* 154c–d) and considers love to be the only thing he really knows anything about (*Phaedrus* 257a; *Symposium* 177e). Although Socrates practically never left the confines of the city, apart from his military service (*Crito* 52b–c, *Phaedrus* 230e), he strikes his fellow Athenians as *atopos* – out of place, or strange – on many dimensions (*Tht.* 175a; *Symp.* 215a, 221c–d; and at *Phdr.* 230c6, 'most strange'). In addition to his uncanny sobriety and steadiness of character, Socrates has a host of socially awkward habits that betray a disconcerting indifference to social judgement. Not a rich or well-born man, nor a particularly attractive man (*Symposium* 215a–c, 221d–e; *Theaetetus* 143e), Socrates has no shame or embarrassment in his poverty or plainness. For Socrates, making a special effort with his appearance, for a celebratory occasion with fine folk, consists merely in having a wash and putting on his best sandals (*Symposium* 174a). Plato's Socrates even openly declares that 'one shouldn't care what all men think, but only what good men think' (*Crito* 47a; *Laches* 189a; *cf. Symp.* 194b–c). So it is evidently nothing to him to stand stock-still if he is puzzled about something, refusing to move on until he knows which direction he ought to go in (*Symposium* 174d–175c, 220c–d). He does not mind that he has acquired no fame for Great Deeds (leaving him open to Callicles' charge that he is unmanly for pursuing philosophical conversation with teenagers, *Gorgias* 485d–e). And he knows that his adherence in conversation to what is best rather than what is pleasant will do him no favours in life or in the law courts (*Tht.* 172–7, *Gorgias* 521d–e). This same obliviousness or disregard for social censure means he does not hesitate to ask awkward questions of public figures as they do their morning's shopping (e.g. Anytus at *Meno* 89e–94e), or work out at the gym (*Charmides* 155c–d). Even visiting dignitaries or celebrities are not spared from being publicly called to account by Socrates (such interrogations are the basis of both the *Protagoras* and the *Gorgias*).

This particular kind of disregard for social censure is disconcerting, for it is invariably accompanied by implicit critique of the censurer: Socrates would be receptive to the critique if it were well founded (*Gorgias* 487e–488b); that he is not thus receptive implies the critic is the one who has got his values mixed up. Surely, whether virtue can be taught, and how, is more important after all than whether people watching think you 'won' – right? This is why Socrates' questions, as Plato describes them, are so awkward for so many interlocutors. Socrates asks about things that really matter – *and he insists on treating them as if they really mattered*. He asks about virtue and justice and friendship and courage and beauty – and expects his interlocutor to engage seriously with the question. Glib answers are returned to sender unopened. Indeed, he is so serious about it that he says nothing is more important than virtue, and nothing can be good without it (*Apology* 28b–30b); and that what is truly good is the only thing worth knowing. Not only does he mean it, but he says it as if it were obvious that everyone agrees. Anyone at that moment concerned rather about his standing or reputation is forced to shift uncomfortably in his seat.

This discomfort is accentuated by the fact that Socrates so obviously does not just *say* virtue is important – he lives it, thus showing up the lives around him as lived differently, as if money or fame or pleasure were more important. In addition to Socrates' refusal to participate in injustice, at great personal risk, he refuses to appeal (as was the norm) to the needs of his family and youth of his children when defending himself against charges of impiety (*Apology* 34d–e). He refuses to beg. Socrates then refuses to run away from prison when sentenced to death for a crime of which he knows himself to be innocent, even when his friends arrive with the money to bribe the guard to look the other direction. And while this looks like a formidable instance of sticking to what one knows to be right in the face of strong temptation to do otherwise, Plato's Socrates almost perversely eschews claim to any knowledge – in particular any knowledge of good and bad, of virtue and vice, and therefore any knowledge that he is, in fact, doing right when he acts by what appears to his best reflective critical evaluation to be right. In spite of all his seeking, Socrates insists he knows nothing (*Gorgias* 506a, 509a; *Apology* 21d) and has nothing to teach (*Apology* 33a–b) – yet Plato shows him as adept at making anyone with pretensions to knowledge look even more ignorant and foolish.

People around him interpret this as obscene arrogance (*Apology* 37a; Thrasymachus in *Rep.* I; Alcibaides at *Symp.* 215c, 219c), as a mocking of others ('That's just Socrates' usual irony', Thrasymachus snarks at *Republic* 337a; cf. *Symp.* 216e, and *Gorgias* 489e), and find it absolutely infuriating. But others find it magnetic, and find in Socrates a true and reliable friend (Crito and Phaedo in the *Phaedo*; Nicias and Laches in the *Laches*), an inspiration to self-improvement through self-examination (Hippocrates in the *Protagoras*, Aristodemus and Alcibiades in the *Symposium*), and 'the best, and also the wisest and most upright' person they have known (*Phaedo* 118a).

This is the portrait Plato gives us of Socrates. It is a vivid and artfully drawn portrait of an unusual and charismatic personality – someone who is constantly searching, and whose search is necessarily a collective one, though it is not a comfortable one for his neighbours. He puts himself on the line by putting others to the test (*Gorgias* 467c, 487e–488b). His unselfconscious embodying of what it is to take virtue seriously exposes those around him as merely paying lip service to virtue, and this makes him out of place, odd, even when most at home.

Plato's masterstroke is that while drawing this portrait of Socrates he simultaneously presents an explanation of this remarkable personality. Over several dialogues, Plato develops and explores a philosophical psychology that offers an analysis of what people are like in general, what they are like when they are virtuous and do good things, and what they are like when they are vicious and do bad things. The details of the account he arrives at – both its plausibility and the reasons offered in favour of it – need not concern us here. Our focus is just the fact that this account offers an explanation of Socrates' extraordinary and *atopos* goodness in terms of unity of the soul, or of the personality.

Across the dialogues, when Plato looks inside human beings, he sees a seething mess. Countless desires, wayward and wilful, struggle against each other, with no promise of practical consistency – indeed, impulses not even aiming to cooperate in forming a harmonious personality. Desire for truth jostles alongside pride and envy, and these rub up against our bare animal aversion to physical pain, and desire for pleasure. That is what human beings are like 'by nature' – that is, without the benefit of a certain kind of education which might form the character otherwise.[1] When we are in this condition, our actions tend to be wayward and contradictory, self-defeating and harmful.

But when all the various forces and factions within us can agree on a common goal, then they pull in the same direction. I may love fame and food and finger-puppets, and pursuit of these several things will often point in contrary directions. If, however, one of these is overriding, then I can begin to order my values and the actions based on them: if food is more important than finger-puppets, eat first and then go to the theatre. If my pursuit of food does not leave much time for the theatre, that latter desire will go unsatisfied. My practical actions acquire a sort of de facto coherence by leaving things out. For any arbitrarily chosen highest good, any arbitrary alternative aims may be forced out as incompatible. But if I win coherence in action at the cost of reducing myself to a single desire, leaving the others unaddressed, I am unlikely to be fully persuaded myself of the overriding value of that arbitrarily chosen good, returning instead to the condition of a thousand clamouring desires competing for attention, prominence and satisfaction. Rather than integration, we are left with the dynamic of suppression and conflict.[2]

That we desperately need some ordering principle in our lives, and what happens when we lack this, preoccupies Plato throughout the dialogues. His verdict is that only love of the good can encompass and coordinate the whole soul – and to love the good in this way is to care that it is the true good, and not merely an inferior approximation or a facsimile. When the whole soul is united by this aim, and relates its partial aims to this overall good, there is nothing left to operate as a 'countervailing desire' or value. This explains why, for Socrates at least, there really is no weakness of will. Pressures to conform just because that is what people expect carry no weight, since they do not track real goodness in any way. Making oneself attractive just for the sake of it, without concern for whether and how this expresses real commitment to what is truly good, just does not show up on the radar. Physical attractions and pleasures might be felt, but so long as they are detached from living rightly, they carry no weight. Power divorced from reason (and thereby from truth and goodness) is frightening in others and pitiable (*Gorgias* 469a–b; *Philebus* 49b–c); it is not even remotely attractive.

On Plato's account of it, Socrates was never tempted by the pleasures and pains of the flesh because he had succeeded in disciplining his physical desires with the authority of wisdom, which respects only the good overall. If we want to know how he had the moral clarity to see what virtue demanded when it demanded difficult things – risking his life, for instance – and how he had the tenacity to persist with it, even at great cost, again it is because he had no desires pulling him in any other direction. While he had the same range of feelings as the rest of us, in Socrates these were all integrated into his prioritizing love of goodness. His constancy over time and through circumstance rests on the fact that he so integrated his manifold desires and values that there was no inconsistency between *them*, and so whatever circumstances arose, there was no source of variation in his understanding of what virtue demanded – nor, more importantly, in his commitment to the primacy of virtue above all else (*Gorgias* 482a, *Apology* 30b).

But notice now how the same thing explains Socrates' eccentricities: his lack of respect for power structures in social relations; his failing to catch the tone of social gatherings (being *serious*, for heaven's sake, at a dinner party, or at the gym); his disregard for money; his maddening insistence that people converse plainly, leaving themselves nowhere to hide among fancy words, while admitting freely that he cannot answer his own questions. All of these behaviours are just obviously going to be what someone does who has genuinely ordered the whole of his outlook and aims around the overriding priority of grasping true goodness. At least, this is Plato's claim.

One might, of course, dispute Plato's theory of human nature, of virtue, or even his explanation of Socrates. But the fact that Plato explained these many striking features of Socrates' distinctive personality by appeal to a single phenomenon – and that phenomenon was one of an integrated unity of the whole person around love of the real good – set the stage for grouping together under a single category of integrity just this range of character traits: constancy; unwavering commitment to the good; steadfast commitment to truth; incorruptibility; absolute aversion to prevarication, to evasiveness, to being compromised; and consistency in values and coherence between values, words and actions.

And Plato may have at least this much claim to be onto something: His explanation of Socrates, and of what integrity is, also explains why we – like the Athenians two thousand five hundred years ago, and countless others in between – are desperately *discomfited* by real integrity, and deeply divided about whether the person of outstanding integrity is, in fact, mad, sad or even, perhaps, bad.

If all we had were Xenophon's *Memorabilia*, we would be perplexed indeed about how it could ever have come to the Athenians executing Socrates. It is Plato who enables us to feel 'no wonder they gave him the hemlock'; for his dialogues are full of Socrates being provocative and of his interlocutors being provoked. Indeed Plato's Socrates seems to have a talent for provoking people just by *being* there, without doing anything at all. Laches and Nicias, Theaetetus and Theodorus, Aristodemus and Appolodorus are enthralled; Thrasymachus and Polus, however, Callicles, Protagoras, Anytus and Alcibiades all become positively exasperated with Socrates – with his questions, his plainness, his directness, his unflustered pursuit of the argument and refusal to bluster.

Plato's dialogue form enacts that frustration. It reveals how it is not just Socrates' questions that are exasperating, but the way he *actually listens* for an answer. Undistracted by the ordinary concerns of ego and esteem, if Socrates asks a question, he simply listens for the answer and takes that answer seriously. But that is just not the done thing. At a dinner party, or a casual encounter in the corridor or on the street or at the gym, you expect a certain sort of polite chit-chat – you might make any old throwaway remark in full confidence that it would be just that: thrown away. So it doesn't really matter what you say, and you need not consider what you actually think.

But with Socrates it is not like that. He asks what you think – and then listens to your reply as if you actually *meant* what you said. His focus on what really matters never wanes; he cannot be flattered into letting a point go if it is an important one, because he genuinely is not trying to score points or be liked. Since he values only the attainment of a shared and true understanding of what really matters, there is no place conversationally for his interlocutor to hide. No matter how banal or trivial the conversation may start out, before you know it, you are having to give an account of yourself, your way of life, your choices (*Laches* 187e–188b, *Theaetetus* 169a–b[3]). And although it may just be a chat between friends, the accounting of oneself – and the prospect of failure – are very real, and very serious. Because Socrates holds firmly within the shared conversational space the paramount importance of truth and goodness, what is at stake is not the mere social standing that usually distracts us, but one's value in one's own eyes – one's ability to be straight with oneself and look oneself in the eye, so to speak.[4]

That Socrates has this effect on people is explained in the same way that his strange goodness itself is explained: he has fully united his whole soul and oriented everything around goodness. The effect itself is conveyed through the dialogue form. This form reiterates the effect in the relationship Plato establishes between the text and the reader. Readers are often *provoked* by Socrates, one way or another – not by Xenophon's Socrates, but by Plato's. They are unsettled, annoyed, indignant, frustrated, sometimes stimulated, inspired, agitated. Suddenly, they are no longer satisfied, for Socrates' single-mindedness reveals their own actions and choices as possibly corrupt or compromised. Sometimes, like the Sophists, they try to put that dissatisfaction onto Socrates (*he* is being ironic, *he* is being arrogant, *he* is like this or like that, fully warranting my annoyance); sometimes, they recognize the dissatisfaction is with themselves, with their own inability to come up with a better account of things that they themselves know are of utmost importance. The portrait Plato offers us of Socrates is at the same time a portrait of integrity under construction, and revision and rejection, as it challenges the reader to forego a natural complacency, hypocrisy and pride in order to recognize her own psychic disintegration.

Recommended reading

Hackett publishes readable and reliable translations of Plato's dialogues into English, separately or collected together in the *Complete Works* (John Cooper, ed.). Plato's depiction of Socrates' character comes across especially strongly in his *Apology*; but see also the *Charmides* and *Phaedrus*. Plato's *Gorgias*, *Symposium*, and Book I of the *Republic* depict prominently the provocative effect he had on others. The *Republic* – especially books VI to IX – are the *locus classicus* for Plato's analysis of virtue as the integration of an otherwise conflicted soul; the *Phaedus*' famous chariot analogy vividly presents the same idea. Hannah Arendt captures well the uncanniness and moral significance of Plato's Socrates in 'Thinking and Moral Considerations', §II, *Social Research* 51 (1984). Alexander Nehamas offers searching discussion of the layers of provocation in Plato's use of Socrates, in 'Platonic Irony' (*Art of Living*, University of California Press, 1998, Ch. 1). M. M. McCabe's '"It goes deep with me": Plato's *Charmides* on Knowledge, Self-Knowledge and Integrity' (in Craig Taylor and Melinda

Graefe (eds), *A Sense for Humanity* Monash University, 2014) insightfully explores Socrates' integrity; essays collected in R. Barney, Tad Brennen and Charles Brittain (eds), *Plato and the Divided Self* (Cambridge: Cambridge University Press, 2012) explore the disintegrated *psychē* in Plato.

Notes

1 If the *Phaedo* depicts this otherwise – as conflict between body and soul, rather than conflict within the soul – this distinction is not significant here. In the *Phaedo* it is the bodily *pleasures* that are the sorcerers (81b 'bewitched'), and cause the confusion about goodness and the bad action which follows from that (*Phaedo* 82, rivets). The phenomenology of conflict is as present in the *Phaedo* as in the *Republic*.

2 The account in this paragraph and the next draws primarily from the *Republic*. But the allegory of the charioteer with a white and a black horse, from the *Phaedrus*, and the exchange with Callicles in the *Gorgias* prominently display different parts of this picture.

3 Interestingly, in the classic places where this is explicitly thematized, it is Socrates' *friends* who report this phenomenon. Rossbach (this volume) describes how conversation with Socrates was 'like being rubbed against a touchstone (187E–188B), making it impossible to hide the truth of one's life'. His discussion of the effect of Gandhi's presence on others bears a strong similarity to features highlighted about Plato's Socrates here.

4 See the anguish Plato puts in the voice of the brilliant Alcibiades – finest flower of Athens, and her most notorious traitor (*Symposium* 215c-216a).

2

Boethius

Integrity as attunement to reality

Matthew Maguire

To live a life of integrity in a stubbornly imperfect world often seems to ask for the squaring of a circle. No one gave more precise expression to that troubling perception than Anicius Manlius Severinus Boethius (AD 480–525/6). Yet he did not stop with acknowledging the challenges of ethical and existential geometry: for him, the only solution for living a life of integrity in an imperfect world is to affirm not a circle of righteous self-enclosure, but a circle that both transcends the self and sets it in ongoing and constant relation to a living and infinite reality, evoked simultaneously in poetic creation and reasoned argument.

Born to an illustrious Roman family as the Western Empire slowly disintegrated, Boethius became a remarkably successful scholar and public servant. While he was still in the prime of life, both his sons were made consuls of the Empire on the same day, even as he himself held an important office under the barbarian emperor Theodoric. Enjoying civic prestige, abundant wealth and political power were only a few of his blessings. He was a philosopher of prodigious learning, at ease in both Greek and Latin and a translator of Aristotle, as well as a writer on philosophy, music and theology. If that were not enough, he enjoyed a happy family life. Boethius must count among those most favoured by fortune in his age or any other. His position in Roman life might be compared to that of a fairly young Regius Professor at Oxford who also serves as a major adviser to the prime minister, and enjoys the boon of domestic happiness. Yet he abruptly lost all of it.

The circumstances are clouded by time and Boethius' rapid exit from the scene. He appears to have upheld the prerogatives of the Roman Senate – and established Roman families – against the emperor and his allies; more controversially, he may have worked with the emperor in Constantinople to undercut and perhaps to depose the barbarian emperor in Rome. These are all more or less conjectures, complicated by religious questions – Theodoric was an Arian Christian, and Boethius was an orthodox Christian. Whatever the exact circumstances that precipitated his fall from favour, he was arrested and imprisoned hundreds of miles from Rome; his extraordinary good fortune was at a sudden and definitive end. Apparently unsure of his ultimate fate – he would be clubbed to death – he languished in his cell, tormented by thoughts that his life had been laid waste not for any wrong he had done, but precisely because he had tried to act justly, to fulfil his civic duty regardless of cost. The wages of integrity were his ruin.

It was in these circumstances – behind bars and possibly without books – that Boethius composed *The Consolation of Philosophy*. Its influence on thinking about living a life of whole-souled commitment to the good was extraordinary, with Boethius exalted as an example of integrity exceeded by very few, among them Socrates and Christ. *The Consolation* drew admiring reference from Chaucer and from Dante; for over a millennium, Boethius' images and metaphors became part of a shared idiom for thinking about how the self finds its unity in virtue.

Yet how can such a virtuous unity be lived? It would take a rash reading of the text to accuse Boethius of wishing away its difficulties. In a poem at the outset of the *Consolation*, Boethius writes of how he is tortured by his suffering, and that death would be preferable to his present disgrace – yet does not come to him. Soon he is greeted by a woman personifying Philosophy, at once young and old, small and then suddenly grand like a goddess. In a book without explicit reference to revelation, references to the divine start early, and remarkably include Boethius' own reflection that his past life of astonishing success was that of a god.

Yet now he lives confined, in exile and disgrace. He laments that the gifts of fortune have been taken away because of his goodness, while opportunistic and evil persons prosper. Most people, he says, inevitably take sides with the successful, and when they are no longer so, they impute fault to the victim of personal misfortune: 'It is always the unfortunate who are first to be deserted by the goodwill of men.' Somehow, the victims are to blame for their suffering, and Boethius claims to know from recent experience that human beings easily succumb to a conviction that those who suffer individually in some way deserve it. The evidence for these claims is so widely available that for Boethius, to assert them is enough for the evidence to appear in one's own life.

Philosophy will have none of his despair, even as she agrees with his decidedly dry-eyed observations about the all-too-common bases of human judgement and behaviour. She tells him that he has lost himself, and that is his greatest misfortune. He has indulged in a poetry of lament that magnifies his sorrows rather than soothing them. A life of integrity will, it seems, be inevitably displeasing to those who live by material and social desires.

Philosophy asks Boethius why he laments the loss of the goods of fortune. Power, fame, money, pleasure, status; all of these admittedly answer to deep desires within us. But like our very existence, they are not truly ours. They can be taken from us with ease and at any moment, and maintaining them requires constant care. The loss of good fortune simply shows us what fortune is – perpetually and uncontrollably inconstant. Human beings who seek the goods of fortune above all live upon a wheel of fortune (an image that Boethius did not invent, but popularized). Fortune can tantalize us with the material and social satisfactions for which we yearn, and raise us near the top of her wheel; but it is in the nature of wheels to turn, and inevitably, our anxious hopes and still more frantic expedients to maintain our good fortune do us no good, as the wheel descends. If Boethius is offering a kind of philosophical therapy to his readers, it is not the kind of therapy that offers some technique for acquiring the political, material and social blessings of life, as one would later find variously in Francis Bacon or Machiavelli. It is an integral part of Boethius' argument that wealth, position, power, pleasure and similar goods of fortune do not deliver what they promise even when good fortune appears to be ours. Far from insulating its beneficiaries from care and sensitivity to failure, worldly success makes one more anxious and sensitive to suffering. Furthermore, our desires for good fortune are insatiable; the notion that we would enjoy a continuous fullness of being were we to acquire some sought-after position, attachment, income, or status is an illusion of those very desires that beguiles us and leads us to live ever more completely under their sway. Even posthumous fame for leading virtuous lives – which Boethius might have plausibly hoped to aspire, even in his prison cell – accomplishes very little, for 'Where lies unbending Cato, Brutus, where?/ A little fame lives on inscribed in stone, a line or two of empty reputation:/we know their splendid names but not their selves.'

At times Philosophy administers her 'medicine' to Boethius with an excessively Stoic astringency; he is enjoined not to count even the gifts of a happy family life as ultimately satisfying, or properly his own – though she acknowledges that with his wife's constant love and her grief at his misfortune, there is 'one thing in which I would concede that your happiness is diminished'. Nonetheless, Boethius is expressly advised by Philosophy that the cure for his suffering requires that he 'rid [him]self of joy and fear/put hope to flight', for 'if first you rid yourself of hope and fear' you are free. There are kinder words for friendship than for power, for example, but really any hope or happiness found in relations to other human beings and the created world appears to be an illusion, best dispensed with dispatch. A 'whole-souled self' – that is, a person with integrity – finds happiness supremely in the intellectual ascent to God and the reasoned practice of virtue that necessarily accompanies it. Boethius takes care to affirm that we are free to ascend towards this true and reasoned happiness through virtue, but it appears to involve an ascent *from* creation, rather than a relational participation *in* that creation. In this way, the *Consolation* appears to offer the consolations most appealing to an exacting martinet of the soul.

Certainly Boethius' account of a virtuous life has often been read as one of hard demands etched in granite, a thoroughgoing repudiation of not only the pleasures and hopes but (as Philosophy says directly) of the joys of life and with them, of other people. As a model of integrity, Boethius can thus easily serve as one of the early testimonials for a broadly shared if not always articulated sense that integrity is a moral ambition for cold, remote souls, quick to renounce evil but not to love their fellow creatures, in which a rigorously reasoned detachment supplants the love of neighbour, the living self encased and hence immobilized in an invulnerable adamantine rectitude.

Indeed, there is something of this sort of integrity in Boethius' own account of his life, and of what consolation is available to us in our suffering. But one reads him very incompletely if one reads him only as one of several ancient exemplars of austere moral grandeur, one made perhaps rather uncertain by the possibility that his political decisions were not quite as unambiguous as he presents them.

Lady Philosophy began by lamenting Boethius' turn to the poetry of lament; yet she is also a poet. Her poetry recalls Boethius not away from creation, but towards it in a different way, specifically to the objective and beautiful order of the cosmos, the magnificent, revolving array of stars, planets and seasons, no less circular but infinitely exceeding the self-centring ambit of fortune's wheel. Even in the first Book, it is 'the Creator of the starry heavens,/Lord on thy everlasting throne,/Thy power turns the moving sky/and makes the stars obey fixed laws.' The beauty of the universe in motion, in seasons, in stars, intimates the love that continuously animates all being and beings. In Book II, change is constant, but it has a beautiful – and only superficially impersonal – harmony: 'And all this chain of things/in earth and sea and sky/One ruler holds in hand:/ If Love relaxed the reins/All things that now keep peace/ Would wage continual war/And wreck the great machine/Which unity maintains/With motions beautiful.'

At this point in the *Consolation*, Boethius has asked us to consider two circles: the Wheel of Fortune, and the cosmic cycles of nature around us in earth and the heavens. For Boethius, we must trust that the impersonal beauty of earth and sky reveals a universal, ultimate and infinite love, however imperfectly our individual lives and the lives of our communities participate in it; that anything at all *is*, and rationally and beautifully so, is the primal origin of gratitude, which precedes and supervenes any discontent with 'the way things are'. With the exception of a single citation from the Book of Wisdom, throughout the *Consolation*, Boethius avoids biblical citations in favour of a philosophical defence of a life of integrity. But to do so, he unmistakably has recourse to the notion that sun and rain fall equally upon the just and the unjust, and that is not a refutation of God's love for his creatures, but testimony to it.

Boethius remains torn, however, and in Book II of the *Consolation*, Philosophy warns Boethius that the beauty of the world can easily come to be seen as if it were our possession, whereas all we can truly possess is our own virtue. Philosophy, in the same book, claims in prose that true goods are those that are not diminished by being shared, so that generosity is superior to the accumulation of goods. All the beauty of nature, however, and the sharing of its bounty 'are of an inferior rank to you as a more excellent creature, and cannot in any way merit your admiration'.

Boethius goes further as the *Consolation* continues, following Plato's arguments in the *Gorgias*. He claims that injustice and wickedness make people unhappy, and all the more so if they are not punished. To be happy is to be unambiguously aligned with divine love and the good. That happiness is alone worthy of the name, rather than a consuming avidity for material and social surfaces, or the gratification of a momentary vanity; that consuming, self-regarding anticipation of satisfaction can be enjoyed by the unjust, even the vicious consists.

In this we find the unmistakable impress of certain themes with great resonance in ancient philosophy, especially Platonism. The Good is one, and all instances of good participate in that supreme Good; the rational soul of human beings is the highest good of creatures and creation. If Philosophy's poetry allows room for the beauty of creation, and she is willing to concede philosophically the value of some creaturely love, it remains her firm contention that the rational soul's adhesion to the fullness of good in God is the true happiness, to which earthly fortune is entirely irrelevant, and earthly attachments mostly so.

We seem to have returned to the uneasy feeling that integrity requires a kind of enclosure that to many people does not feel entirely human – not just in relation to our creaturely needs and limitations, but in relation to our most admirable creaturely calling and possibilities. Boethius can thus appear to be among the purveyors of syllogisms depending upon a unity of meaning (for words like 'good'), for example, that does not survive later developments in the philosophy of language, or the notions of competing goods and variable 'values' that comes so naturally to the inhabitants of post-nominalist, philosophically liberal and contractual orders of political economy, social life and thinking.

Yet for Boethius – unlike Plato, for example – it is indispensable that the ultimate Good is not an impersonal form, but a personal being that loves us, even if that love finds expression in an objective rigour sometimes quite different from creaturely love, a rigour that could only be wielded without corruption by a being endowed with infinite intellect, before whose gaze all possible outcomes are present, and in which past, present and future alike are open. Divine intellect works within dimensions of understanding beyond those available to any human being, dimensions in which unity and multiplicity are infinitely reconciled. To align oneself with that love is finally not to be encased in one's own rectitude, but to revolve the thoughts and actions of one's life around the love that animates all, rather than to revolve them around the goods of fortune, and at their worst, the goods of fortune as a means to our own aggrandizement, in which we intend for the created order to revolve around ourselves.

To achieve the transition from revolving around self to revolving around God and the Good requires an openness to what transcends ourselves – that Boethius the author speaks of figuratively when urging his readers to 'look up' – that also requires an intention and an effort to seek the upward journey. For Boethius, we are awakened for that journey of reason towards love not simply by some abstemious inward resolve, but by attending rigorously to creation made by love, and here Philosophy the poet and Philosophy the purveyor of argument come at last to a full agreement. By Book V, the penultimate poem of the *Consolation*, living creation evokes the intellect that seeks transcendence, for

> When comes this powerful understanding/That all things sees and all discerns?/... passivity in things/that live precedes the calling forth/And stirring of the power of mind;/As when light strikes upon the eye/Or voices clatter in the ear:/The active power of mind then roused/Calls forth the species from within/ to motions of a similar kind.

The way towards the Good in Boethius is hence neither mummified in immobility, nor loveless, nor without need for other beings and nature. It includes conversation with others and within oneself, and relations to the world, to open the participation of the intellect with creation, and ultimately with its creator. At the last, this is the hope that Philosophy, speaking in prose, can commend rather than asking for hope's abandonment. At the conclusion of the *Consolation*, the reader is told that God 'constantly adapts' to 'the future quality of our actions', respecting our freedom, loving us always. In this way, 'Hope is not placed in God in vain and prayers are not made in vain, for if they are the right kind they cannot but be efficacious.' If we, as Philosophy the poet puts it, can raise our 'head upon high' we may stand freely upon the earth without being earthbound: we 'can stand with body upright and disdain the ground', a strength to stand drawn at once from Philosophy's demands and the aesthetic and impassioned ministrations of verse. In this early exemplar of integrity, we find that the way of integrity is, indeed, hard; yet with its rigour, Boethius comes to understand that integrity requires multiple, harmonious, affectionate and self-transcending relations beyond ourselves, to seek out and live what is good without reserve.

Recommended reading

Margaret Gibson (ed.), *Boethius: His Life, Thought, and Influence* (Oxford: Blackwell, 1981), offers a helpful, wide-ranging and erudite introduction to its subjects. Douglas Langston (ed.), *The Consolation of Philosophy: A Norton Critical Edition* (New York: W. W. Norton and Co., 2010), includes helpful notes and a well-chosen sampling of scholarly essays and interpretation. C. S. Lewis, *The Discarded Image* (Cambridge: Cambridge University Press, 1964), gives the reader a vivid, learned account of the cosmological, philosophical and psychological horizons of the pre-modern West, and offers some insightful accounts of the *Consolation* specifically. Finally, John Marenbon (ed.), *The Cambridge Companion to Boethius* (Cambridge: Cambridge University Press, 2009), is an important introduction to relatively recent scholarship addressed to Boethius, including his diverse writings on logic, philosophy and theology.

3

Rāma

The imperfections of the perfect man in the Vālmīki *Rāmāyaṇa*

Emily T. Hudson

The Vālmīki *Rāmāyaṇa* is one of the most popular stories ever told. Countless retellings of the story have dominated the religions, art and literature, as well as the social and political thought of much of Asia for over two thousand years. One reason for the epic's enormous popularity is that it tells the story of the morally perfect human being: Rāma. The epic overtly presents Rāma as the ideal son, husband and king, and his behaviour has served as a model for countless generations of people living in the South Asian cultural complex and beyond. Indeed, with the possible exception of the Buddha, Rāma is the pre-eminent example of what may be described as integrity in the South Asian literary tradition.

In addition to telling one of the most popular stories ever composed, the Vālmīki *Rāmāyaṇa* has another claim to fame: it is considered by the Indian tradition to be the very first work of narrative poetry (*kāvya*). But what precisely is *kāvya*? According to Daniel Ingalls, *kāvya* is that which holds the interest of the audience through the evocation of mood (*rasa*) or suggestion (*dhvani*) rather than through plot. Another way to put this is that understanding how *kāvya* works entails distinguishing between two levels of meaning: the literal (what the text says) and the suggested (how what the text says engages the emotions of the audience), and seeing the second level as the most important. In what follows, we will investigate the text's depiction of Rāma's integrity in light of these two levels of meaning. While it is clear that the literal level depicts Rāma as a paragon of integrity, a careful reading of the text reveals that the suggested level characterizes him in a different manner.

The Vālmīki *Rāmāyaṇa* begins when the ascetic Vālmīki, the author of the text, asks a seer named Nārada if there is a human being in the world who is truly virtuous. Nārada declares that there is such a person and that person is Rāma. Nārada continues, 'All men know of him, for he is self-controlled, steadfast, and masterful' (1.1.8).[1] After extolling Rāma's virtues, Nārada summarizes the entire story of Rāma including the following episodes: Rāma's banishment from the kingdom of Ayodhyā on the eve of his coronation; his departure to the forest accompanied by his wife Sītā; Sītā's abduction by the *rākṣasa* (ogre) Rāvaṇa; Rāma's defeat of Rāvaṇa and recovery of Sītā; and finally the return of Rāma to Ayodhyā where he is crowned king.

Additionally, Rāma is praised for his moral perfection throughout the text. In the first two books alone, the narrative voice devotes twenty-five stanzas to enumerating Rāma's many virtues. Additionally, characters repeatedly extol Rāma's truthfulness, self-discipline and equanimity, and Rāma himself professes that he has one concern and that is with *dharma*, or righteousness. While there is no Sanskrit term for 'integrity', what emerges from the statements is a fairly straightforward notion of the concept. According to its dictionary definition, integrity means 'soundness of moral principle', 'uprightness' and 'honesty'. Likewise, as it is associated with Rāma in the Vālmīki *Rāmāyaṇa*, integrity involves firmness, sticking to one's principles and control of one's emotions. It is also closely associated with the concept of *dharma*. While Rāma interprets *dharma* as consisting almost exclusively of truth-telling and obedience to his father, what the text ultimately says about *dharma* remains open to question.

Paradoxically, despite the consistent statements affirming Rāma's moral perfection in the text, Rāma repeatedly behaves in morally problematic ways. Two types of ethically questionable actions pertain to Rāma: (1) actions that are explicitly presented as morally reprehensible and (2) actions that are called into question at the 'suggested' level of the text. Both types of acts serve to undermine the audience's confidence in Rāma's status as a moral exemplar, but, for the most part, only the first type has captured the attention of modern scholars of the text. However, it is the second type that is the most damning with respect to the text's own claims concerning Rāma's perfection.

With respect to the first type, three episodes stand out: Rāma's slaying of the monkey king Vālin in a dishonourable manner; Rāma's cruel rejection of his wife Sītā after his defeat of Rāvaṇa; and Rāma's decision to abandon Sītā in the forest after he learns that she is pregnant. These episodes are marked by three common features: (1) strikingly egregious behaviour by Rāma, (2) characters in the story who express their disapproval, and (3) justifications provided by Rāma that are unconvincing or unsatisfactory. For example, Rāma angrily rebukes Sītā after his defeat of Rāvaṇa by informing her that since she has lived in the house of another man, he wants nothing to do with her (6.103.19-21). The narrative voice explicitly calls into question Rāma's behaviour by noting that characters in the story are troubled by Rāma's treatment of Sītā here (6.103.25). Further, Rāma's justification for his behaviour is notably unsatisfactory: He professes that he rejected Sītā because he feared a public scandal. In short, Rāma admits that he treated Sītā cruelly solely for political expediency, a reason that explains his behaviour but does *not* put to rest the moral concerns it raises.

Turning to the second type of morally problematic acts, ones that are called into question by the text's suggestions, it becomes apparent that once we scrutinize Rāma at this level, virtually *every* act he commits from Book 3 onwards is morally questionable. Let us take a look at one of the virtues for which he is most famous and which is closely associated with his purported integrity: self-control. We will consider briefly what the text does with it at the suggested level.

The paradigmatic example of Rāma's perfect control of his emotions occurs in Book 2, when Kaikeyī, Rāma's stepmother, summons him to inform him on the eve of his coronation that due to a promise that his father Daśaratha had made to her, he, Rāma, must leave the kingdom at once and live in the forest for fourteen years. Rāma, without a trace of emotion, proclaims, 'So be it, I shall go away to live in the forest to protect the promise of the king' (2.16.28). With regard to Rāma's status as a moral exemplar, his reaction has been viewed by the tradition as a moment that frames all other moments involving his moral behaviour. For example, the noted scholar Robert Goldman writes, 'Rāma's unemotional acquiescence to his wrongful disinheritance marks the central moment of the epic, and it is this willing renunciation of this inheritance and apparently perfect control of his emotions that is the reason for the enormous esteem in which he is held.'[2]

Keeping Goldman's statement in mind, we are surprised to discover that from Book 3 onwards, Rāma is subject to almost total loss of self-control. For example, at the end of Book 3, Rāma loses control when he learns that Sītā has been kidnapped by Rāvaṇa. He excessively laments her loss, angrily rebukes Lakṣmaṇa for leaving her alone in the hermitage, and in a fit of madness threatens to destroy the universe. In Book 4, he laments his separation from Sītā on three different occasions, and in Book 6, as previously mentioned, when he is reunited with Sītā after the war, he angrily tells her he wants nothing to do with her 'with rage in his heart' (6.103.1). Finally, in Book 7 after Sītā enters the earth and disappears forever, he grieves and threatens to destroy the earth.

Confoundingly, even though the text consistently shows us that Rāma is no longer a master of his senses from Book 3 onwards, it never explicitly declares that Rāma has lost control of himself. Perhaps because neither characters nor the narrative explicitly draw attention to Rāma's sudden shift in behaviour coupled with the fact that the text virtually hits us over the head with the idea that he is the perfect *dharma*-knowing person, this second type of morally problematic behaviour on the part of Rāma has gone virtually undetected by modern scholars of the text.[3] However, if we take into account *both* types of problematic actions – explicit *and* suggested – then an inescapable conclusion follows: the text is deliberately undermining its own claim concerning Rāma's moral perfection. But why would it promise us a moral paragon only to call it into question? And what does calling into question its promised exemplar have to do with what the text is really saying about integrity, if anything?

To answer these questions, I want to take us on two very brief detours, one into Sanskrit literary theory, where we will deepen our understanding of how *kāvya* works, and the other into the

Rāmāyana's own reflections on itself as a work of literature. According to perhaps the most influential thinker in the tradition of Sanskrit literary theory, Ānandavardhana, the *Rāmāyana* is a pre-eminent example of narrative poetry (*kāvya*) because it conveys meaning through suggestion. How does suggested meaning become apparent if it is not directly stated? Ānanda likened the appearance of the suggestion to the resonance of a bell after it is struck. First comes the stroke by which the literal meaning of the word enters the mind. Then, the mind is suddenly aware of something related but distinct – an overtone or suggestion. For Ānanda, the most important messages of a work of literature are delivered through suggestion.

There are two points worth underscoring: First, according to Ānandavardhana, suggested meaning is *not* located on the page. It takes place in the mind of the sensitive audience member, the '*sahṛdaya*' (literally 'the with-hearted audience member').[4] Second, the suggested meaning of a work of literary art may be the opposite of the literal meaning.

Now for our second brief detour, let us return to the prologue where the epic offers an important clue as to how it functions as a work of literature. I have already mentioned that the *Rāmāyaṇa* begins with a prologue in which Vālmīki asks Nārada the question 'Is there a person who is truly virtuous?' Shortly after, Vālmīki goes to bathe in the Tamasā River. As he is bathing, he sees a pair of birds mating. Suddenly, a hunter, hiding in a blind, shoots the male bird. When the female bird sees the bloody body of her mate writhing on the ground, she utters a heartbreaking cry. As Vālmīki hears the cry of grief from the female bird, compassion (*kāruṇyam*) wells up in him. From the intensity of his compassion, he utters a curse which is in verse. This verse is the very first line of poetry according to the *Rāmāyaṇa*.

In this scene, Vālmīki's compassion caused by hearing the cry of grief (*śoka*) of the female bird gives birth to the metre of lyric poetry (*śloka*), and the proximity of the two terms (*śoka*, grief and *śloka*, a kind of poetic metre) is intentional. Further, Vālmīki composes the entire story of the *Rāmāyaṇa* in this *śloka* metre. The fact that the emotion of grief is transmuted through Vālmīki's compassionate response into a poetic metre, the metre in which the entire *Rāmāyaṇa* is composed, implies that sorrow is at the very base of the entire *Rāmāyaṇa*. To hit home just how important grief is in the text, the word *śoka* appears ninety-four times in Book 2 alone.

Thus, the *Rāmāyaṇa's* prologue clues us in to the fact that the *Rāmāyaṇa* is about two themes that seem to be at cross purposes. On the one hand, the opening scene where Vālmīki asks his famous question and Nārada gives his famous answer sets the audience up to expect a straightforward tale about a moral exemplar. However, the prologue's subsequent scene where Vālmīki's empathetic response to the crane episode gives birth to the metre of the poem alerts its audiences to the fact that the central aesthetic-emotive tenor of the text will be that of grief. These two scenes taken together raise an essential question: Why would a text about the perfect *dharma*-knowing human being be told in such a way as to evoke sorrow?

Let us return to our original question: Why would the text give us a moral paragon only to call it into question? Knowing the text's intense interest in the emotion of grief, let us very briefly turn to the text's most heartbreaking scene: Rāma's rejection of Sītā after he has defeated Rāvaṇa. By turning to this scene, I want to highlight not only Rāma's cruel treatment of Sītā but also the immense work that the text does in the episodes leading up to this scene to encourage its audience to expect one outcome, namely that Rāma will be overjoyed to see Sītā, and what it delivers on the other.

I have already alluded to Rāma's descent into grief in response to the abduction of Sītā in the context of arguing that the text implicitly undermines its own claim concerning Rāma's self-control. Now, I want to return to this component of Rāma's characterization for a different reason. I want to focus on the expectations that Rāma's many expressions of grief create in the audience. Rāma's laments in Books 3–6 are heartbreaking. Rāma delivers more than ten lengthy laments in these books over his separation from Sītā. Two things are noteworthy about these laments. First, Rāma's grief over his separation from Sītā *never* wanes. Second, the text does not provide one hint that Rāma is concerned with public opinion and that he will reject Sītā. Therefore, we see that the text, through its depiction of a ceaselessly lamenting Rāma, is carefully manipulating its audience to expect a specific narrative outcome, namely that Rāma will be overjoyed when he is reunited with Sītā.

Therefore, the moment of Rāma and Sītā's reunion is the singular dramatic event in the text. It is the moment where the fact that the text has worked hard to set the audience up to expect one outcome coalesces with the fact that it delivers something quite different. Given the innumerable laments that the audience has heard Rāma utter, it is utterly shocking to witness him first laying eyes on Sītā and exhibiting not joy but anger. Even more shocking are the harsh words that Rāma speaks to Sītā informing her that he won her back solely to protect the reputation of his lineage, and that since her virtue is now in question, her presence is disagreeable to him, and she should go wherever she likes (*Rāmāyaṇa*, 6.103.15-21).

This moment is a revelatory one in the text. While Rāma has disappointed the audience's expectations of him before, here the emotions of the audience have been carefully manipulated so that the heart and not just the mind is invested in Rāma's reaction to Sītā. Therefore, Rāma's behaviour is not merely disappointing. In watching him break Sītā's heart, he breaks our hearts. And it is in this breaking of the heart that the disjuncture between what the text has explicitly promised and what it actually delivers is experienced to the fullest.

What then is the purpose of the compromised moral exemplar in the Vālmīki *Rāmāyaṇa* and what does it have to do with what the text is ultimately communicating about integrity? By promising to give its audience members a moral exemplar and then superficially giving them one at the literal level only to call it into question at the suggested level, the text points its sensitive audience members (the *sahṛdaya*-s) in the direction of where its real messages about *dharma* and integrity lie. This process of giving and then calling into question creates a space in the audience for intense moral reflection. This space encourages the audience to realize that the crux of the matter lies in the following question: If Rāma is the morally perfect person, then why is he the source of so much separation and sorrow? For example, consider the consequences of his fateful decision to go to the forest: it kills his father, brings suffering to his mother, and places his brother and wife in vulnerable positions that culminate in the kidnapping of Sītā. Once the text's sensitive audience members come to this realization, they are engaged in the kinds of moral questions that the text's suggestive elements encourage. They realize that the crux of the matter is not only what Rāma *does*, but also what he fails to do. They realize that it is not only the attributes present in Rāma's character that are the ethical centre of the text, but also those attributes that are absent in him.

What exactly is absent in Rāma's character? Two points are relevant. First, when one is reading the *Rāmāyaṇa*, one cannot avoid being struck by how much quiet attention the text devotes to minor characters advising other characters to think carefully about the actions that they plan to take, factoring in the relevant contextual variables, and weighing the consequences of each option *and* its potential ill effects. When one places these instances of advice on the part of peripheral characters in the quiet moments of the text next to the 'louder' scenes depicting the central protagonist Rāma making the fateful decisions that he does, one realizes that one type of action that is absent in Rāma is deliberation. Rāma's so-called integrity is based on an adherence to a rigid set of formalistic principles, and based on these, he makes blind decisions whose consequences are almost always disastrous for those dear to him.

Second, in promising to deliver a story about a moral exemplar at the literal level and then delivering something quite different at the suggested level, the text carefully engages the emotions of its sensitive or 'with-hearted' audience members. When Rāma cruelly rejects Sītā, the audience is encouraged to feel distance towards Rāma and compassion towards Sītā. Compassion, according to the Sanskrit literary theorists, is the dominant mood (*rasa*) of the Vālmīki *Rāmāyaṇa*. It is what the sensitive audience members of the text feel when they engage with the emotions of grief expressed by the characters.[5] Remember that when Vālmīki witnessed the painful scene of the hunter killing the male bird and heard the sorrowful cry of the female bird, he was overwhelmed with compassion and this led to the birth of the *śloka* metre. Similarly, the painful separations of fathers from sons, brothers from brothers, and wives from husbands that dominate the narrative are carefully orchestrated to engender this same emotion in us. Indeed, the prologue provides a model for how the with-hearted audience member is supposed to emotionally react to the poem.

Where then do the *Rāmāyaṇa*'s real messages about integrity lie and what precisely are they? At the literal level, the text presents its audience with a portrait of a man who possesses a high degree of integrity precisely because he sticks to his principles no matter what the cost. For example, when Rāma reacts with calm acceptance to the news of his banishment, he does so because he feels bound by his most cherished moral principles: truth-telling and obedience to his father. Therefore, he spends no time assessing the situation before he agrees to go to the forest, even though the fate of virtually every character in the book hangs in the balance. However, the text makes it clear that there were many factors going into the banishment order, making the situation far more complicated than Rāma's cut and dried assessment allowed. Indeed, the text implicitly criticizes Rāma's rigidity and coldness, aspects that are closely associated with his purported integrity. By showing the audience that Rāma's unyielding commitment to his principles has turned his heart to stone, the text provides a suggested argument that awakens its audience to a deeper understanding of integrity, which involves sensitivity, compassion and flexible, contextual thinking.

Finally, it must be underscored that the form of this argument is as important as its messages. The text does not spoon-feed its ideas about integrity. Instead, it makes its sensitive audience members work for their insights, thus requiring a kind of integrity in them. What the *Rāmāyaṇa* is ultimately saying about integrity does not exist in any five lines of the text. It exists rather in the opened, compassionate heart and activated, attentive and flexible mind of the with-hearted audience member.

Recommended reading

Goldman (Princeton University Press, 1984–2016) offers a full English translation of the Critical Edition of the Vālmīki *Rāmāyaṇa* and a general overview and introduction to each book by noted scholars in the field. Sattar (Penguin Global, 2003) is an abridged readable translation of the text that is a great place to start for newcomers to the story. Shulman (Oxford University Press, 2001) offers an excellent and sensitive discussion of the literary features of the *Vālmīki Rāmāyaṇa*, and Ingalls (Belknap Press of Harvard University, 1968) provides a brilliant introduction to Sanskrit literary theory.

Notes

1 All citations refer specifically to the Vālmīki *Rāmāyaṇa*. All translations of the text are based on G. H. Bhatt and U. P. Shah (gen. eds), *The Vālmīki Rāmāyaṇa: Critical Edition*. 7 vols. (Baroda: Oriental Institute, 1960–1975). I closely follow the translations of Robert P. Goldman (gen. ed.), *The Rāmāyaṇa of Vālmīki: An Epic of Ancient India*. 7 vols. (Princeton, NJ: Princeton University Press, 1984–2016).

2 Robert P. Goldman (trans.), *The Rāmāyaṇa of Vālmīki*, vol. 1: *Balakāṇḍa* (Princeton: Princeton University Press, 1990), 50.
3 Notable exceptions are Sheldon Pollock, 'Rāma's Madness', in Sheldon Pollock (trans.), *The Rāmāyaṇa of Vālmīki: An Epic of Ancient India*, vol. 3. (Princeton, NJ: Princeton University Press, 1984–2016), 55–67; Arshia Sattar, *Lost Loves: Exploring Rama's Anguish* (London: Penguin Books, 2011).
4 For a discussion of the role of the sensitive audience member in the apprehension of *dhvani*, see Emily T. Hudson, *Disorienting Dharma: Ethics and Aesthetics in the Mahābhārata* (New York: Oxford University Press, 2013), 56.
5 For an excellent discussion of *rasa*, see Daniel H. H. Ingalls, 'General Introduction', in *Sanskrit Poetry from Vidyākara's Treasury* (Cambridge: Belknap Press of Harvard University, 1968). For an insightful discussion of the poetics of the Vālmīki *Rāmāyaṇa*, see David Shulman, 'Towards a Historical Poetics of the Sanskrit Epics', in *The Wisdom of the Poets* (New Delhi and New York: Oxford University Press, 2001).

4

Antigone

Staging integrity through sorority

Valentina Moro

Antigone is probably the most famous female character of Sophocles' dramas. The eponymous play has become a staple in the critical literature of many fields. As Sophocles' play opens, Antigone's uncle, Creon, acting as the king of Thebes allows the mourning and burial of only one of Antigone's two dead brothers. By doing so, Creon introduces to the public gaze two opposed characters: the hero who fought for the collective (Etheocles) and the public enemy who put the *polis* at risk (Polynices). His aim is to put an end to an awful civil war by inviting the citizens of Thebes to celebrate the soldiers who fought for them and to disgrace the memory of those who, despite belonging to the same community, battled against them. For Creon, the unburied body of Polynices should be an exemplary reminder for the citizens to be loyal to the State. The king claims that such a distinction between the friend and the enemy has to be made for the sake of the city. Moreover, Creon's law also constitutes the common good: obedience to it signals membership in the new community. In defiance of the king's edict, Antigone decides to bury Polynices and tries to convince her sister Ismene to help her. Ismene refuses, so Antigone acts alone. She gets caught by the king's soldiers and publicly confesses in front of Creon and the citizens. Unexpectedly, Ismene declares that she actively helped her sister with the burial, but Antigone refuses to share any responsibility with her. The king states that Antigone will be buried alive in a cave, with no honours. Therefore, while Polynices is a corpse among the living, Antigone is fated to be a living creature among the dead. Despite the fortune-teller Tiresias' advice to free Antigone and bury the corpse, Creon does not change his mind and Antigone hangs herself in the cave, willing to be the one to decide whether to live or die.

Scholars have thought about Antigone as a dissident, a migrant, a criminal, a civil disobedient. Almost all portray her as the champion of kinship relationships over State authority, of her dead brother's singularity over a political ideology, which casts citizens of the *polis* as interchangeable soldiers. The famous line 523, where Antigone declares that 'It is not my nature to join in hate, but in love', is often seen as a paradigm of her refusal of the military duties required by the State of the citizens. Despite the feminist theorists' strenuous efforts to highlight Antigone's agency, her character is often understood as acting in accordance with a claim that seems to *speak through her* – and in devotion to which she eventually sacrifices herself. The idea of Antigone acting according to *her own* claim allows us to think of her as a figure of integrity – but it also may be read as an interpretation of her desire and actions as being useless and dangerous. This is precisely Ismene's critique of her sister: 'You crave the impossible' (line 90).

But what if Antigone is *not* a claimer? What if she is not someone who stands for a project that comes into being and ends with her, beginning with her own criminal birth (as the product of incest) and culminating with her own death (as a result of her crime of burying Polynices)? Bonnie Honig[1] offered an interpretation of Antigone as a *plotter*, who conspires both with Ismene and with the audience itself, by using linguistic devices such as irony to make her appeals undetected. In doing so, according to Honig, Antigone *does* initiate an action in concert and shares a communal project.

In the centuries since Sophocles' play was first staged in 442 BCE., Antigone's action has continued to resound. If we consider the reception of *Antigone* (the play), we see that it created many *publics* and that it continually inspires myriad political initiatives and artistic performances. Most recently and relevantly, *Theater of War Productions*[2] staged *Antigone in Ferguson*, a reading of the play at Normandy High School in Ferguson (Missouri), two years after Michael Brown was shot dead by a policeman. The idea that inspires the reading is that Michael Brown's dead body, left for four hours on the road, recalls Creon's exposure of the body of Polynices, which represented a 'lesson' given to the citizens. In the wake of the ensuing protests in Ferguson, the theatre company aimed to problematize the relation between the precarious lives of black citizens in the United States and the authority of the law (and those who are supposed to act in the name of it and to defend the community).

Must integrity isolate its subjects? Antigone invites a critical re-interrogation of that habitual assumption. In order to have a grasp on Antigone's integrity, it will be necessary first to *dis-integrate* her.

Why does Antigone not obey the law, which would be the only *rational* thing to do, according to her sister?[3] Unable to bear the thought of her brother's body, left out for birds and dogs to feast upon, Antigone refuses to compromise and, as the Chorus points out, 'she shows herself the wild offspring of a wild father' (line 471). She claims to act only in compliance with the gods' laws. As she tells Creon: 'Nor did I think that your decrees were of such force, that a mortal could override the unwritten and unfailing statutes given us by the gods. For their life is not of today or yesterday, but for all time, and no man knows when they were first put forth' (lines 453–457). Although she refuses Creon's political authority and his legislation, this is not all that she does; if it were, her action would be just a *criminal* one. Instead of listening to her sister, who asks her to keep her intentions covered and to act secretly, Antigone goes *public*. Indeed, she both performs the burial out in the open, under the noonday sun, and then loudly claims responsibility for her own act (lines 84–87):

> Ismene: Then at least disclose the deed to no one before you do it. Conceal it, instead, in secrecy–and so, too, will I.
> Antigone: Go on! Denounce it! You will be far more hated for your silence, if you fail to proclaim these things to everyone.

Like her father in spirit, devoted to the gods in practice, Antigone seems to many scholars like the perfect example of integrity: isolated, willing to flout law and power, even at her own peril, in order to do what is right; steadfast in her moral vision and commitment. But the conventional idea of integrity isolates the moral actor, while Antigone's exemplarity prompts us to think about integrity as a necessarily collective project. Indeed, Antigone's refusal addresses the entire community, through three specific public performances: (1) her conspiracy with Ismene and with her fellow citizens, (2) her public avowal, and (3) her suicide by hanging.

At the beginning of the play, Antigone tries to get Ismene involved in her plan and, in so doing, to pair herself with her sister. Why does she need a partner in crime? A corpse is heavy to move and, by asking Ismene to help her, Antigone seems to display intentionally the weakness of her own female body. But she is also looking for allies; thus she tries to convince Ismene to cooperate by reminding her about their own sororal tie. For instance, at the very first line she addresses Ismene by using a periphrasis[4], which refers to the fact that they are born from the same womb, while expressing affection. Afterwards she asks Ismene: 'Will you join your hand to mine in order to lift his corpse?' (line 43). While pairing herself with her sister, Antigone keeps referring to their bodies (first, Ismene's head; then, her own hand) – a physicality they have *in common* as sisters, but also as women. Indeed, Antigone knows that she cannot take the sororal tie for granted as if Ismene were obliged to support her with all of her choices. Her appeals to their shared embodiedness underwrite her request for help.

She needs to build an alliance with her sister, and in so doing, she acts like a plotter who organizes a covert military act, or a mutiny. Indeed, she has to convince Ismene with strong arguments, while speaking to her in private outside the house. Just as she relies on their embodied sisterhood to serve as the locus of a conspiracy, Antigone denies gender roles. She seems to have the ambition to deny those distinctions that allow 'gender' to function as a concept. Indeed, when Ismene points out that 'we must remember, first, that ours is a woman's nature, and accordingly not suited to battles against men' (lines 61–62), Antigone claims that she is looking for a beautiful death – that is, a male ideal of the hero's sacrifice in battle (according to Homer's account). Antigone, in this way, makes gender *inoperative*.

Does Antigone achieve her goal of getting her sister on her side? After the first exchange with her (lines 1–99), she seems to have failed, since Ismene refuses to help her. Nevertheless, at lines 536–537 Ismene seems entirely willing to share with her sister responsibility for her criminal act, as she says to Creon: 'I performed the deed—as long as she concurs—and I share and carry the burden of guilt'. Eventually, Antigone's quest for a partner in crime was successful, inasmuch as Ismene is ready to pair with her.

The second relevant moment of Antigone's 'performance of refusal' is her public avowal: 'I declare it and make no denial' (line 443), she says, in front of Creon, the guard and the Theban citizens (the Chorus). Afterwards, when Creon asks her 'Did you know that an edict had forbidden this?' (line 447), she replies 'How could I not? It was public' (line 448). She not only claims responsibility for the act, which is considered a crime. She contests also the legitimacy of that very legislation – while stressing its publicness – and Creon's authority itself. Acting openly, without covering her own intentions – she performs an act of *political exemplarity*. Had she acted covertly, as Ismene advised, Creon's regime might have easily framed Antigone's deed as a crime. But Antigone's aim is to act for the sake of a collective, by inaugurating a new political possibility. Offering her fellow citizens her exemplarity, she creates an alternative to the only supposedly rational choice the regime offers – namely, to dishonour the public enemy and leave his corpse unburied as a partisan reminder. Showing that a law can be unjust, Antigone makes the case that it is an obligation for everyone to protest against an unjust law, and even to risk themselves for the sake of the community.[5]

Creon understands that Antigone is dangerous precisely because she is able to involve a collective in her open acts of refusal and 'resistance'. Indeed, as his son Haemon reminds the king, while blaming him for acting like a tyrant, 'dread of your glance forbids the ordinary citizen to speak such words as would offend your ear. But I can hear these murmurs in the dark, how the city moans for this girl' (lines 690–693). Therefore, Creon decides to punish Antigone in a peculiar way: by ordering her to be buried alive, he deprives her of her public visibility. Even isolated and alone in her cave, though, Antigone finds a way to stage a public performance. Her suicide *counteracts* Creon's privatizing move. She takes back the control on her own body and life, after *publicly* telling her own story the way she wants her fellow citizens to remember it. She does this by singing her own dirge[6] framing her acts in relation to her alleged claim. Her aim is not only to bury Polynices and to contest an unjust law by performing an act of civil disobedience.[7] She also *refuses* an entire regime and its narrative, according to which there is no other choice – for either a citizen or the entire community – than to follow the leadership in order to avoid civil war. In so doing, she refuses the patriarchal authority of both the tyrant and the father as well as the emergency politics by which so many have consolidated their power throughout the ages.[8]

In his essay *A Critique of Utilitarianism*, Bernard Williams provides a definition of 'integrity' as one's 'moral identity' – those feelings, desires, projects and especially commitments that constitute one's moral self. Instead, we might think, politically, about integrity as an effort not just to be at home with oneself by protecting oneself from a demanding and cruel world, but also as an effort to build the world in which one's integrity *can* be at home. This calls us to attend, *beyond* the terms of the choice itself, to the idea of integrity as involving a political promise for a collective. A *political* consideration of integrity would take into account the larger contexts of social and communal networks (which implies *other people's* projects, desires, interests, commitments and so on) in which one is situated. If we think about integrity this way, then we are invited to think about Antigone as acting on behalf of a collective instead of her own moral commitments and identity.

Antigone's integrity is not fully expressed – or betrayed – by one single unified act of refusal. Indeed, she acts as a political organizer of an action in concert. She enlists an ally, she acts in public and she claims responsibility for the burial in front of the political authority, while reasoning in ways designed to move others to act as well. From a political perspective, Antigone's choreography of integrity is inaugural inasmuch as it is *exemplary*. Therefore, Antigone is a figure of integrity, though not for the reasons the scholars usually point out – a sort of individualistic and rigid moral posture. Instead, her integrity depends on her embedment in a network of sororal and communal relationships that she actively transforms.

Acknowledgements

I owe many thanks to Bonnie Honig, Nancy Duke Lewis Professor of Modern Culture and Media and Political Science at Brown

University. Her grasp on Antigone was crucial for this essay's project – and for my research in general. She encouraged me to be brave enough to *dis*-integrate Antigone, and then to let her speak again.

Recommended reading

The best-known annotated and translated edition of the play is R. C. Jebb, *Sophocles: The Plays and Fragments, with Critical Notes, Commentary, and Translation in English Prose. Part III: The Antigone* (Cambridge: Cambridge University Press, 1900). The readers can find a general introduction to the play and an overview of its reception and interpretations in D. Cairns, *Sophocles: Antigone* (London: Bloomsbury Academic, 2016). *Antigone* is a staple in the critical literature of many fields (Classics, Philosophy, Political Theory, Dramaturgy, Feminist Theory and more). Scholars have thought about Antigone as a dissident, a migrant, a criminal, a civil disobedient. A broad spectrum of feminist readers became interested in her as a heroine with a gendered agenda of caring. For those who are interested in a 'humanist' reception of female voices in ancient Greek tragedy, see for instance: N. Loraux, *The Mourning Voice* (Ithaca: Cornell University Press, 2002), focusing on lamentation as related to the fifth-century polis. Readers interested in Judith Butler's famous references to the play should check in *Antigone's Claim: Kinship Between Life and Death* (New York: Columbia University Press, 2000) and *Precarious Life: The Powers of Mourning and Violence* (New York: Verso 2004).

Notes

1 B. Honig, *Antigone, Interrupted* (Cambridge, New York, etc.: Cambridge University Press, 2013).
2 See http://theaterofwar.com/projects/new-projects/overview.
3 See, for instance, lines 44 and 47.
4 'Ismene's head, born from the same uterus as me' (my own translation).
5 M. Walzer, *Obligation: Essays on Disobedience, War and Citizenship* (Cambridge, MA: Harvard University Press, 1970), 7, highlights the

fact that someone who performs an act of civil disobedience feels it as an obligation, due to her commitment to being part of a community ('willful membership') – which could be also the 'human community'.

6 See Honig, *Antigone, Interrupted*, 129: 'All are part of Antigone's *agon*, part of her effort to frame her story and control the field of interpretation by which she will be judged. ... It is Antigone's conspiracy with language and it is language conspiring with her.'

7 See H. Arendt, *Civil Disobedience* in *Crises of the Republic* (New York: Harcourt Brace & Company, 1972), 74): 'Civil disobedience arises when a significant number of citizens have become convinced either that the normal channels of change no longer function, and grievances will not be heard or acted upon.'

8 As Antigone recalls while lamenting: 'Oh, the horrors of our mother's bed! Oh, the slumbers of the wretched mother at the side of her own son, my own father! What manner of parents gave me my miserable being!' (lines 863–6).

5

Job

'And still he holdeth fast his integrity'

Katharine J. Dell

The figure of Job is the epitome of integrity. The first adjective used to describe Job in the opening to his book is תָּם *tam* (perfect/complete/blameless).[1] This same word *tam* is also translated as 'integrity'. We are told in the opening line of the book: 'There was a man in the land of Uz, whose name was Job; and that man was perfect (*tam*) and upright, and one that feared God, and eschewed evil' (Job 1:1). It is essential to the story of Job and to the plot of the book that he is, indeed, perfect, a man of integrity first and foremost. The conjunction of integrity with uprightness is also found in the Psalter, for example Ps 25:21 as a plea to God: 'Let integrity and uprightness preserve me; for I wait on thee.' It is only a man of such a character that can suffer completely innocently. Indeed, a key theological theme of the book is that Job is totally undeserving of the suffering that God and the Satan inflict upon him in the prologue. In that prologue, Job loses all he has – his possessions, his livestock and finally his children – everything except his wife. The friends – Eliphaz, Bildad and Zophar – who come supposedly to comfort him, tell him that he must have sinned and so is being punished, but Job is adamant that he has not sinned. Interpretations of Job's story have often focused on his legendary patience, but his refusal to admit to sins that he had not committed testifies less to his patience than to his integrity.

The information conveyed about Job is brief: location, name and then essential character, followed by the information that he 'feared God, and eschewed evil' (Job 1:1). In this sense he is the epitome of the ideal of the just man, as described in Proverbs: 'The just man walketh in his integrity (*tam*): his children are blessed after him' (20:7). After an opening scene describing Job's status, his wealth, his offspring and his piety (1:2–5), all the result of his 'integrity' as befits the 'just man', the action moves to heaven where God and the Satan are having a conference concerning Job. Again Job's integrity is at the centre of the debate, with God's opening question to the Satan being, 'Hast thou considered my servant Job, that there is none like him in the earth, a perfect (*tam*) and an upright man, one that feareth God, and escheweth evil?' (1:8). These words echo the opening line of the book but also hold Job up as a paradigm of integrity – like no other on earth – Job is a paragon of virtue, ripe for a test. This gives the perfect opportunity for the Satan to ask his penetrating question: 'Doth Job fear God for nought?' (1:9). This question sets up the tension that will also characterize the book, between Job's true integrity and the questioning of his motivation for it. Why is he such an upright man, so pious that he even sacrifices on behalf of his children in case they might have sinned (1:5)? What motivates his character? Is he only in this relationship with God and other people for what he can get out of it, notably for the wealth, prosperity and blessings that he has already received and goes on enjoying? This is at the heart of the Satan's question. The Satan goes on to accuse God of coddling Job, of having 'made a hedge about him, and about his house, and about all that he hath on every side' (1:10). Satan's challenge is that if the nurturing hand of God is turned into one that inflicts suffering then Job's attitude will change – his integrity will vanish and he will 'curse thee to thy face' (1:11). And so the stage is set and God responds to the challenge by allowing the Satan to afflict Job in any way that is external to Job's own body (1:12). Thus follows the first set of trials in four events: two the result of marauding enemies – the Sabeans and the Chaldeans;[2] and two natural disasters – fire and hurricane. At first it is Job's possessions, his oxen and asses, his sheep and his camels that are struck down, with their accompanying servants, but ultimately his children are killed when the house in which they are feasting falls upon them (1:13–19).[3] Job's response is one of mourning and yet also of blessing. Instead of cursing God, as hoped by the Satan, he says: 'Naked came I out of my mother's womb, and naked shall I return thither: the Lord gave, and the Lord hath taken away; blessed be the name of the Lord' (1:21). This represents a suitably pious response from a man of integrity, who expected nothing although blessings came, and still expects nothing now that calamity has struck. One is reminded of another proverb: 'Better *is* the poor that walketh in his integrity, than *he that is* perverse in his lips, and is a fool' (Prov. 19:1). Instead of wordy complaints and curses, Job here is concise in his words and chooses them carefully: 'In all this Job sinned not, nor charged God foolishly' (1:22). His integrity and piety are intact.

We then find a second round in heaven in which the same question is asked by God: 'And the Lord said unto Satan, Hast thou considered my servant Job, that there is none like him in the earth, a perfect (*tam*) and an upright man, one that feareth God, and escheweth evil? and still he holdeth fast his integrity (תֻּמָּה[4]), although thou movedst me against him, to destroy him without cause' (Job 2:3). These words again echo the opening line and God's opening question from round one, but then uses *tam* again in an additional emphasis on Job's tenacity after the first set of trials. But Satan exploits the same loophole as before – afflict Job in his body and he will complain, he says. So again God gives the Satan permission to afflict Job, but not so as to cause his death. 'So went Satan forth from the presence of the Lord, and smote Job with sore boils from the sole of his foot unto his crown.' Now Job has an unpleasant disease to cope with on top of his grief at his losses and so we find him scraping at his sores with a potsherd as he sits on a pile of ashes,[5] the traditional pictorial scene of Job in centuries of artistic tradition.[6] At this point his wife enters the scene and advises the same as the Satan: 'Curse God and die'. She also refers to Job's integrity, and is incredulous that he holds on to it: 'Then said his wife unto him, Dost thou still retain thine integrity?' (2:9). Job scolds her, calling her a foolish woman, and again he utters the kind of response one would expect from the 'complete' man. He says: 'What? Shall we receive good at the hand of God, and shall we not receive evil?' Again, he is resigned to God's apparent ability to deal out good and bad – it is almost as if he expects some evil to counterbalance the good. One could again make a comparison to Proverbs and its insightful words: 'The integrity of the upright shall guide them: but the perverseness of transgressors shall destroy them' (Prov. 11:3). The basic traditional assumption is that good things come to the righteous and evil to sinners, but here Job is allowing his integrity to guide him and so even in his darkest hour he is following the wisdom that has been passed down to him. He accepts good or bad from God not in a strict retributive sense, since he knows he is innocent, but as an acknowledgement that God is capable of both. It is an acknowledgement of God's power and of human helplessness in the face of that power (anticipating the speeches of God and Job's responses later in the book). The narrator is keen to tell us that Job 'did not sin with his lips' (2:10) – his integrity is intact. At this point the friends come to comfort him and they remain silent until Job speaks at the opening of chapter 3.

At this point the seemingly straightforward picture of the character of Job becomes more complex.[7] The first thing we are told at the opening of chapter 3 is that 'Job opened his mouth, and cursed his day'. Is he not, then, now doing the very cursing that was predicted by the Satan and advised by his wife? It sounds remarkably like it, although we are told that Job is specifically cursing 'his day', that is, the day of his birth. It does appear, though, to be a sudden character change – the pious accepting Job of the prologue is apparently replaced by a more vociferous, complaining figure who suddenly becomes more real as a human being, plumbing the depths of his lament and pathos.[8] He curses the day he was born and even the day of his conception and wishes that he had never been, such is his suffering, both mental and physical.[9] The dialogue between Job and the friends is long, containing three cycles of speeches,[10] but the theme of 'integrity' is never far away. The main issue of the speeches turns on whether Job deserved this suffering because he had sinned, even if inadvertently, or whether he is, indeed, as blameless as he maintains. In Eliphaz's opening speech he asks, 'Is not this thy fear, thy confidence, thy hope, and the uprightness of thy ways?' By 'this' Eliphaz is referring to Job's fear of God, referring back to the ground of Job's integrity, that is, his confidence that God was his support. Suddenly the reason for Job's uprightness – his fear of God – has been undermined. Eliphaz restates the traditional view that the innocent do not perish and he suggests that Job is arrogantly challenging the justice of God in persisting in his view that he is, indeed, just and blameless (Job 4:17). Bildad, the second friend, says much the same thing when he holds: 'Behold, God will not cast away a perfect man, neither will he help the evil doer' (Job 8:20). It is all back to front that the 'complete' man should suffer in this way. This is a breaking of God's own rules and so, in their view, Job must be in the wrong to maintain his innocence.

Job reacts angrily to the friends' accusation when he responds to Bildad:

> If I justify myself, mine own mouth shall condemn me: if I say, I am perfect (*tam*), it shall also prove me perverse. Though I were perfect (*tam*), yet would I not know my soul: I would despise my life. This is one thing, therefore I said it, He destroyeth the perfect (*tam*) and the wicked. (9:20–2)

Here he uses *tam* three times. Job realizes that he cannot win – if he says he is 'perfect' – a man of integrity as he knows himself to be – then he is considered 'perverse'. On the other hand, his suffering despite this knowledge leads him to self-loathing. He has realized one overwhelming and deeply worrying fact: God destroys *both* the person of integrity and the wicked. Traditional proverbs such as 13:6 – 'Righteousness keepeth him that *is* upright (tam) in the way: but wickedness overthroweth the sinner' – are simply wrong. There is no distinction between righteous and sinner when it comes to God's punishment. Job's quiet acceptance of good and bad from the hand of God seems far away at this point. In chapter 19 he asks for a 'redeemer' to judge between himself and God, since God appears to be the accuser as well as the judge. In chapter 21 Job describes the prosperity of the wicked: 'Their seed is established in their sight with them, and their offspring before their eyes. Their houses *are* safe from fear, neither *is* the rod of God upon them. Their bull gendereth, and faileth not; their cow calveth, and casteth not her calf' (Job 21:8–10). Job is adamant in his refusal to listen to the accusations of the friends and he holds on to his integrity above everything: he says: 'God forbid that I should justify you: till I die I will not remove mine integrity from me' (27:5), and in his final lament (chapters 29–31) he challenges God to respond: 'Let me be weighed in an even balance, that God may know mine integrity.'

After Job's words are ended, and a fourth friend, Elihu, has had his say,[11] God appears in a whirlwind, ostensibly to defend His actions, but no mention is made of the issue of just rewards and punishments that has so occupied the dialogue. No mention is made of Job's integrity either and there is a long description of animals that God has created (chapter 39) and of the great monsters Behemoth and Leviathan (both real creatures, the hippopotamus and the crocodile) and mythological creatures overcome by God at creation (40–1). The message from God is clear, though: there are many great and wonderful things that Job does not understand. The technique of rhetorical questions is employed, with God asking continuous questions to which the answer is clearly 'no' (chapter 38). The inference is that Job is attempting to make God too small in challenging him to conform to human ideas of justice. Job responds to God first by putting his hand over his mouth and second by acknowledging that there are many things he did not, indeed, understand: 'therefore have I uttered that I understood not; things too wonderful for me, which I knew not' (42:4). Job is seemingly vindicated at the end (in 42:7) when he is said to have spoken 'the thing that is right' as opposed to the friends. Exactly what 'the thing that is right' is remains unclear: Is this a reference back to Job's pious words in the prologue about accepting good and evil alike (since here we are back in the prose narrative)? Or is it about his being 'right' to question God's actions and to protest?[12] The Epilogue (42:7–17) or ending is a happy one – after all, Job is restored and has a new set of children, with three beautiful daughters given especial mention with names and an inheritance (42:14–15),[13] and he lives a long life, living to see four generations of his offspring. This is integrity's reward – wealth, offspring and longevity – and the traditional view of God's blessing upon the righteous seems to hold in the end. And yet, questions have been raised about the worth of integrity and its ultimate value – after that trial will Job ever be the same?

Integrity is an absolute quality that Job is said to have had from the outset (hence the other translations of *tam* as 'perfect', 'complete' or 'blameless') and God recognizes that Job has this above all others such that there is 'no one like him on the earth' (1:8). This concept of integrity in the wider Hebrew Bible is often used in conjunction with 'heart' to describe 'integrity of heart' (Gen 20:5–6; I Kings 9:4; Ps 101:2), hence referring to one's deepest conscience and inner motivation. Yet one wonders if Job's integrity has been modified or improved by his trial. We are told at the start in Job 1:5 that such was Job's concern that his sons and daughters were overindulging on their feast days that he would send for them, sanctify them and offer sacrifices daily on their behalf. This is an example of his scrupulous integrity and attention to all aspects of his familial piety. One wonders how he could possibly have improved on this. In a similar scrupulous vein also is his attention and charity to others as described in Job 29. In Proverbs, integrity is linked to the behaviour of the upright in contrast to the crookedness of the wicked (e.g. Prov. 11:3; 14:32). The path of integrity is a secure one (Prov. 10:9; 20:7), and better to be poor and walking along such a path than to be rich and deceitful (Prov. 28:6). Punishments lie in wait for such people, while the person of integrity will be safe (Prov. 28:18). However, one of the goals of wisdom is constant examination and self-improvement and the wise person should never be complacent (Prov. 18:4; 19:8) – wisdom is a deep well that can never be fully plumbed (Eccl 7:23–5) and its mainspring is ultimately from God (Prov. 2:6). So maybe there was a sense in which the overscrupulous Job might have benefited from a dose of modesty. The trial has certainly put his integrity to the test and any hint of superficiality has now disappeared. Job has come face to face with the stark reality of God's capricious nature and yet, according to the Epilogue, he remains relatively unchanged by the experience. Perhaps after such a rollercoaster of changes life can never be the same again, and yet one gets the impression of a calm acceptance and a carrying on with everyday life and its blessings. Just before the Epilogue, Job capitulates in the face of such a deity – in that sense he is not a tragic figure because he accepts his lack of understanding and bows in reverence, offering further sacrifice on behalf of others in Job 42:8. There is a certain circularity here that suggests that Job's integrity has remained constant throughout and despite all his anguish. Perhaps the most vital aspect is that God recognized Job from the start as a man of integrity, blameless and upright (1:1) and that integrity is ultimately rewarded by God despite all that has happened in between.

It is interesting to note, as an addendum, that Job's integrity has not been the focus of the history of interpretation of Job; rather, mainly under the influence of James 5:11 in the New Testament, which refers to the 'patience of Job', the emphasis has been on his legendary 'patience'. This word is never used to describe Job within the book itself, but has come to characterize Job's 'saintly' attitude, a view promoted by the Septuagint translation of Job which omitted some of his more impious remarks and the Testament of Job, a first-century Christian text. As the Testament of Job puts it: 'Patience is better than anything' (T. Job 27:7). By the time of the fourth century AD Apocalypse of Paul, Job is one of the saints that Paul meets in heaven. An elevation, indeed, for the exemplar of integrity! Job, this exemplar, regarded by many as 'everyman', suffered and came face to face with his God. He held on to his integrity by a shred and was encouraged to abandon it by his wife, but he ultimately won through, sufficient for his tale to become a paradigm of virtuous behaviour in the face of troubles both human and divine. Integrity is arguably a more important virtue than patience in its absolute quality and centrality to character in the face of such a trial as that faced by Job.

Recommended reading

The text of Job (cited here using the King James Bible version) is a good starting point. An excellent three-volume commentary upon the text is found in David J. A. Clines, *Job* (Dallas, Texas: Word Books, 1989, 2006, 2010). For more of a daily reading and modern application approach to the text of Job, see Katharine J. Dell, *Job, The People's Bible Commentary* (Oxford: Bible Reading Fellowship, 2002). For an introduction to scholarly issues around the interpretation of Job, see Katharine J. Dell, *Job: Where Shall Wisdom Be Found?* (London: Bloomsbury, 2016). For the history of interpretation of Job, see Samuel Terrien, *The Iconography of Job through the Centuries: Artists as Biblical Interpreters* (University Park: Pennsylvania State University Press, 1996); and Samuel E. Balentine, *Have You Considered My Servant Job? Understanding the Biblical Archetype of Patience* (Columbia, SC: University of South Carolina Press, 2015).

Notes

1 תֹּם n.[m.] completeness, integrity; adj. complete, perfect.

2 These are both legendary enemies and real ones at various times in Israel's history. Since this tale is set outside Israel, in 'Uz', they are probably legendary.

3 The regular feasting of the children of Job is an enigma. They seem to regularly celebrate their 'days' (birthdays perhaps) and gather together without their parents. Job is concerned that they might have sinned which may suggest inappropriate partying.

4 תַּמָּה, n.f. integrity (late).

5 This is probably the ash-heap or dungheap that accumulated outside a town. This was the burnt remains of the waste of the city and it was a place where outcasts were taken.

6 See Samuel Terrien, *The Iconography of Job Through the Centuries: Artists as Biblical Interpreters* (University Park: Pennsylvania State University Press, 1996).

7 See Bruce Zuckerman, *Job the Silent: A Study of Historical Counterpoint* (Oxford: Oxford University Press, 1991).

8 His laments resemble psalmic laments, and at times parodies them – see Katharine Dell, *The Book of Job as Sceptical Literature* BZAW 157 (Berlin: Walter de Gruyter, 1991).

9 Katharine Dell, 'What Was Job's Malady?' *JSOT* 41 (September 2016): 61–77.

10 The third cycle of speeches appears to be dislocated and people seem to say the wrong things at times. There is also a hymn to wisdom in chapter 28 that may be separate. These are the subject of intense scholarly debates, see Katharine Dell, *Job: Where Shall Wisdom Be Found?* Phoenix Guides to the Old Testament (London: Bloomsbury, 2016).

11 These chapters (32–7) are often regarded as secondary since the fourth friend, Elihu, is not introduced and since much of the material is a repeat either of the arguments of the friends or of God's.

12 See Dell, *The Book of Job as Sceptical Literature*.

13 This is an unusual detail as the women do not normally inherit, nor are they often named in the Hebrew Bible as a whole.

6

Ella Baker

Leading with integrity in the service of a cause

Robin Zheng

Although she was a key leader in several of the most influential organizations of the US civil rights movement, Ella Baker remains relatively unknown – perhaps in part because, in her words: 'I never worked for an organization but for a cause.'[1] In her six decades of activism, Baker was affiliated with more than forty different political organizations (much to the bewilderment of the FBI agents writing her file), a history that reflected her tendency to eschew narrow ideological purity in favour of pragmatism. It might also be due to clashes with prominent figures such as Walter White and Martin Luther King, Jr., which led to her resigning from top positions in the National Association for the Advancement of Colored People (NAACP) and the Southern Christian Leadership Conference (SCLC). These conflicts were prompted by the way she trusted in the intelligence and self-determination of the black community she served, especially the poor and uneducated, rather than the leadership of a Messianic few. Finally, Baker's lack of fame very likely has to do with the all-too-common erasure of women's voices, along with her dedication to performing the vital but undervalued work (like much women's work) of movement-building. Baker's life thus represents a model of what it means for a person to have *political integrity* – to work for a cause – that is very different from the iconic hero narratives that tend to populate history books.

In numerous ways, Ella Baker was a paragon of what we ordinarily think of as integrity. First of all, her devotion to improving the lot of those made vulnerable by injustice was complete, unwavering and lifelong. Born in 1903 in Norfolk, Virginia, Baker moved to her mother's hometown of Littleton, North Carolina, at the age of seven. As a child, she helped feed, wash and care for the poor and sick under the tutelage of her mother, who was an active leader in the black Baptist women's missionary movement. In her twilight years, she continued to work with local, national and international activist organizations, even as her memory and health began to fail. She passed away in 1986 on the day after her eighty-third birthday.[2]

Baker defied social expectations and underwent considerable personal sacrifice in order to perform this work according to her own understanding of how it needed to be done. As a young woman with a middle-class background and a college degree, it was almost 'inevitable' that she should become a teacher like her mother, who greatly desired that she do so.[3] But Baker refused. According to her, a woman 'couldn't teach unless somebody in the white hierarchy okayed your teaching', which she found 'a demeaning sort of thing, and I resented this, and I refused to teach'.[4] This attitude was the product of her upbringing within the vibrant and self-contained black community in Littleton: the Bakers lived in a black neighbourhood of mostly educated professionals and skilled artisans, and shopped at black-owned stores.[5] Baker's childhood was thus exceptional in being relatively insulated from explicit acts of white racism, though she remained highly attuned to it. She was especially close to her maternal grandfather – a former slave who refused to let his children work for white people or to eat foods reminiscent of slavery.[6] These early experiences instilled in Baker a powerful recognition of her own and her people's worth, which became a crucial ingredient in her distinctive brand of integrity. Yet Baker would eventually reject the 'Talented Tenth'[7] mentality that characterized her family's relative social position, choosing to work for and among the poorest and most stigmatized margins of the black community.

Another reason Baker did not want to teach was that, in her experience, 'I had seen generations of graduates also go out and teach. And sometimes there had been people who had shown spirit fighting back in school but after they taught they came back and they were nothing. They had no spirit.'[8] Rather than risk compromising her own fighting spirit, Baker chose to forego a safe and respectable teaching career. This sense of integrity drove her to make similar choices throughout the rest of her life. After working a variety of odd and part-time jobs in New York, she succeeded in becoming director of branches of the NAACP in 1943. But she eventually resigned in 1946 because, in her words:

> I came to the Association because I felt that I could make a contribution to the struggle for human justice and equality. I am leaving because I feel that there must be some way to do this without further jeopardizing one's integrity and sense of fair play.[9]

With that Baker gave up the last position with a steady salary, benefits and long-term security she would ever hold, spending the next forty-one years of her life making ends meet through multiple jobs, borrowed money and funds from a supportive network.[10] Indeed, Baker told a friend that if she wrote a memoir it would be called 'Making a Life, Not Making a Living'.[11]

Why did Baker leave? The answer lies in another element of her conception of integrity: a flat rejection of elitism and hero worship. While NAACP director Walter White wanted a highly centralized programme that issued top-down national directives (e.g. organizing federal voting drives, fundraising for expensive legal challenges to Jim Crow legislation), Baker insisted on working with local branches on their own terms, towards whatever concerns were most pressing to them. Her strategy was to build neighbourhood-level structures promoting rank-and-file members' ongoing participation in local actions, and to hold regional leadership conferences providing training for promising grassroots leaders.[12] Baker's chosen title for these conferences, one of which was attended by Rosa Parks in 1946 (nine years before the Montgomery Bus Boycott), was 'Give Light and the People Will Find a Way'.[13] Baker's relationship with White deteriorated, in part because she saw him as someone who 'went out of his way to remind everyone around him how important he was'.[14] Yet even after a personally acrimonious departure, she did not publicly disclose her criticisms of the NAACP, so as not to undermine its future ability to perform valuable political work.[15]

In 1958, Baker was hired as the first full-time staff member of the SCLC, a temporary job which she held until 1960 when the organization found a permanent director – a position for which she was never seriously considered. During her tenure, she ran into fierce disagreement with Martin Luther King, Jr., who had initially been reluctant to hire her because he believed that other clergymen would expect a (male) minister in this leadership role.[16] With regards to King, Baker stated: 'I had no capacity for worshipping the leader'.[17] She was, as ever, committed to protecting the integrity of others through encouraging indigenous leadership. 'I firmly believe in the right of the people who were under the heel to be the ones to decide what action they were going to take to get [out] from under their oppression',[18] she insisted, and 'the Negro must quit looking for a savior and work to save himself.'[19] Baker found the culture of hero worship around King not only unhelpful, but positively harmful. While King said that he allowed it because it was what the people wanted, Baker thought that it obscured and obstructed the self-directed, bottom-up efforts of the community at large – efforts that she believed to be the true drivers of social change.[20]

Baker recognized, however, that the problem did not lie with King specifically, but with a wider individualist and masculine culture that attributed social change to charismatic male leaders – exemplified in the model of (male) minister leading his flock. She was acutely aware of the many dangers of this model. In her words: 'I have always felt it was a handicap for oppressed peoples to depend so largely upon such a leader [because] the media made him, and the media may undo him', and that 'such a person gets to the point of believing that he *is* the movement'.[21] Most importantly, she warned against 'succumb[ing to] the failures of what I call the American weakness of being recognized and having arrived and taking on the characteristics and the values, even, of the foe'.[22] In short, Baker recognized that 'we on the outside, we want to be important ... so we ape the insiders' – and hence achieving success was itself a tremendous risk to political integrity.[23]

Baker thus advocated a genuinely radical programme of social transformation: for her, the ultimate goal was not for blacks to merely ascend the social hierarchy, but to dismantle it altogether. It was, in her words, a matter of being 'radical in its original meaning – *getting down to and understanding the root cause*'.[24] And this entailed willingness to soldier on with the gruelling and inglorious work of day-to-day organizing, akin to the kind of unrecognized but life-sustaining labour to which women have long been accustomed – for example, the work of taking down lists of people's names and what they needed, rather than making speeches at the front of the stage. Baker said: 'You didn't see me on television, you didn't see news stories about me. The kind of role that I tried to play was to pick up pieces or put together pieces out of which I hoped organization might come. My theory is, strong people don't need strong leaders.'[25]

Because Baker believed that the power to bring about social change belonged fundamentally with the masses, she staunchly rejected the notion of 'respectability politics', wherein a discriminated group seeks to be extra 'respectable' to counteract the stigma with which they are all saddled. Baker recognized that respectability politics leads to *internal* distancing, neglect and even blaming (e.g. for hindering the race) of the most vulnerable members of the group. She frequently criticized middle-class leaders whom she described as being 'against the idea of going to battle for the town drunk who happened to have been brutalized when being arrested, because who was he?'[26] Baker, who worked closely with at least one actual town drunk (nicknamed 'Papa Tight'), gave both moral and pragmatic reasons for doing so. Morally speaking, fighting for equal rights entailed rallying behind even the least respectable of persons, on pain of hypocrisy; practically speaking, elitism undermined the kind of mass organizing that was crucial for radical social transformation.

From 1960 to 1966, Baker finally came into her own as the primary mentor of the Student Nonviolent Coordinating Committee (SNCC). Black students around the country had been conducting sit-ins at lunch counters to protest against segregation, and Baker quickly arranged a leadership conference for them; by steering them away from the hierarchical church-led model, she persuaded them to bring her political vision to life. SNCC organized sit-ins and Freedom Rides throughout the Mississippi Delta, adopting Baker's model of investing time and effort into gaining the trust of local communities before taking direct action. In 1964, the Mississippi Freedom Democratic Party sent a historic slate of black delegates to the all-white Mississippi Democratic Party, which intransigently refused to seat them; this marked a turning point for many young SNCC leaders. Although Baker (the 'Godmother of SNCC') began to withdraw from SNCC and focused her energies elsewhere in the late 1960s and 70s, her unmistakable influence lived on in former SNCC luminaries such as Diane Nash, Julian Bond, Bob Moses and Bernice Johnson Reagon.

For all her extraordinary accomplishments, Baker's life also exemplifies some of the limits, complications and challenges of political integrity. One of the few mistakes that Baker owned up to in her life, for example, was a failure to come out strongly against anti-communism in her earlier years with the NAACP. While she did not like restrictions on civil liberties, Baker expressed support for excluding communists from the NAACP for the pragmatic reason of protecting the organization from government persecution;[27] this, perhaps, allowed her to rationalize her role in the NAACP's communist purge in the late 1950s. Yet such a position runs counter to Baker's lifelong 'big tent' approach to embracing allies of all stripes, and her later explanation that 'I followed a national office directive to the letter, and I should not have' belies her famous willingness to buck organizational authority.[28] As leftist and other social movements continue to struggle in the shadow of anti-communism, it seems a mistake, indeed – not committed only by Baker, of course. Walking the line between principle and pragmatism thus presents great risks to political integrity: arguably, civil rights and labour leaders' willingness to offer up communist allies in exchange for respectability represents a *lack* of integrity, to detrimental effect.

To her credit, however, Baker was willing to acknowledge and learn from her earlier actions. Between 1960 and 1963, she joined the staff of the Southern Conference Educational Fund (SCEF) and, working closely with Anne and Carl Braden, organized a series of events on free speech and civil liberties. She would continue to criticize the House of Un-American Activities Committee (HUAC) throughout her later work, including extensive efforts on behalf of the 'Free Angela Davis' campaign. Ultimately, this too is a form of integrity.

However, Baker may have missed or been unable to take the opportunity to cultivate a different sort of integrity, which harkens back to a second meaning of 'integrity' as a kind of integration, of unified wholeness. Baker's lifelong policy was to excise her personal life from her political work, rather than incorporating it. Her refusal to discuss her marriage – many people, even among her friends, never even knew that she had married and divorced – was likely a way of 'defining herself as something other than a traditional wife and mother ... [in a way that] refocused attention on her ideas', according to historian J. Todd Moye.[29] Perhaps Baker felt that the best way to combat sexism was to reject these feminine roles. Indeed, for pragmatic reasons, she may have been wise in choosing to totally distance herself from her identity as a woman. Yet another – more radical, according to Baker's own use of the term – approach might have been to embrace and subsequently *redefine* the role of 'wife and mother' itself in less stereotypically feminine ways. It is striking that, in a 1969 speech on 'The Black Woman in the Civil Rights Struggle', Baker opened with the following:

> I was a little bit amazed as to why the selection of a discussion on the role of black women in the world. I just said to Bernice Reagon that I have never been one to feel great needs in the direction of setting myself apart as a woman. I've always thought first and foremost of people as individuals.[30]

Although Baker often emphasized that the freedom struggle aimed at the liberation of all people, not just African Americans, consider how strange it would be for her to say 'I have never been one to feel great needs in the direction of setting myself apart as a Black person. I've always thought first and foremost of people as individuals.' After all, while it is surely true that people must be thought of as individuals, both racial and gender identities acquire undeniable political (and sometimes personal) significance when they form the basis of systematic oppression. Hence sexism deserves to be explicitly called out and publicly challenged, and may serve grounds for political solidarity, just as much as fighting racism. In historian Barbara Ransby's analysis, Baker – despite being the living incarnation of feminist values, and keenly critical of the gender discrimination she faced within the civil rights movement – 'often downplayed gender issues' and might be better characterized as a 'profeminist', that is, a 'strong advocate of gender equality ... without a self-conscious investment in the term "feminist" or its attendant theories'.[31] Perhaps Baker's reluctance to set herself apart as a woman might be traced to the strict division between personal and political in her own life. Had they been more integrated, she might have been motivated to act more directly and radically (rather than indirectly, which she undoubtedly did)[32] against gender-based oppression.

In the final analysis, however, there are very few figures who can lay claim to have embodied so fully the virtue of political integrity as Ella Baker. As Plato famously suggested, the best ruler is the *reluctant* ruler – one who leads out of duty and in pursuit of virtue, rather than for the sake of fame and power, which easily corrupt. Baker was precisely such a leader: a leader who strove above all to empower her people, to mobilize that power for radical social change, and to give her life wholly and completely to the cause.

Recommended reading

Interested readers are advised to begin with historian Barbara Ransby's masterful biography *Ella Baker and the Black Freedom Movement: A Radical Democratic Vision*, which blends biographical detail with historical analysis and a reconstruction of Baker's political philosophy. Two other full-length biographies include *Ella Baker: Community Organizer of the Civil Rights Movement* by J. Todd Moye and *Ella Baker: Freedom Bound* by Joanne Grant. Grant, a journalist and activist who reported on the civil rights movement during the 1960s, also produced a documentary entitled *Fundi: The Story of Ella Baker*. Younger readers can be encouraged to read *Ella Baker: A Leader Behind the Scenes* by Shyrlee Dallard and *Freedom Cannot Rest: Ella Baker and the Civil Rights Movement* by Lisa Frederiksen Bohannon.

Notes

1 Barbara Ransby, *Ella Baker and the Black Freedom Movement: A Radical Democratic Vision* (Chapel Hill and London: The University of North Carolina Press, 2003), 209.
2 Ibid., 10.
3 Ibid., 62.

4 Ibid., 63.
5 Ibid., 39, 42.
6 Ibid., 36, 40.
7 The 'Talented Tenth' was W. E. B. Du Bois' conception of a class of exceptional 'race leaders' among the black community whose achievement of 'leadership status, a badge of respectability, and membership in the middle class' would lead the way to uplifting the rest of the race (Ransby, *Ella Baker and the Black Freedom Movement*, 51).
8 Ransby, *Ella Baker and the Black Freedom Movement*, 62.
9 J. Todd Moye, *Ella Baker: Community Organizer of the Civil Rights Movement* (Lanham: Rowman & Littlefield, 2013), 64.
10 Ibid., 6, 65.
11 Ransby, *Ella Baker and the Black Freedom Movement*, 261.
12 Ibid., 118, 126.
13 Moye, *Ella Baker*, 62.
14 Ransby, *Ella Baker and the Black Freedom Movement*, 143.
15 Ibid., 161.
16 Ibid., 180.
17 Moye, *Ella Baker*, 107.
18 Ransby, *Ella Baker and the Black Freedom Movement*, 195
19 Ibid., 188.
20 Ibid.
21 Carol Mueller, 'Ella Baker and the Origins of "Participatory Democracy"', in Vicki L. Crawford, Jacqueline Anne Rouse and Barbara Woods (eds), *Women in the Civil Rights Movement: Trailblazers and Torchbearers, 1941–1965* (Bloomington and Indianapolis, IN: Indiana University Press, 1990), 51–70, p. 64.
22 Moye, *Ella Baker*, 61.
23 Ransby, *Ella Baker and the Black Freedom Movement*, 191.
24 Moye, *Ella Baker*, 166.
25 Mueller, 'Ella Baker and the Origins of "Participatory Democracy"', 51.
26 Ransby, *Ella Baker and the Black Freedom Movement*, 120.
27 Ibid., 407, fn. 98.
28 Ibid., 161.

29 Moye, *Ella Baker*, 6.
30 Joanne Grant, *Ella Baker: Freedom Bound* (New York: Wiley & Sons, 1998), 227.
31 Ransby, *Ella Baker and the Black Freedom Movement*, 34, 367.
32 Indeed, the young women Baker mentored found it 'liberating' to follow her example, undertaking their own actions and expressing their own opinions without feeling tied to their partners (Ransby, *Ella Baker and the Black Freedom Movement*, 9).

7

'Albert'

Transformational agency and integrity in the workplace

Lisa Herzog

This chapter does not portray a famous model of integrity. Rather, it presents an anonymous interviewee, whom I call Albert.[1] He stands for all those of us who work in large organizations. In such organizations, individuals face various psychological pressures that can compromise their integrity. After all, what does it mean to be a person with integrity when one is the proverbial 'cog in the wheel'? Dealing with these pressures requires a reflective attitude towards one's organizational role: neither unrealistic attempts to remain completely unaffected by one's role, nor a complete identification with it, are promising strategies for safeguarding one's integrity. The term 'transformational agency' describes moral agency in organizations by individuals such as Albert, who combine a willingness to live up to basic moral norms with knowledge about what the applications of these norms means in practice, in their specific field of work. Albert's example illustrates what transformational agency can mean, by taking up Hirschman's classic distinction of 'voice' and 'exit': Albert tried to challenge existing practices and spoke up against immoral behaviour, but would also exit from jobs, even very prestigious ones, if he felt he could not square the expectations that came with them with his moral convictions.

Modern work life is dominated by large-scale organizations. They are characterized by divided labour within delineated spheres of responsibility, bound together by rules, and embedded in hierarchical structures.[2] Although their concrete forms (and the jargon for describing them) have varied over time, such organizations continue to be ubiquitous both in the private economy – with the business corporation as the most obvious example – and in the public sector – where hospitals, universities or civil administrations all function more or less along these lines. The vast majority of jobs are integrated into such organizations. The individuals who hold them are faced with specific moral questions. For example, should they always stick to the expectations of their organization's roles or might it be morally legitimate, or even required, to sometimes deviate from them? Do they have a right to stick to their own moral convictions if these are in tension with what their boss wants them to do?

Moreover, workplaces are social spaces in which individuals with different world views meet. As Cynthia Estlund reminds us, in our religiously and morally pluralistic societies, workplaces are the most important meeting point for individuals from different backgrounds.[3] This means that individuals cannot simply assume that all their colleagues will share their moral views down to the last detail – reasonable people can disagree about various moral issues. But the fact of pluralism should not blind us to the equally important fact that there are many moral issues on which individuals from different backgrounds can agree. These can be captured in basic norms such as the Golden Rule or the prohibition against harming others without good cause. What follows adopts the picture drawn by John Rawls, who emphasized that even in pluralistic societies there is an 'overlapping consensus' of shared moral norms.[4] The question that then poses itself is this: How can individuals follow these basic moral norms when they act as employees of organizations? What does it mean to possess moral integrity in such contexts?

Albert, the interviewee portrayed here, asked himself such questions throughout his career. He worked in banking, and he was well aware that the world of finance had its morally grey areas. He was convinced that banking practices should not be harmful to others, for example, by exploiting a lack of financial literacy. Nor should they harm society, for example, by creating huge, uncontrollable risks in the shadow banking system, as had happened before the Great Financial Crisis. These are views that are probably shared by most members of society, but not sufficiently many bankers seem to have carried them into their professional contexts. Albert combined these moral convictions with his insider knowledge of how the world of banking worked. In conversations with like-minded bankers, but also outsiders, he developed a sense of what it would mean to fill his role as a banker *well*. And he tried to make a difference, transforming the practices he was part of – sometimes successful, sometimes not. His credo was: 'I am always the same person, whether in the office or in my private life, with the same moral standards.'

Other individuals, however, seem to relate to their organizational roles in rather different ways. Some speak of them explicitly as roles that they play, but that have nothing to do with them as private persons. In what follows, two psychological pitfalls are contrasted with a middle path that seems more promising, which emerged from my conversations with Albert and other practitioners.

A first approach towards one's organizational role is to try to remain as unaffected by it as possible – to deny the very fact that one has taken on a role, as it were, and to try to behave exactly as one would in one's private life. But this approach is likely to run into problems. For one thing, one may encounter moral questions that are outside the scope of what one encounters in one's private life, and for which one lacks guidance. And one foregoes an opportunity for moral learning: the imperatives of one's role might, after all, encompass moral insights and the best solutions for difficult moral problems in one's specific fields of work. Moreover, not taking on one's role might not be the best recipe for motivating oneself to make a moral difference in one's organization: if it is nothing but a 'coat', as some people have described it,[5] why bother about its moral qualities, rather than focusing exclusively on keeping one's hands clean? The most important point, however, is that it is simply psychologically unrealistic that one would not be affected by one's role. If one spends eight or more hours a day, week after week, month after month, in a certain job, can one really assume that it wouldn't have an impact on one's perceptions and beliefs? Isn't it more likely that it will *gradually* change us, in invisible steps that we can do nothing against precisely because we deny their existence? This is a possibility that we need to acknowledge, in order to take active steps against it.

The second strategy takes the opposite approach: it suggests a complete immersion in, or identification with, one's role. One thinks of oneself as 'a doctor' or 'an administrator' or 'a banker', and buys into the moral imperatives of such a role. In a sense, that may be tempting – one might simply adopt the imperatives of the role and stop thinking about whether or not these imperatives are right. But this is precisely the problem: strong identification with one's role can lead to the loss of an independent perspective on the moral quality of one's actions. One risks turning oneself into a passive tool, doing whatever one's role requires – which, in practice, often means doing what one's boss wants one to do. A quote from a study by Robert Jackall, based on interviews with corporate managers, has become famous for capturing this attitude: 'What is right in the corporation is not what is right in a man's home or in his church. What is right in the corporation is what the guy above you wants from you.'[6] Even if the attitude of all employees is not as drastic as that, there is a real danger of being *too* involved with one's role, and thereby lacking the distance that might be required for exercising moral judgement. If my identity is tied up with *being* a good administrator, or doctor – or even a good 'employee of company x', or 'a good Techie' – then it is understandable that I react with anxiety if I realize that morality might require me to act *against* the requirements of my role. The French term *deformation professionelle* describes how gradually, one sees *everything* from one perspective, without any corrective from other perspectives. But in societies with divided labour, with highly differentiated jobs, it is true almost by definition that no perspective can *fully* capture all that matters for complex moral questions.

Rather than adopting either of these extreme positions, people who work in organizational roles need to retain the capacity to think critically about their roles, their moral standards, and the relation between them. This also implies closely watching how one's own standards are shifting – and whether these shifts are cases of moral insights and deepened understanding, or of becoming complacent with bad practices and complicit with moral corruption. Individuals like Albert and others interviewed regularly asked themselves questions about their roles: How do their day-to-day activities relate to basic moral norms? Are there elements of their jobs that they would not be comfortable sharing with people in their private lives, and if so, why? And what would it mean to fulfil one's role *well*, in accordance with moral principles?

Albert used various strategies for preventing his perspective from becoming too narrowly focused on his professional concerns. In contrast to many of his colleagues, he remained rooted in the local community and many of his friends and acquaintances were non-bankers. This helped him, he said, to critically scrutinize himself and his activities. It was also very important to him to stay in touch with employees on all levels of hierarchy as his career moved him up the corporate ladder. The multiplicity of perspectives helped him ask himself what he was doing, why he was doing it, and whether it was compatible with his moral commitments.

This is, arguably, a form of integrity: holding up one's ideals in the face of adversity, being willing to undergo painful processes of reflection about one's role and one's activities and how they relate to one's moral principles, struggling to avoid the various biases that might creep into one's moral perspective over time. Such a form of integrity may seem mundane compared to the great role models many of us see as paragons of integrity. But what would our work life and our organizations look like *without* people who act as transformational agents, and stand up for moral principles and values in their organizational roles? Arguably, it is the work – both the reflection and the actual activities – of individuals like Albert that prevents organizations from derailing morally, and that can help bring them back onto more moral paths. It is the combination of inside knowledge and involvement, and the willingness to critically scrutinize one's own actions, which makes the integrity of transformational agents so important for organizations.

Several people I interviewed also reported that they had specific moments of moral insights about their jobs, often in response to the reactions of outsiders. For example, a consultant told me about a time when he worked in a 'downsizing' project, crunching numbers without giving any thoughts to its moral dimensions. His mother saw on the evening news that there were huge protests because of the planned layoffs. She called him and asked, in shock: 'Is that you guys who are doing this?' Such moments offer individuals with a choice: Do they push the critical voices away, ignore them and maybe have a drink to forget them? Or are they willing to critically engage with their arguments, even if this may lead to the conclusion that one has not done the right thing? Many organizations *want* individuals to identify with their roles, to have employees who smoothly integrate themselves into the machine. But even from an organizational perspective, this is a dangerous strategy in the long term: if employees don't ask critical questions and engage in moral discussions, organizations miss an opportunity to detect and address morally sensitive issues early on, and might only discover them when it is too late – when the scandal is on the front page of the newspapers, or the prosecutor is on the premises.

But reflection is only the *precondition* for acting on one's moral commitments from within one's organizational roles. What also matters is to put the results of one's reflection into action – or 'transformational agency'. It can be understood as a form of integrity of individuals in roles that are part of morally problematic practices. Hirschman's distinction between 'voice' and 'exit', which he does not use for describing *moral* phenomena, can be easily adapted for describing these forms of agency.[7] 'Voice' means to speak up about problems, and to insist on being heard; Hirschman describes it as *political* action *par excellence*. 'Exit', by contrast, means the decision to leave if one disagrees with the practices of an organization, but feels one cannot change them; by exiting, one might at least succeed in sending a message to the organization. Often, voice and exit can be combined, or voice can be directed at different audiences to create indirect pressures.[8]

Albert told me about various instances in his career in which he successfully raised his voice, out of moral concerns. For example, in one job as a manager in a bank, he managed to reform the bonus schemes for service representations. The new system factored in the value *to clients* rather than focusing only on value *to the bank*. However, after a few months, just when the culture started to change, a new board of directors came in and scrapped the scheme, returning to incentive structures that focused on aggressive short-term profit maximization. For Albert, this was a defeat, and a clear sign that the organization was taking a route that he could not square with his understanding of good banking and basic moral norms. He started looking for a new job. But in other jobs, he had similar experiences: having to fight against powerful players with vested interests, and failing to convince them to change banking practices.

At some point, Albert realized that if he continued his career in large banks, the pattern would very likely repeat itself: a few months or years in a position, then there would be some moral conflict with his employer, and he would probably have to leave. Instead of continuing this pattern, he decided to take some risk: together with some colleagues who shared his moral commitments, he started a small financial company. He forwent the high salaries he could have earned in corporate roles, working, instead, on his vision to implement sustainable, environmentally friendly, socially useful banking practices and thereby to show that banking *can*, indeed, be different. He used his competences and his knowledge to build an alternative organization that he hoped would serve as a moral inspiration for the rest of the banking community.

Albert's transformational agency was a failure in some respects: he did not manage to abolish certain practices; he did not accomplish a revolution in the incentive structures of mainstream banking.[9] But in other respects, it was (and continues to be) highly successful, inasmuch as Albert and his colleagues established a viable finance company, committed to the moral standards that he could not find in his previous jobs. By doing so, they showed that other ways of being a banker are possible, even in a difficult market environment. The company thereby stands as a model for others, which can encourage more transformational agency. And Albert managed to remain true to his credo: he stuck to his standards, and he tried to ensure, through intense reflection and conversation with others, that his role would not corrupt his integrity.

To be sure, Albert was in many ways in a privileged position. He not only had a strong and independent character, but also valuable skills and a good network in the financial industry, and he had kept his standards of living low in order to make sure that he would not become dependent on a high-income job. Many individuals are in more vulnerable positions, and it is much harder for them to stand up against organizations if they encounter moral wrongdoing or want to make morally questionable practices public. Integrity can carry a high price if it means being willing to give up a good job (or maybe even a bad job) – this is something many individuals simply cannot afford.

But the price of integrity in the world of work is not set in stone. It is, at least in part, a question of the social structures in and around organizations: these structures determine, for example, what rights and responsibilities employees have and what steps they can take to protect themselves against pressures to violate their moral principles. It is also a question of the public reaction to organizational behaviour. For example, is there a critical press that is willing to take up issues raised by whistle-blowers? Are internal critics right to point out that organizations face public resistance and legal risks if they choose immoral practices? And last but not least, do we, as societies, see organizations as spaces in which at least certain basic moral norms remain intact – or have we bought into the narrative of organizations as 'morality free' zones in which only financial imperatives matter?

Whether or not individuals are able to maintain their integrity when entering their organizational roles as 'cogs in the wheel' is thus not only a question of individual morality – it is also a question of social and political norms and institutions. Instead of relying on a small number of outstanding models of integrity, in an age of divided labour we need to empower each other, as many of us as possible, to mutually support our integrity.

Recommended reading

Naturally, there is no further reading on 'Albert', but there are a number of works that deal with related aspects and questions about integrity in organizations. For example, Kimberley Brownlee discusses civil disobedience, including disobedience on the job, in *Conscience and Conviction: The Case for Civil Disobedience* (Oxford: Oxford University Press, 2012). Patricia Werhane provides an analysis of moral decision-making in organizations in *Moral Imagination and Management Decision-Making* (New York: Oxford University Press, 1999). Another angle from which similar themes can be approached is professional ethics; see for example, Larry May's *The Socially Responsible Self: Social Theory and Professional Ethics* (Chicago and London: The University of Chicago Press, 1996) or William Sullivan's *Work and Integrity: The Crisis and Promise of Professionalism in America* (San Francisco: Jossey-Bass, 2005). Recently, Bernardo Zacka has analysed the ways in which 'street level bureaucrats' deal with moral dilemmas in *When the State Meets the Street: Public Service and Moral Agency* (Cambridge, MA and London: The Belknap Press of Harvard University Press, 2017). My own book on ethical agency in organizations is *Reclaiming the System. Moral Responsibility, Divided Labour, and the Role of Organizations in Society* (Oxford: Oxford University Press, 2018).

Notes

1 The interview with Albert took place in 2012 in the context of a project on ethics in organizations. The arguments described below can also be found, in more detail, in chapter VIII of my book, *Reclaiming the System: Moral Responsibility, Divided Labour, and the Role of Organizations in Society* (Oxford: Oxford University Press, 2018).

2 The classic description of bureaucracy can be found in Max Weber, *Economy and Society: An Outline of Interpretive sociology*, ed. Guenther Roth, vol. III (New York: Bedminster Press, 1968), 956ff.

3 Cynthia Estlund, *Working Together: How Workplace Bonds Strengthen a Diverse Democracy* (New York: Oxford University Press, 2003).

4 However, Rawls uses this term for describing a theory of *justice*, while I look at *moral* norms. See esp. John Rawls, 'The Idea of an Overlapping Consensus', *Oxford Journal of Legal Studies* 7 (1) (1987): 1–25.

5 See for example, Joris Luyendijk, Joris, *The Banking Blog*, 2011–2013. Available at http://www.theguardian.com/commentisfree/joris-luyendijk-banking-blog, entry of 16 May 2013.

6 Robert Jackall, *Moral Mazes: The World of Corporate Managers* (New York and Oxford: Oxford University Press, 1988), 6.

7 Albert O. Hirschman, *Exit, Voice, and Loyalty: Responses to Decline in Firms, Organizations, and States* (Cambridge, MA.: Harvard University Press, 1970).

8 This alternative is also articulated in Plato's *Crito*. See the portrait of Plato's Socrates in ch. 1 of this book.

9 It is worth noting, however, that at a minimum, Albert managed to carry moral conversations into the organizations he worked for. He was an experienced banker with high professional credentials, and so his voice had more weight than that of outside critics. Perhaps some of his arguments had a long-term effect, slowly working on his colleagues' convictions, facilitating the work of the next Albert who would, hopefully, come along and try to morally improve things.

8

Huang Zongxi

Making it safe not to be servile

Sandra Leonie Field

We revel in the stories of moral heroes, stories of people who hold strong in their commitment to what they see to be right, regardless of the pressure on them to yield. They are moral saints, or even moral martyrs: for them, 'virtue is its own reward', above any other possible reward and against any possible penalty. But the moral good feelings from such stories quickly convert into outrage and anger when we contrast these moral heroes with the more common failures of integrity that we witness in everyday life. Nor is there a clear solution to the familiar everyday failures of integrity: if the essence of integrity is moral heroism, all we can do is vainly hope that more people might come to be more morally inspired.

The seventeenth-century political theorist Huang Zongxi (1610–1695) thought we could do better than wish earnestly for more moral saints and martyrs. He presents to us a portrait of a different sort of integrity, something more commonplace and reasonable to expect ordinary people to live up to. In his essay *Waiting for the Dawn: Advice for a Prince*,[1] Huang invites us to think more broadly about institutional conditions that *make it safe* for ordinary people, who are not moral saints and who do not want to be moral martyrs, to act with integrity. Perhaps there is a joy in acting with integrity, and for everyone virtue is its own reward, at least to some small degree. The problem is that often there are contrary incentives that outweigh that reward. Any optimism regarding human nature needs to be supported by a clear-eyed view of the various other desires and fears that weigh upon ordinary individuals as they make decisions in their lives. In particular, Huang shows us there needs to be attention to the drivers of *servility*: to the desires and fears that lead individuals to pander to the will of the powerful. A portrait of ordinary integrity will be one that is framed by a broader picture of a political ecology that allows servility to be overcome and integrity to shine through.

The dying days of the Ming dynasty form the backdrop for Huang's impatience with non-institutional approaches to integrity. In theory and in ideal, Ming dynasty China (1368–1644) was ruled by an Emperor, supported by an imperial court. The court comprised the ministers and other officials of the civil service. All members of the imperial civil service were Confucian scholars, whose knowledge of the classics would enable them to facilitate governance in accord with the Confucian Way of virtue. In practice, however, Emperors resented any constraint that the imperial civil service brought to bear on their ambitions and desires. They centralized Imperial power, and sought to achieve a docile and compliant civil service; suspicious of roles that might limit or compete with Imperial power, they eliminated the post of prime minister.[2]

The case of Scholar Fang (1357–1402), perhaps the most famous Confucian martyr in Chinese history, would have offered Huang an example of heroic integrity. The Yongle Emperor (1360–1424), an early Ming emperor, wanted the great Confucian scholar, Scholar Fang, to assist him by drafting imperial ordinances. The Yongle Emperor had, in fact, illegitimately usurped the throne; Fang did not approve of it and therefore he thought it was inappropriate to cooperate. Scholar Fang arrived at the court in mourning clothes, and declared that he preferred death to assisting the new Emperor. The Emperor was not prepared to tolerate this ostentatious display of virtue. He promised to deny Fang's wish: if Fang continued not to assist him, he would not satisfy Fang's desire for death, but, instead, he would kill his 'nine families'. The killing of nine degrees of kinship was the most serious punishment in ancient China, but Fang was undeterred. Refusing to back down, he invited the Emperor to kill his ten families, and then continued to defy the Emperor's command. He wrote just one sentence for the Emperor – 'The Bastard Prince Di of Yan usurped the throne' – on a piece of paper that he threw back in the Emperor's face. Even as the Emperor gathered together Fang's nine families, Fang continued to upbraid the Emperor. To silence Fang's insolence, the Emperor ordered that Fang's tongue and cheeks be cut off. Fang, unable to talk, spurted blood on him. The Emperor dismembered Scholar Fang's body and killed his nine families, as well as his friends and disciples, a total of 873 people.[3] In the face of this exemplar of heroic integrity, far from being inspired to virtue, many scholar-officials were cowed into submission, as, of course, was the Emperor's intention. If Fang's case teaches the cost of not being servile, small wonder if decent upstanding people choose servility instead.

Bloody though he was, at least the Yongle Emperor was effective. Subsequent Ming emperors combined a similar hostility to criticism with a sybaritic lifestyle of luxury and concubines, allowing for the rise of the eunuchs as a political force. Eunuchs had long played a role in Chinese imperial rule. They were responsible for the imperial household and the Emperor's personal needs; they could be put in charge of the Emperor's harem without the Emperor facing any risk of becoming a cuckold. Their intimacy with the Emperor allowed them to pander to his whims. In return for this, favoured eunuchs were increasingly entrusted with carrying out his political business, thus sidelining and subverting the civil service.

Between the submissive civil service and the pandering of the eunuchs, there was little check on Imperial power within the Imperial court. Traditional Confucianism proposed a model of politics in which virtue naturally rules. In Confucius' words, 'One who rules through the power of Virtue is analogous to the Pole Star: it simply remains in its place and receives the homage of the myriad lesser stars' (*Kongzi*, 2.1)[4]. A good ruler learns virtue by reflecting upon the examples of the sage-Kings of the ancient Confucian golden age; his subjects gladly obey.

But where does this leave upstanding subjects whose emperor is indifferent to virtue? In the late Ming period, a group of scholars formed the Donglin academy, an oppositional force characterized by its rigorous adherence to Confucian precepts of virtue, even at great personal cost. The Donglin academy found many sympathizers within the Imperial civil service: all civil servants, after all, were trained in the Confucian classics. The late Ming period became riven by conflict between the Donglin faction and the eunuchs, and amidst this conflict the governance of the country was neglected and misdirected, and famine fell upon the land. The peasants rose up (1628–1644), the Ming dynasty collapsed, and Manchurian invaders from the north inaugurated a new dynasty, the Qing (1644–1912).

Huang Zongxi was born in the final decades of the Ming dynasty, and received a good Confucian education. But what could he make of the traditional Confucian idea of the people naturally bowing to the gentle influence of virtue? His own father was a virtuous Confucian scholar-official in the Donglin faction, but in reward for his noble efforts, he was murdered by a eunuch. Beyond this intense familial experience of a corrupt political system, Huang was also in other respects uniquely well placed to analyse politics. His personal circumstances freed him to be acutely critical of all contemporary political powers. Despite all the Ming dynasty's flaws, Huang was a loyalist, fighting in guerilla resistance against the Qing for more than a decade until all hope of a Ming restoration was lost. He did not need to please the Qing, because as a loyalist, he could never hold office in the Qing regime. But the Ming dynasty had collapsed, so it too was fair game for criticism: What were the causes of its fall? His reflections on this topic are compiled in his best-known work, *Waiting for the Dawn*.

Waiting for the Dawn proposes a fundamental and intuitively appealing criterion for good politics, expressed through an analogy with the relationship between master and tenant. A tenant works for the benefit of the master. Applying this to the political relationship between the prince (emperor) and all-under-heaven (the populace), Huang contrasts the golden age of virtuous Confucian kings with the present. Whereas 'in ancient times, all-under-Heaven were considered the master, and the prince was the tenant', now the situation is reversed: 'the prince is master, and all-under-Heaven are tenants' (*Waiting*, 92).

In other words, good politics serves the common benefit, whereas bad and corrupted politics serves the personal interest of the ruler. Whereas generations of Confucians had exhorted subjects to uphold the virtues of obedience, deference and filiality, even to the worst ruler, Huang boldly embraces the revolutionary possibilities of distinguishing between good and bad politics. He explicitly endorses a famous passage of the classic text the *Mengzi*, which was often suppressed in his time (*Waiting*, 92-93): if a ruler is a tyrant, then he fails truly to be a ruler. He has become nothing better than a 'mutilator and a thief' (*Mengzi*, 1B8), and correspondingly deserves punishment, including execution.

But Huang is under no illusions that this willingness to distinguish tyranny from proper rule, and willingness to punish it accordingly, amounts to a sufficient theory of good politics. The benefit of all-under-heaven does not take care of itself: when a bad form of politics is removed, then the task of establishing a good form still faces us. Nor is this straightforward: ruling well is hard, exhausting work for the prince, and contrary to all humans' natural inclination to ease and pleasure (*Waiting*, 91-92). The critical question will be this: How to bring about good rule?

Huang's answer begins with a detour: let us start by considering what a good minister should do. '[W]hen one goes forth to serve, it is for all-under-Heaven and not for the prince' (*Waiting*, 94). This follows from our fundamental criterion of good politics: even though a minister works for the prince, his[5] activities should not serve the prince's desires. When one acts for the sake of all-under-Heaven and its people, then one 'cannot agree to do anything contrary to the Way even if the prince explicitly constrains one to do so' (*Waiting*, 94). To put this in other words, a good minister should act with *integrity*.

Notice a striking feature of Huang's analysis: the main threat to integrity is not self-interest. Self-interest may be a problem, but Huang is primarily concerned about combating a different phenomenon, namely, *servility*. The exemplar of servility is a house-servant. Such a servant does not act for their own interest. But neither do they even act for their master's interest. Instead, they act to satisfy whatever wish or desire their master has; indeed, a good house-servant seeks to satisfy the desires even before the master has articulated them. Crucially, they do not pass judgement on these desires. Servility is this total submission to the master's whim. Huang allows that servility has its place in the domestic sphere, but it is fatal to politics: 'To act solely for the prince and his dynasty, and attempt to anticipate the prince's unexpressed whims or cravings – this is to have the mind of a eunuch or a palace maid' (*Waiting*, 95, see also 166).

The solution to bad political orders is to have ministers, most especially prime ministers, who are not servile. When ministers act with integrity rather than servility, then they pass judgement on the prince's desires and judgements. They place virtuous pressure on the ego of the prince, bringing his decisions back in line with the Way, and thereby benefiting all-under-Heaven.

This solution to the problem of securing a good political order may appear to be no solution at all. Certainly, if ministers act with integrity, then the prince is somewhat constrained to rule in accordance with the Way. But recall that our starting point was the problem that princes are sometimes tempted not to exert themselves with virtue. How much more of a problem it is for ministers! Remember what happened to Scholar Fang: if integrity comes at the cost of such spectacular martyrdom, we can predict that there will be few ministers of integrity. Nor is it clear that integrity is even particularly efficacious in the end. Think of Huang's own father and the other leaders of the Donglin faction: their virtuous remonstrances were certainly irritating for the imperial court so long as they lasted, but ultimately they were crushed. The lesson for future ministers was clear, even for those of virtuous disposition: the only safe route is servility. And perhaps this is also the route of efficacy: hopefully you can make some small positive contributions to good rule within the confines of your servile role, and these positive contributions amount to something, in contrast to the utter futility of heroic martyrdom. Surely this is the best way to serve all-under-heaven, given the circumstances.

The cautious counsel of virtuous servility may be prudent and necessary, but it amounts to entirely abandoning integrity as a real political value. And this is not something that Huang is prepared to do. Could there be a different way to think about integrity? Huang wonders, what if it were possible to *make it safe not to be servile*? After all, Huang is a Confucian who is confident that there is some inner reward and satisfaction for us when we act virtuously; if only the harsh incentives against integrity can be lessened, then we can have integrity as an everyday realizable moral value. We can realistically call for ordinary integrity to characterize the conduct of ministers.

The key to Huang's proposal is the institutionalization of integrity: we need established practices that protect and guard the space for individual political actors to behave with integrity. These practices cover a full gamut of political forms. There are ritual practices in which political actors regularly symbolically perform and display respect. Huang tells us, for example, that 'in ancient times the prince treated his ministers with such courtesy that when a minister bowed to the emperor, the emperor always bowed in return' (*Waiting*, 94).

There are laws that serve the public interest and therefore do not force officials into a hard choice between the Confucian Way of virtue and the prince's will (*Waiting*, 97-99). And there are institutional schedules and patterns of interaction that require the prince to expose himself to the criticism of ministers and scholars: every day, he hears presentations and submissions from his ministers, according to the agenda that they decide; once a month, he visits the Imperial College in the status of a student, listening in deference to the judgement of the most eminent scholars (*Waiting*, 103, 107). All of these dissipate a power that would otherwise be centralized in the prince's unfettered will.

In Huang's view, for most of us, whether prince, minister or ordinary citizen, virtue is not a free-floating possibility, unrelated to the institutional structure in which we live. But we can have insight into the kind of conditions that will support our virtue. In particular, we might hope that a reasonable prince could be persuaded of the need to establish an institutional system that curbs his whims and desires, and which subjects his judgement to scrutiny. Central to this system is the protection of space for all other political actors to be non-servile, without facing martyrdom for doing so. And within this space, these other actors will rise to the occasion, enjoying the inherent satisfaction of acting with integrity.

The optimism of this proposal might appear not to be supported by the historical record. How would Huang's optimism explain the Ming emperors' consistently striving to establish a system of centralized power supported by eunuchs and servile ministers? Why did these emperors not maintain the model of the Confucian golden age, where the prince deferred to the virtuous judgement of ministers and scholars? It was not for want of scholars explaining to them that they should! Huang provides a sharp diagnosis of the temptations of servility, both for master and slave.

[W]henever ministers of state opposed the emperor's misguided desires, the eunuchs would say, '... How can they be so disrespectful?' ... So [the emperor] said '... It seems as if the household ministers really love me, while the state ministers only love themselves!' Thereupon, those who served as ministers took this as an indication of what pleased the emperor and what displeased him. As a result, they abandoned the true way of teacher and friend, hastening to adopt the manners and appearance of slaves (*Waiting*, 166).

If the prince is so absorbed in his own desires that he is unable to recognize the possibility that his desires and judgements are misguided, then he will not permit the development of a political order in which ministers are safe not to be servile. This narcissism always remains a possibility and a temptation for a ruler. In a bad political order that is organized to support rulerly narcissism, subjects face an unsatisfactory choice between heroic integrity and servility. Under such conditions, servility becomes a reasonable path: well-intentioned individuals are reduced to making occasional small positive contributions within their servile roles, where it does not directly conflict with rulerly intentions. But a good political system eliminates this constraint, and makes space for us all to cultivate our ordinary integrity.

Recommended reading

There is not a lot written about Huang in English. The scholar who has done the most to bring Huang's story and his philosophy to Anglophone audiences is Wm. Theodore de Bary: readers might helpfully start with de Bary's introduction to the text of *Waiting for the Dawn*. De Bary provides further analysis in a recent article: 'Waiting for the Dawn: Huang Zongxi's Critique of the Chinese Dynastic System', in Wm. Theodore de Bary (ed.), *Finding Wisdom in East Asian Classics* (New York: Columbia University Press, 2011); as well as in his classic study, *The Liberal Tradition in China* (New York: Columbia University Press, 1983). For readers wanting to compare Huang's view to the categories of Euro-American political theory, see Elton Chan, 'Huang Zongxi as a Republican: A Theory of Governance for Confucian Democracy', *Dao: A Journal of Comparative Philosophy* 17 (2) (2018). Volume 7 of C. C. Low's *A General History of China* (Singapore: Canfonian Pte Ltd, 1995) retells the history of the relevant period of Chinese history in graphic novel format.

Notes

1 Huang Zongxi, *Waiting for the Dawn: A Plan for the Prince*, trans. Wm. Theodore de Bary (New York: Columbia University Press, 1993).
2 C. C. Low et al., *A General History of China, Vol. 7: Ming Dynasty* (Singapore: Canfonian Pte Ltd, 1995), 20–2. In what follows, I provide a rough caricature history of the period, with the purpose of supporting Huang's own analysis of politics. For a history of the period meeting proper scholarly standards, see Dennis C. Twitchett and Frederick W. Mote, *The Cambridge History of China, Volumes 7 & 8: The Ming Dynasty, Parts I & II* (Cambridge: Cambridge University Press, 2008).
3 Low et al., *A General History of China*, 42–3.
4 The *Kongzi*, in Philip J. Ivanhoe and Bryan W. Van Norden (eds.), *Readings in Classical Chinese Philosophy* (Indianapolis: Hackett, 2005).
5 There was no possibility of women holding political office in this period.

9

Lambert Strether

'What plays you least false' in a life with others

Danielle Petherbridge

Although Henry James did not write a philosophical treatise on moral experience, as Cora Diamond suggests, 'he was a great observer and painter of that variety' and his late novels provide a rich canvas upon which the textures and nuances of integrity are explored.[1] The late novels such as *The Wings of the Dove*, *The Golden Bowl* and *The Ambassadors*, offer ways of thinking about integrity that are not about major historical figures or extraordinary heroic deeds in extreme social and historical conditions, but rather portray characters for whom everyday circumstances give rise to issues or struggles with integrity. Such portraits thereby indicate the complexity and ambivalence associated with integrity and conflicts about interpretation and judgement in regard to 'right' and 'wrong' action in everyday life.

James' novels offer a historicized version of moral categories; they portray a new constellation of moral dilemmas with the rise of capitalism and materialism that challenge conventional forms of (self)evaluation and moral concepts, including questions of integrity. The novels also raise the question of whether forms of integrity might be socially or historically specific rather than necessarily universal or general. In this sense, his literature is instructive for the way in which it explores morality understood as a matter of habits or mores rather than as universal principles, and it therefore draws attention to the forms of moral particularism at play in a given situation.[2]

The late novels of James, then, offer a means to explore the nuances of philosophical categories and to break open rigid forms of moral understanding.[3] As Richard Rorty suggests, James offers his readers 'a sense of the possibility of a new level of consciousness, the chance to enter a world … different from the one we usually inhabit', and to notice things we do not usually notice.[4] James does so by employing techniques of interior monologue from the view of individual characters, which are juxtaposed against one another in order to reveal differences of perception, insight and interpretation in regard to a given situation.

The Ambassadors deals with questions not only of individual but also of relational integrity, especially the way in which the characters are tempted to compromise themselves or build instrumental relations with others in order to achieve their goals, desires or needs. The most fundamental experience for James' characters is one of entanglement with others. The dilemma they are continually confronted with is how to live a life of one's own within these interdependent conditions; how to navigate or negotiate 'living all you can' (181), as Lambert Strether puts it in *The Ambassadors*, in the context of relations with others.

In James' later novels, 'integrity' is often associated with a notion of freedom and reflexivity, as well as a sense of an individual's life having some sort of meaning. For characters such as Lambert Strether, however, meaning and the 'getting of wisdom' is often achieved only after the fact, that is, after the realization that he has been deceived by others or has been living a life constructed or shaped by others. Rather than invoking a kind of 'puritanism' or moralism in response, though, James demonstrates the ways in which these characters incorporate the actions and interpretations of others into new forms of moral understanding.

The Ambassadors continually explores the tension between subjectivity and dependency, including understandings and interpretations based on the consciousness of others. This, however, does not necessarily represent a form of self-deception, but as the novel suggests, refers to a form of 'double-consciousness'. We see this ambiguity captured poignantly at the beginning of the novel, where Strether is characterized by ambivalence and conflicting intentions and is described as 'burdened with ... a double consciousness'. 'There was', the narrator tells us 'detachment in his zeal and curiosity in his indifference' (7). It is this kind of ambiguity and the conflict of emotions that resonates throughout the novel, as Strether gradually moves towards a realization of his own integrity and independence.

Like the other late novels, *The Ambassadors* revolves around the triadic character structure of a wealthy heir(ess), a mediating friend and a seemingly opportunistic suitor.[5] Lambert Strether is the mediating loyal 'ambassador' for his wealthy (widowed) American fiancé Mrs. Newsome. At the behest of Mrs. Newsome, Strether is sent on an ambassadorial mission to bring back her wayward son, Chad Newsome (the heir to the Newsome fortune), who had left New England for Europe five years earlier. His mother, Mrs. Newsome, is convinced that the only reason he has not returned home to Woollett, New England, to take up his responsibilities is that a corrupting and ill-intentioned French woman has seduced him and is keeping him in France under false pretences. Mrs. Newsome makes it clear to Strether that her impending marriage to him is entirely conditional upon his successful mission in Paris to carry out her will and to retrieve her lost son. Accordingly, Strether travels to Europe as Mrs. Newsome's representative, and the novel unfolds as he begins his journey to fulfil his ambassadorial task.

Upon disembarking first in London and then in Paris, Strether is struck by old memories of Europe and the associations it held for him in his youth, that is, of a type of life that might be worth living, one of purpose and integrity. Within this context Strether begins to experience a consciousness of his freedom, and a sense that he has escaped the moralistic confines of Mrs. Newsome as well as Woollett and all that it represents, a life that has reduced him to a mere 'little scrap of identity' (56). He begins, as he puts it, to experience 'the strange logic of finding himself so free' (60). For Strether, there is an ongoing struggle throughout the novel between independence and dependence; heteronomy and autonomy, and of living a life that is not his own in contrast to one that might be. One of the questions of the novel is this: What might such a life look like?[6] In part, this process unfolds in the company of Maria Gostrey who Strether meets en route to Paris. She acts as a reflexive voice that encourages him to find his own truth and independence, and challenges him to confront the issue of his own integrity.

This sense of living a life that is not his own is exacerbated by the way in which Strether begins his journey informed by 'Woollett' moral categories and forms of understanding. He sets out, for example, with the standard Woollett views about Chad and his French lover, Madame de Vionnet, who is considered to have entrapped Chad and with whom it is assumed he is having an unvirtuous affair. Upon reaching Paris and speaking to Chad's friends, particularly Little Bilham, Strether is in fact led to believe that the relation between Madame de Vionnet and Chad is nothing but 'virtuous' and Platonic, a friendship of a beautiful sort and of the highest order (168). Strether later learns that he has been deceived when he accidentally comes across the two lovers boating upon a river and also learns that Madame de Vionnet is, in fact, married (458–467). However, instead of being outraged by the deception or the adulterous affair in which his future son-in-law is involved, Strether avoids taking the 'Woollett moralistic view'. As such, he becomes not only accepting but also supportive of the couple to such an extent that he tries to encourage Chad to remain true to his own convictions and stay in Paris to be with Madame de Vionnet instead of returning to New England.

Throughout this process of 'getting of wisdom' there are several important events and transformations that occur for Strether, particularly in regard to forms of interpretation, self-reflection and the recognition of his own freedom and integrity.

First, throughout the novel Strether worries about the manner in which the actions of Chad and Madame de Vionnet should be judged. He constantly tries to come to terms with competing interpretations of their relationship: those that accord with the 'Woollett point of view', and the subtle reinterpretations of virtue that mean their relationship does not neatly fit into standard moral truths or categories. This is complicated later in the novel when Strether realizes that Madame de Vionnet is, indeed, virtuous in regard to the relationship and that, in fact, it is Chad who is disingenuous. The question revolves around how we, or rather how the characters in the novel, understand the term 'virtuousness' in their judgement of Chad and Madame de Vionnet. Moreover, we witness how Strether eventually tries to judge the relationship 'for itself' or 'as it is' rather than according to the Woollett point of view.

The second important transformation is captured in the interactions between Little Bilham and Strether at a garden party of a well-known sculptor in Paris. At this point in the text, Strether makes an impassioned speech to Little Bilham, indicating that he has begun to reflect upon the matter of his own integrity and the importance of one 'having one's life'. He begins by offering advice to Little Bilham to live the fullest life possible, indicating that to neglect to do so means one is neither free nor freely 'formed'.

Strether goes on to reflect upon what he terms the affair of life; contrasting two alternative metaphors for life he says:

> [I]t's at the best a tin mould, either fluted and embossed, with ornamental excrescences, or else smooth and dreadfully plain, into which, a helpless jelly, one's consciousness is poured – so that one 'takes the form', as the great cook says, and is more or less compactly held by it: one lives in fine as one can. Still, one has the illusion of freedom; therefore don't be, like me, without the memory of that illusion. (181)

James understands this sense of consciousness as externally shaped as though poured into a tin mould as 'strange' and 'pitiful'. He also seems to suggest that integrity cannot easily be understood in terms of the purity of identity, or as a rigidly conceived form of self, isolated from or unaffected by others. The fact that one rarely looks at life for oneself and is moulded by conventional mores and values means one often lives in a false state of consciousness, thinking of oneself as free without any memory of the true value of freedom. For James, the important point is that one must become reflexive about this condition and become conscious of one's condition in the midst of a life with others.

It is in this context that Strether asks what is perhaps the central question in the book. In response to a compliment about his character from Little Bilham, he retorts: '*Impayable*, as you say, no doubt. *But what am I to myself?*' (182). It is precisely this question that drives Strether to explore his conscience in the closing scenes of the novel. There he suggests that although in conventional terms the views of others may be deemed 'priceless', the real question is this: How do I value myself? He comes to realize that even within the constellation of relations with others one must have one's own life.

After gradually embarking on a reflexive journey, Strether ultimately rejects his ambassadorial role and the inauthentic

Woollett life that he has been living. He also comes to realize that his dependence on Mrs. Newsome is based purely on her money and power, and he is prepared to lose it all in order to maintain some kind of integrity – even if this is a somewhat complicated form of integrity, one that is always characterized by a double consciousness or a way of 'living doubly'.[7] However, Strether also leaves Maria Gostrey, of whom he had originally become rather fond and who acted as his voice of conscience, so to speak. Maria beseeches Strether to stay with her at the close of the novel. However, in the end he realizes, as Maria does too, that his feelings for her have been compromised by his growing affection for Madame de Vionnet, which he vows not to act upon out of a sense of responsibility and decency towards Chad. This makes staying in Paris unthinkable: he eventually returns to Woollett but does so on his own terms independent of any former arrangements with Mrs. Newsome and with a certain realization about his relations with others.

Within the novel, important questions are raised about the basis upon which the actions and integrity of the characters can be judged, or on what grounds such judgements are made possible.[8] Throughout this work, James is particularly concerned with the notion of 'consciousness' and the development of 'conscience' or the getting of wisdom. However, there is a double logic operating here: on the one hand, there is a sense in which perception and interpretation are particular and highly subjective, often with issues being portrayed from the point of view of a particular character or of the narrator. Yet, on the other hand, there is a sense that our moral perspectives are also highly dependent upon others and are socially embedded. In contrast to standard philosophical views that often understand integrity as a fidelity to one's personal projects and commitments or as a harmonious union of one's desires, volitions and motivations, James seems to offer a very different sense of what awareness of one's own internal states and judgements might involve and how this awareness relates to others.

The figure of Lambert Strether raises the issue of whether integrity should be conceived as oriented around the individual, or whether it might be conceived in social or relational terms. It also suggests that integrity cannot simply be understood as a form of integrated self or a steadfast and unwavering commitment to one's own projects without any consideration of others. In this sense, it raises questions about integrity understood as a form of moral puritanism or fanaticism, of sticking to one's guns or commitments, no matter what the consequences. Integrity, in *The Ambassadors* is not understood as a rigid form of morality or moral personhood that is maintained at all costs, or as a commitment to a sense of core identity to which one dedicates oneself absolutely or dogmatically. Rather, integrity here is painted as a kind of 'coming to integrity', of acquiring a certain self-awareness and self-knowledge while not sacrificing others on the basis of puritanical viewpoints or commitments. James paints Strether as a figure faced with ambivalence, inconsistency and contingency, who at times is confronted with value systems that conflict with one another, yet who attempts to shape and maintain subtle forms of integrity.

James' account is further complicated at the end of the novel when he leaves open the question of whether or not Strether does come to achieve 'a life of his own' or whether he does so only imperfectly; that is, whether his integrity is maintained only by abandoning his relations with others. Yet, in the closing passages his decision not to stay in Europe is made after a knowing discussion with Maria Gostrey when the two agree that he 'must go' in order for it '[t]o be right' (518). That is Strether's 'only logic', as he explains, '[n]ot out of the whole affair, to have got anything for myself' but to have remained virtuous towards others (518). This suggests that 'integrity' cannot simply be thought of as an individualistic or subjective category but is one of intersubjective complexity. In other words, we can only understand ourselves in particular contexts of meaning; our desires, motivations, commitments and values are constructed in the context of our relations with others. This complicates the notion of integrity and questions its conventional meaning. In this respect, James' novel suggests that integrity might be understood as 'what plays you least false' (482) in the context of a life with others.

Recommended reading

A full exploration of Lambert Strether's struggle with integrity can be found in Henry James, *The Ambassadors* (New York: Modern Library, 2011). Further studies on portraits of integrity in the work of Henry James can also be found in other late novels, including *The Wings of the Dove* (New York: The Modern Library, 2003) and

The Golden Bowl (London: Penguin Books, 2009). These novels, like *The Ambassadors*, explore complex relations and portray characters who are confronted with their own integrity or for whom everyday instances of integrity are raised within the context of personal relations. An illuminating study of Henry James' work that situates his characters within the context of the rise of new forms of capitalism and materialism and new moral dilemmas is provided by Robert Pippin, *Henry James and Modern Moral Life* (Cambridge: Cambridge University Press, 2000). Martha Nussbaum also provides interesting observations about James' late work and the ways in which his novels explore the question of what it is to live a good life. Her comments on the relation between literature and philosophy in this context are also valuable (See Nussbaum, *Love's Knowledge: Essays on Philosophy and Literature* [New York and Oxford: Oxford University Press, 1990]).

Notes

1 Cora Diamond, 'Henry James, Moral Philosophers, Moralism', *The Henry James Review* 18 (3) (1997): 243–57, p. 243.

2 See Robert B. Pippin's discussion in *Henry James and Modern Moral Life* (Cambridge: Cambridge University Press, 2000), 147, 5.

3 Also see Martha Nussbaum, '"Finely Aware and Richly Possible": Literature and Moral Imagination' and 'Perceptive Equilibrium: Literary Theory and Ethical Theory', in *Love's Knowledge: Essays on Philosophy and Literature* (New York and Oxford: Oxford University Press, 1990), 148–67, 168–94.

4 Richard Rorty, 'Redemption from Egotism', in C. J. Voparil and R. Bernstein (eds), *The Rorty Reader* (Chichester: Wiley-Blackwell, 2010), 393, 399, 401.

5 See also Pippin, *Henry James*; ibid., 149.

6 Ibid., 152.

7 See Pippin's discussion in *Henry James*.

8 Ibid., 7.

10

Confucius' village worthies

Hypocrites as thieves of virtue

Winnie Sung

'Village worthies', says Confucius, 'are the thieves of virtue' (*Analects* 17.13). Village worthies are those who are popular and respected in their villages as virtuous, conscientious, truthful and incorruptible in their conduct. Confucius (c. 551–479 BCE) particularly detests the village worthies for outwardly acting in ways that people commonly regard as moral but inwardly lacking the relevant virtuous character that substantiates their behaviours. But why detest them so much as to call them the thieves of virtue? Although it is not ideal that one does not have a virtuous character, it is at least better for one to perform virtuous acts than to perform vicious acts – or so the thought goes.

Confucius does not say more about the village worthies than this. But Mencius (c.372–289 BCE), one of Confucius' most prominent interpreters, sheds some light on the matter, by telling us more about what the village worthies are like. According to Mencius:

> If you would blame them, you find nothing to allege. If you would criticize them, you have nothing to criticize. They agree with the current customs. They consent with an impure age. Their principles [appear to be] right-heartedness and truth. Their

conduct [appears to be] disinterestedness and purity. All men are pleased with them, and they [deem themselves to be right, but one cannot] proceed with them to the principles of Yao and Shun.[1] On this account they are called 'The thieves of virtue.' (*Mencius* 7B:37, trans. Lau, modified)

We may understand the village worthies as a special kind of hypocrite. These village worthies would say and do anything in order to please others.[2] Although their words and actions might happen to be in line with ethical standards, such convergence is accidental. Should others' expectations and likings be a little bit off from the ethical standards, the village worthies would cease to speak and act ethically.

One distinctive feature of these village worthies is that they do not have a hidden side. Fictional hypocrites like Iago, Tartuffe and Uriah Heep also act in ways that appear to be virtuous, but we readers know what these fictional hypocrites are really like deep down. We may call these fictional hypocrites *inner-outer inconsistent* hypocrites. Their appearances are like masks that conceal their real faces. The village worthies, by contrast, do not have a real face that is inconsistent with the image they project. Instead, they take on whatever face is considered attractive or laudable by the people they want to appeal to. The village worthies are like chameleons: they respond to the environment but do not have a colour of their own. Such people are *appearance-only* hypocrites.

The appearance-only hypocrite puts us in a special predicament, for someone who does not wear a mask cannot be *unmasked*. One may unmask Tartuffe and expose his profane side; but there is nothing that we can expose when it comes to the village worthies because there is nothing underneath.[3]

We might think of the village worthies, then, as lacking integrity in a distinctive sort of way. This may account for Confucius' severe disapproval. We might see the difficulty by considering Gabriele Taylor's notion of the person of integrity as someone who preserves her identity – that is, 'what identifies the person as essentially the person he is' or 'what is truly hers'[4]. On such an understanding of integrity, one who lacks integrity is someone whose actions or words do not reflect the kind of person she really is. Assuming that having identifications is necessary for having an identity, the village worthies' lack of identifications means we cannot say what kind of persons they really are. They do not have anything that they identify with, and hence do not have what is *truly* theirs. We cannot in their case say that there is any break between their practices and their true identity. The village worthies lack integrity not in the sense where one's identity is corrupted or concealed but because they do not even have their own identifications.

One might wonder whether being a village worthy itself can be the village worthy's identification, so that for a village worthy to have integrity is for him or her to live like a true village worthy. The problem is, there is nothing that it is to be a village worthy. Someone who identifies with a set of values associated with a particular role would be willing to bear possible losses to self-interests and accept constraints on what she can or cannot do in defence of her identifications. The village worthies, by contrast, will take on any role to reflect others' values and expectations. There is no way of conducting the role, nor values proper to it.

The village worthies' lack of integrity also prevents others from engaging in meaningful personal relationships with them. In the cases of inner-outer inconsistent hypocrites, the hypocrites still have their own views, it is just that these views are masked. A relationship with the inner-outer inconsistent hypocrites is, of course, defective because their audience is being kept from the truth; yet there *is* a truth of the matter, and so it is possible that the audience may somehow discover what the inner-outer inconsistent hypocrite actually thinks. The possibility of unmasking implies the possibility to really get to know the person under the mask and therefore a choice of whether one wants to be acquainted with the real person. In the case of village worthies, however, since there is not even the possibility of unmasking them, there is not even the possibility of really getting to know them, for there is no one there to get to know. Since the village worthies do not have their own character, there is no ground to even begin a personal relationship with them. The audience will never get to see the genuine side of them, for there is not any. There is nothing underneath, so to speak, that the village worthies' audience can latch on to, to establish some sort of bond with the village worthies.

The impossibility of genuine relationships, though unfortunate, may not seem so grave. Some might prefer their acquaintances to continue the pretence, or prefer to interact with others in a superficial way so as to promote or preserve their own public image and self-esteem. It seems that Confucius, as Mencius understands him, has a broader worry about the presence of these village worthies aside from their inability to engage with others. On a larger scale, Confucius thinks that the presence of people who have no identity of their own, and merely reflect others' values, is a threat to the moral system. Mencius quotes Confucius as saying:

> I detest what is specious. I detest the foxtail for fear it should pass for seedlings. I detest flattery for fear it should pass for what is right. I detest glibness for fear it should pass for the truthful ... I detest purple for fear it should pass for vermilion.[5] I detest the village worthy for fear he should pass for the virtuous. (*Mencius* 7B:37, trans. Lau, modified)

Just as the colour purple, which closely resembles vermilion, easily confuses people and misleads people in their choice, the village worthies, who look just like the virtuous people according to our current conceptions and appear attractive to the audience, easily confuse their audience and mislead them into thinking that they have the more attractive character than the genuinely virtuous people. The village worthies will pretend to have moral qualities that appeal to their audience, and will not pretend to have moral qualities that do not appeal to their audience. Hence, the village worthies will never fail a moral test from the perspective of their audience. Although a small group of genuinely virtuous people might be able to detect the village worthies' hypocrisy, they will not be able to convince the village worthies' audience that these seemingly gracious and attractive people are not what they appear.

The village worthies pose a special sort of risk to moral community: they stand in the way in morally complex and urgent cases because they merely propagate the public's confused moral judgements and potentially undermine certain moral judgements that are essential to moral community. In a morally complex situation where certain moral qualities are called for, but the complex nature of the situation prevents the audience from finding those moral qualities attractive, the village worthies will not exhibit those moral qualities. In a morally urgent situation, the village worthies side only with popular opinion. If they think the kind of act required in a morally urgent situation is deemed laudable by the general public, they might still do the morally right thing. A problem occurs, however, when there is a divergence between public opinion and what is, in fact, called for in a morally urgent situation. Suppose it is morally wrong for officials to accept bribes but the majority or dominant group of the community thinks that it is acceptable. In this case, the village worthies may take bribes without causing their audience to think that they are immoral. In an attempt to protect themselves from possible criticism by the group of people who defend rectitude, they might, in turn, criticize the morally upright for being too stringent and impractical in practice. The village worthies will mock those who firmly hold moral values for being inflexible and not knowing how to engage with people. Such mocking or criticism of the morally upright will further reinforce the majority's misguided thinking on moral issues. Hence, in cases where we have an unstable moral system and the general public are in the process of working out their views on certain moral issues, the pretence of village worthies who perpetuate confusions over moral issues only accelerates the collapse of an already unstable moral system.

This brings us to the point that the presence of village worthies also harms the genuinely virtuous people in a community. We may figuratively speak of the hypocrite as a thief of virtue who free rides on the virtues of the genuinely good people for self-serving purposes. If the qualities of the genuinely virtuous people align with the preference of the majority or dominant group, the village worthies will imitate the qualities of the virtuous people. In such cases, the village worthies are not only being credited with qualities they do not deserve; more problematically, the village worthies feign the virtuous qualities only for self-serving purposes that are against the nature of these qualities. Even if the genuinely virtuous people themselves are not bothered by the village worthies' stealing their qualities, the village worthies are still a threat to the genuinely virtuous people because the village worthies subvert the moral system that the genuinely virtuous people are committed to building and preserving. And as mentioned earlier, if the qualities of the genuinely virtuous people do not align with the preference of the majority, the village worthies will criticize the genuinely virtuous people. In doing so, the village worthies distract the general public from recognizing and crediting the genuinely virtuous people with the praise they deserve. Hence, we may take Confucius' comment that the village worthies are the thieves of virtue to have two senses: the harm they pose to the system of morality and the harm they pose to genuinely virtuous people.

Although Confucius himself emphasizes the importance of observing ritual practices and maintaining harmony with others, he does not think that one should indiscriminately follow norms and morph oneself in accordance with the preferences of others. For Confucius, one of the significant marks distinguishing the ethically superior person (*junzi*) from the petty person (*xiao ren*) is whether he is committed to ethical standards.[6] The superior person, he says, is versed in righteousness/propriety, whereas the petty person is versed in self-interest (4.16). Ethically superior persons are easy of mind and do not fret about others' perception of them. They seek to be harmonious but do not attempt to be similar to others (13.23). Since the ethically superior person has his own moral commitments and identifications, he is bound to disagree with people sometimes and will inevitably have a certain degree of independence from, not indifference towards, others.

That the ethically superior person is not troubled by others' opinion of him does not mean that he does not care about others. Quite the contrary, the ethically superior person has deep concern for others because he embodies a deep benevolence (*ren*), one of the paramount ethical ideals in Confucian thought. However, if the ethically superior person's environment and the people around him do not share his ethical commitments, he will continue to hold himself to ethical standards. Hence, Confucius famously said:

> In the eating of coarse rice and the drinking of water, the using of one's elbow for a pillow, joy is to be found. Wealth and rank attained through immoral means have as much to do with me as passing clouds. (7.16)

Petty persons, however, are always full of anxiety, worrying about other's views of them and concerned with garnering others' favourable views of them to further their own self-interest (7:37). They seek to be similar to others but they are not harmonious (13:23). The village worthies are a kind of petty person. We can imagine that some other kind of petty person is not as psychologically adept as the village worthies. They might lack some mindreading ability such that they just do not know how to act in a way that pleases others even though they also want fame and power. Either they do not know all the possible means of getting fame and power or they lack the skills to carry out some of the means. The village worthies are the kind of petty person who have heightened psychological skills. What is particularly worrying about village worthies compared to other kinds of petty persons is that the village worthies' attention is predominantly on themselves. For example, a standard petty person might want a promotion in her company and tries to flatter her boss. She might deep down hate her boss and try very hard to suppress her anger towards the boss. Since the standard petty person has her opinion of the boss, which she has to mask, she still has paid some attention to others. By contrast, the village worthy can flatter her boss without having any 'deep down' attitudes towards the boss. She neither hates the boss nor likes him. Rather, the boss is just a stepping stone for the village worthy to get what she wants. The village worthies are so preoccupied with themselves that they are indifferent towards others. Although they might be eager to find out their audience's likes and dislikes, they do not actually care about others, for they cannot pay attention to others in a way that does not make reference to themselves.

Throughout the *Analects*, we find references to how one should not be troubled by others' opinions, but should be troubled by whether one is living up to ethical standards. For example, 'It is not the failure of others to appreciate your abilities that should trouble you, but rather your failure to appreciate theirs' (1.16); and 'Is it not [like a superior person] not to take offence when others fail to appreciate abilities?' (1.1). As much as Confucius emphasizes studying and learning, he laments that 'men of antiquity studied to improve themselves; men today study to impress others' (14.24). It is clear in Confucius' thinking that it is not enough to perform certain good actions. In fact, performing certain actions for the sake of impressing others could be even more damaging than not performing them at all. More importantly, one needs to have the right heart or mind for doing the right thing.

What matters to Confucius is not whether one regards something as the *prescribed* course of action, but whether one regards it as the *only* course of action *for him or her*, even in the face of alternatives. This may happen when something is of the greatest moral significance, so that any other alternative is no longer a viable alternative for the person. Or it may be that the only alternatives to a certain course of action are things that one cannot conceive oneself doing due to some ethical constraints one sees oneself as subject to. Hence, by the virtuous person's own lights, there is only one course of action she can see herself pursuing: the one that aligns with ethical standards. If wealth and rank are only attainable through immoral means, then attaining wealth and rank is not even an option for such a person. Such a mind that cannot conceive options that do not align with ethical standards is necessary for the cultivation of many Confucian virtues.

Our reflection on Confucius' criticism of the village worthies has given us a glimpse of Confucius' view on integrity. In order for a person to have integrity at all, she needs to at least have some identifications, values, traits or attitudes that can be called her own. Otherwise, even if she has acted in a way that is in accordance with moral norms, she will fall prey to a pernicious kind of hypocrisy and lack integrity. This is different from saying that the outwardly right actions have to come from the right kind of attitudes or character. Confucius is making a more basic point: one needs to at least have one's own take on things in order to satisfy the minimal condition for having integrity.

For Confucius, having integrity means that one is both outwardly observing and inwardly identifying with ethical standards. The village worthies' seemingly ethical actions are detached from their inward identification because they do not have any identification. They do not have a mind of their own. Since they do not have their own take on things, they are not even in a position to identify with ethical standards. Their actions are not much different from a fluke. Should their audience cease to endorse ethical standards for whatever reason, they would also stop following ethical standards. What sets ethically superior persons apart from the village worthies is not just that they make better moral judgements, nor that they are more capable of abiding by these standards in their actions, nor even that they possess more virtues; rather, at a more basic level, ethically superior persons have their own take on things. They do not observe the ethical standards simply because others endorse them. Instead, they make up their own mind about, and come to identify with, ethical standards. It is in virtue of such identification that the ethically superior persons are able to hold themselves to ethical standards, so that even if those around them give up ethical standards, they would continue to steadfastly uphold and observe ethical standards.

In order to have a take on something, one needs to turn one's attention to that thing in the first place. The village worthies' main problem is that they cannot turn their attention to that thing because they are preoccupied with themselves.

Recommended reading

It is Mencius who first provided an influential interpretation of Confucius' remark on the village worthies. For a recent reliable translation of the *Mencius*, see Bryan W. Van Norden's *The Essential Mengzi* (Cambridge: Hackett Publishing, 2009), which also includes important commentaries from Zhu Xi, another key figure in the Confucian tradition from the twelfth century. Roger Ames' 'The Classical Chinese Self and Hypocrisy', in Roger T. Ames and Wimal Dissanayake (eds), *Self and Deception: A Cross-Cultural Philosophical Enquiry* (Albany: SUNY Press, 1996) introduces readers to some basic conceptual frameworks and historical background that are crucial to our understanding of the village worthies. Stephen C. Angle's 'Is Conscientiousness a Virtue? Confucian Responses', in Stephen Angle and Michael Slote (eds), *Virtue Ethics and Confucianism* (London and New York: Routledge, 2015) is a stimulating article that explores conscientiousness by drawing on early Confucian sources. It makes the interesting observation that there are resemblances between a village worthy and a conscientious person.

Notes

1 Yao and Shun are the legendary sage-kings who are regarded as moral exemplars in the Confucian tradition.
2 See Shun 2014 for an insightful discussion of the village worthies.
3 See Sung 2016 for further discussion of the village worthies as a peculiar type of hypocrites.
4 Gabriele Taylor, *Pride, Shame, and Guilt: Emotions of Self-Assessment* (Oxford: Oxford University Press, 1985).
5 The colour vermilion is considered as the morally proper colour.
6 Since Confucius' usages of *junzi* and *xiao ren* refer to certain kinds of men, I will use the pronoun 'he' in my following discussion.

11

G. E. M. Anscombe

The false hypocrisy of the ideal standard

Rachael Wiseman

On 1 May 1956, Oxford University's academics met to consider nominations for honorary degrees. Such nominations are traditionally waved through – the consideration and vote are mere formality. However, on this occasion, the dons were expecting something unusual. Rumour had spread that the nomination for Harry S. Truman, former president of the United States, was to be challenged by a young research fellow from Somerville College. The dons from the men's colleges had turned out en masse to ensure that Truman's nomination was passed. In some colleges consciences had been 'greatly exercised' by the challenge of finding a reason to pass over the objection to Truman's award – even before hearing it. In others, like St. John's, it was sufficient to know that 'the women were up to something' to be convinced of the imperative to 'go and vote them down'.[1] In fact 'the women' weren't up to something; just one woman, acting alone. The troublemaker was Elizabeth Anscombe, previously a student of Wittgenstein's and now at Oxford teaching courses on the philosophy of psychology and writing what would become the monograph *Intention*.

Anscombe made a provocative speech, which she later published as a pamphlet and distributed around Oxford bookshops. She argued that when Harry Truman gave the order to drop atomic bombs on Hiroshima and Nagasaki in 1945 he committed mass murder. To intentionally kill the innocent, even during wartime, is murder and in giving the order to bomb civilians Truman made himself a murderer. As such, she said, to bestow honours on him was sycophantic and no different from showing them to Nero or Genghis Khan. The Censor, tasked with replying, attempted to placate Anscombe by conceding that ordering the use of atomic weapons may have been a 'mistake'; however, he went on: 'Truman did not make the bombs himself, and decide to drop them without consulting anyone.' As such it would be unfair to hold him responsible 'just because his signature is at the foot of the order'.[2] Truman's nomination was approved; witnesses recall only one or two dissenting voices. The intervention caused enough of a stir to prompt a *New York Times* journalist to ask Truman what he thought of Anscombe's intervention. Truman stated: 'I made the decision [to use the bombs] on the facts as they existed at the time, and if I had to do it again I would do it all over again.'[3]

The two central claims in Anscombe's speech are simple: Truman is guilty of murder and murderers should not be given honours. Anscombe thinks that anyone who is tempted to deny either claim has lost their grip on the concept of murder. She diagnoses as the cause of that loss the befuddling effect of the doctrine of pacifism on popular thinking about what is to be expected when a country goes to war. Pacifism, she says, 'teaches people to make no distinction between the shedding of innocent blood and the shedding of any human blood'; that is, between killing (which is unfortunate and often wrong) and murder (which is always forbidden).[4] With the loss of that distinction comes both a failure to recognize when the concept of murder applies and a reluctance to condemn murderous acts during war, given that there is so much killing going on.

Anscombe herself thinks that pacifism is a false doctrine because there can be such a thing as a just war, but her objection to the doctrine is not on grounds of falsehood. She recognizes that for those who want to 'draw apart from the world' pacifism may be an adequate and practical form of life – those who take religious orders, for example, or who join a community that lives separately from mainstream society by its own standards and norms. The evil of pacifism, Anscombe argues, lies in its power to corrupt the thinking of those who do not wish to draw apart from the world.

Anscombe identifies a specific sort of threat to integrity: she calls it *the false hypocrisy of the ideal standard*. A hypocrite is someone who feigns the virtues, who falsely professes to have standards that her behaviour belies. Such a person can exist only in the context of a society that cares about virtue and that can recognize when someone is acting well. Just as the liar must be guided by a concern for the truth, so the true hypocrite must be guided by a concern for the good.[5] In contrast to the true hypocrite the *false hypocrite* displays his hypocrisy as a form of admirable pragmatism. He does so by characterizing virtue as an 'ideal standard': a set of norms that can be followed only by those whose privilege or exceptionality allows them to transcend the concerns of ordinary folk. This is a *false* hypocrisy because rather than feigning virtue, it is hypocrisy itself that is feigned. The false hypocrite is to the true hypocrite what the bullshitter is to the liar. As such, Anscombe's analysis of the context in which the false hypocrite thrives poses a challenge to ways of thinking about integrity that begins from the tripartite model of the 'saints, heroes and sages'.[6] It contains a warning against the allure of such 'ideal standards' and a reminder of the way in which the existence of such archetypes in our moral thinking can be a psychological impediment to our acting well.

Anscombe's analysis begins with observations about the view of Christianity, and of the figure of Jesus, that prevails in middle-class secular Western thought. This dominant way of thinking pictures Christianity's norms as setting out a 'beautiful ideal' to which only the actions of an exceptional few can ever accord, and Jesus as a model whose life, though exemplary, is not one towards which ordinary modern people might strive. This status – as beautiful but impracticable – is achieved by 'turning [Christian] counsels into principles'.[7] A principle is an unchanging rule of conduct or behaviour. Principles apply universally and eternally, so one does not need to be sensitive to the facts to know whether a principle applies: it applies, whatever the facts. In contrast, a counsel is a local application of a principle – it is neither universal nor eternal. So one might have a policy of not bombing hospitals in light of the principle that one must not murder, yet counsel bombing this particular hospital given certain facts – for example, that the hospital is now being used as an enemy base – which mean that the principle does not apply (this bombing would not be a case of murder). Anscombe thinks that pacifism arises when the Christian policy of 'turning the other cheek' is elevated to the status of a principle, so that it can be applied independent of any facts, for example, facts about the behaviour of the enemy.

Anscombe identifies two specific forms of corruption in moral thinking that arise when we turn counsels into principles. First, the change encourages the *false hypocrisy of the ideal standard* – the pretence of hypocrisy that undermines the very possibility of a shared moral framework. Second, it allows us to live comfortably with the idea that living an ordinary sort of life with integrity is impossible, and in doing so leads us to accept that some form of corruption or wrongdoing is a necessary part of living a life among others. These corruptions arise because the newly coined principles can only be kept by someone who 'draws apart from the world'. A life governed by those principles is that of a Christian saint. So for those in the world it is pretence to talk as if they are our principles when we cannot act in accord with them; and the fact that we are compelled to act against them leads us to view it as a sign of impractical high-mindedness to object when, for example, someone commits murder in order to pursue the greater good.

These corruptions are not particular to the concept of *murder*. Compare the way in which pacifism undermines the concept of murder with the way in which concepts like *greed* or *dishonesty* can be undermined by turning the evangelical counsel of poverty into a principle against property. '[P]eople would pay lip service to it as the ideal', Anscombe predicts, 'while in practice they went in for swindling.' If absolute honesty meant having no property, then while each might avow 'respect for those who follow that course', in practice all would go in for swindling: in such a situation 'the amount of swindling one does will depend on convenience'.[8] Similarly, we might elevate the counsel of chastity into a principle forbidding sex. This would not promote chastity, but rather make fornicators of us all.

When the House of Commons debated air strikes in Syria in 2015, the conservative MP Richard Benyon preceded his consequentialist defence of bombing by remarking that he had a deep respect for pacifists – in fact, over a dozen speakers who supported the air strikes prefaced their arguments by 'paying lip service' to the ideal of pacifism. Anscombe was prescient in identifying the 'pretence of hypocrisy' with the sort of cynicism 'found ... among the clearer-headed politicians'.[9] The result of 'turning counsels into principles' is, paradoxically, a set of principles that are treated as counsels: guides to action that can be broken, revised or overlooked depending on the circumstances.

In the year after her speech, Anscombe went on BBC radio to attack her Oxford colleagues' moral philosophy on the grounds that it encoded precisely those corruptions of thought she identified in those who failed to see that Truman's murderous actions precluded him from honour. She took Nowell-Smith's comments as illustrative: 'A man *must*, he says ... refuse any non-moral advantage, say a bribe, gained by doing something against his moral principles "unless he can manage to bring acceptance of the offer under some other moral principle"'.[10] Anscombe points out that on this moral philosophy 'people can ... do anything "on principle"'. So long as you have 'a good large stock of principles, and you will be able to manage ... very well indeed; you will always find relevant differences in particular cases, and so maintain your principles with high impartiality'.[11] She suggests that this is 'one reason why the phrase "on principle" stinks so'.

Anscombe goes on to identify this kind of ethics of principles with a particular tenor of moral discourse. When principles are broken, and their breaking justified by appeal to some other principle, the discussion, she says, takes on a 'lugubriously elevated moral tone'. For example, the sort of hand wringing and performance of regret that goes with taking 'difficult decisions', like the decision to bomb a civilian population. This posture of maintaining your principles with high impartiality – but in a context in which those principles are so numerous as to mean one can always bring what one is doing under some principle – is a posture of a kind of moral earnestness that is *false hypocrisy*. This is why Anscombe says that 'if one really wants to corrupt people by direct teaching of ideas, moral earnestness [is] an important item of equipment'.[12]

Anscombe suggests that to counter this corruption we need to replace our false image of Christianity as 'a beautiful ideal' with a true one on which it is 'severe and practicable'.[13] To secularize this thought: we need to replace our portraits of saints, heroes or sages as exemplars of integrity with models of quite ordinary lives that are exemplary only insofar as they were lived well. Instead of turning ourselves towards an unachievable ideal, and then wringing our hands in pretended regret as we fall short, we should begin with the recognition that there are some things that are forbidden absolutely and then seek ways to conduct our lives accordingly. Our morality, thinks Anscombe, must begin with the truth that there are acts such that one doesn't have to consider 'the facts' in order to know that to do them would be bad. Among the acts that are subject to absolute prohibition is murder. A policy against killing is a good rule of thumb if one wants to avoid murder, but it is murder and not killing that is evil.

The suggestion is that this reversal will lead us away from an 'impractical but ideal' ethics to one that is 'severe and practicable'. It is perfectly possible, though of course not always easy, to live a life – an ordinary, everyday life in the world – in which one avoids doing what is forbidden. This practicality makes it reasonable to treat transgressions severely. On the view that evil is unavoidable, a benign attitude towards wrongdoing is reasonable; on Anscombe's view, it is perfectly practicable to live by the dictate: 'Do no evil that good may come!'

To return to Anscombe's intervention in Truman's honorary degree: Anscombe says in her speech that she expects to be accused of being 'disagreeably high-minded'. She imagines her interlocutor – in a 'lugubriously elevated moral tone' – cajoling her, 'The action was necessary, or at any rate it was thought by competent, expert military opinion to be necessary; it probably saved more lives than it sacrificed; it was a good result, it ended the war.' The interlocutor ends with a flourish familiar from moral philosophy textbooks: 'Come now: if you had to choose between boiling one baby and letting some frightful disaster befall a thousand people ... what would you do?'[14]

Anscombe's response is a parody of the principle of doing evil that good may come: 'every fool can be as much of a knave as suits him'. Her point is that the choice that is faced in such high-stakes dilemmas is rarely as it seems in these sketches. Even if expert military opinion was right, the conditions under which it was right were conditions that could be influenced: for example, it was in Truman's power to change the requirement that Japan's surrender be unconditional. It is within our capacity as practical reasoners to find ways out of such situations, to adopt different means, to change our ends, to alter the circumstances that constrain our options for action. In all but the most tragic cases, we can use wit, cunning and wisdom to find a way forward – and in those rare tragic cases the possibility of refusing to do something terrible remains open even in the face of the most dreadful consequences. The accusation that to object to the killing of innocents as a means to an end in war is 'high-minded', stems from a failure to see that Anscombe's objection is not based on queasiness about suffering, or an objection to killing in general. If it were, it would have the status of a 'high-sounding principle' that a sensible adult knows when to break. When Truman says he made his decision based on the facts, he reveals – on Anscombe's analysis – that he saw the injunction against killing civilian populations in this way: as a policy, a rule of thumb. For Anscombe, however, the prohibition is on *murder*.

One of the difficulties that arises if one tries to use the concept of integrity to study the form of a good life is the striking unlivability of the lives of many of the standard exemplars. If we do not want to give up all our worldly belongings, leave our families, eschew pleasure and comfort, or go and fight in the resistance, it seems to follow that we are compromised and corrupted. The exemplars that populate virtue ethics throughout its ancient and recent history, and which serve as touchstones in our practical thought, are often people of *extraordinary* moral character, who have given up many of the things that we – the ordinary folk – would consider necessary to a flourishing human life: friends, family, art, music, good food. Iris Murdoch observed that the subjects of moral philosophy – the saints, sages and heroes – are more often than not autonomous male deliberators operating independently of others with a resolute and brave commitment to bending their wills to the moral law.[15]

Anscombe warns us of the practical consequences of having such moral exemplars central to our ethical thought. First, if the life of a person of integrity is necessarily extraordinary, lonely and hard, is it not reasonable for us – the ordinary folk – to stop worrying about being people of integrity and adopt a more pragmatic – more realistic – outlook? If an ordinary human life means being a bit hypocritical, a bit corrupt, a bit bad, then we should go easy on ourselves and each other when we fall short. And given that a bit of badness is only to be expected, perhaps our ethics should reflect this, and give us a guide for action that involves calculating which of the available actions are least bad, given that we are not morally extraordinary. Second, if being a person of integrity is at odds with being – in an important sense – human, then should we not choose humanity over integrity? Susan Woolf has argued that being a moral saint just is not something we should go in for. Third, the person of integrity ceases to operate as a proper guide for practical reason. The deliberative question 'What would Jesus do?' cannot get us very far, if what Jesus would do is give away all of his possessions, alienate all of his friends and get crucified. Such lives, lives of integrity, can be at best objects of contemplation and admiration, rather than proper guides to action.

There are two suggestions, then, we might take from Anscombe. First, the thought that a life of integrity – a life of good action – is unlivable is itself a kind of corruption. Anscombe insisted that it is practicable to live a life of integrity which is also a quite ordinary life of family, work, friends, politics and compromise. Morality, as she saw it, does not create the sort of obligations and duties that might require one to 'draw apart from the world'; rather, it places limits and restrictions on what is permissible to do. Limiting one's possibilities for acting does not mean adopting standards that only the morally exceptional could meet. In one respect this is a comforting thought, but in another, it is a heavy one to bear. And this is the second suggestion: in turning our gaze to the morally exceptional we must be careful not to let ourselves be comforted by the thought that we have already fallen short of the ideal, and so may be forgiven our trespasses. Once we reject the cynicism that is the *false hypocrisy of the ideal standard* we must confront the fact that very ordinary people – those of us who are neither saint nor hero nor sage – can live with integrity and, as such, so can we. Being a person of integrity does not require the sort of lone-wolf life that we are accustomed to hearing about; you can be a person of integrity and a mother of a large family – as was Elizabeth Anscombe.

Recommended reading

Anscombe's radio-talk, 'Does Oxford Moral Philosophy Corrupt the Youth?' was printed in the BBC's magazine, *The Listener*, Issue 1455 (Thursday, 14 February 1957), 157. The following six editions contain a lively exchange in the letters pages between Anscombe and her critics. Anscombe's writings on ethics and politics are collected in her *Ethics, Religion and Politics* (Oxford: Blackwell 1981). For those wishing to know more about this episode and its connections with Anscombe's philosophy of mind and action, see Rachael Wiseman, *A Routledge Philosophical Guidebook to*

Anscombe's Intention (London and New York: Routledge, 2016). Harry Frankfurt's *On Bullshit* (Princeton: Princeton University Press, 2005) is an accessible and amusing essay on the dangers of those who abandon their interest in the truth.

Notes

1. G. E. M. Anscombe, 'Mr Truman's Degree', in *From Parmendides to Anscombe. G. E. M. Anscombe: Collected Papers Volume III* (Oxford: Blackwell, 1981), 62–71, p. 65.
2. Ibid., 66.
3. 'Oxford Don Fights Honor for Truman', *New York Times*, 19 June 1956.
4. G. E. M. Anscombe, 'War and Murder', in *Ethics, Religion and Politics*, 57. Of course, peace activists and pacificists would not describe their pacifism in these terms and there are many well-worked-out positions on what is and is not acceptable for different pacifists and peace activists. Anscombe's point is about the role the idea of pacifism – particularly for those who are not themselves pacifists – on political and ethical thought.
5. See Harry Frankfurt, *On Bullshit* (Princeton: Princeton University Press, 2005).
6. See, for example, Linda Zagzebski, *Exemplarist Moral Theory* (Oxford: Oxford University Press, 2017).
7. G. E. M. Anscombe, 'War and Murder', 56.
8. Ibid.
9. G. E. M. Anscombe, 'Pretending', in *Proceedings of the Aristotelian Society, Supplementary Volumes*, 32 (1958): 261–94, p. 294.
10. Anscombe, Letter to the Editor, *The Listener* (London, England), Issue 1460 (Thursday, 21 March 1957), 457.
11. Ibid.
12. Anscombe, 'Does Oxford Moral Philosophy Corrupt the Youth?' *The Listener* (London, England), Issue 1455 (Thursday, 14 February 1957), 157.
13. G. E. M. Anscombe, 'War and Murder', 56.
14. G. E. M. Anscombe, 'Mr Truman's Degree', 65.
15. Iris Murdoch, *The Sovereignty of the Good over Other Concepts* (London and New York: Routledge, 1970), 7.

12

Mohandas Gandhi

'My life is its own message'

Stefan Rossbach

Even the earliest biographies, written during his lifetime, imbued Gandhi's life with a religious and civilizational importance. Joseph Doke, an English Baptist clergyman from Devon, was the first to present an account of Gandhi's life to a wider audience. Doke met Gandhi for the first time in late December 1907, while Gandhi was campaigning for the rights and welfare of the Indian community in South Africa, and he proceeded to interview Gandhi in a series of meetings, resulting in a book entitled *M.K. Gandhi: An Indian Patriot in South Africa*. For Doke, the encounter with Gandhi was a significant spiritual experience: 'Our Indian friend lives on a higher plane than most men do,' he wrote, acknowledging that Gandhi's actions were often 'counted eccentric, and not infrequently misunderstood'; yet, 'those who know him well are ashamed of themselves in his presence'.[1]

Doke also inaugurated what would become a prevailing tradition in Western accounts of Gandhi by evoking New Testament imagery in order to situate the 'eccentric' Gandhi within a more familiar framework. It became common to canonize Gandhi as a Christ-like figure, a Christian saint – apart from Jesus, St Francis of Assisi was a frequently used reference. Unitarian pastor John Haynes

Holmes popularized this image in the United States, famously claiming in 1921 that Gandhi was the 'greatest man in the world': 'But when I think of Gandhi, I think of Jesus Christ. He lives his life; he speaks his word; he suffers, strives and will some day nobly die, for his kingdom upon earth.'[2] In Europe, the saintly Gandhi was immortalized by Romain Rolland's book *Mahatma Gandhi* (1924), which in its English translation carried the subtitle *The Man Who Became One with the Universal Being*. Rolland had won the Nobel Prize for Literature in 1915, and was a highly respected public intellectual and writer – Stefan Zweig famously called him the 'moral consciousness of Europe'. At the time of writing his book on Gandhi, Rolland had no personal experience of India or Gandhi and later admitted that he had brought to the subject his very own 'European preoccupations, the spectre of war which had raged over Western fields', hoping that 'the little St. Francis of India' could provide the remedy for the self-destructive tendencies inherent in European culture: 'The path to peace is through self-sacrifice. This is Gandhi's lesson. Only the Cross is missing.'[3]

Those who encountered Gandhi as a political opponent were unlikely to share those impressions. To them, Gandhi's eccentric asceticism was a façade, behind which lurked a shrewd, manipulative and relentless political agitator. British officials generally found him a strange and tricky adversary. Some respected him for his spiritual and moral aspirations, while others were more hostile, calling him a hypocrite. All of them, whether sympathetic or hostile, struggled to hide their exasperation when dealing with the 'seditious Middle Temple lawyer' posing as a 'half-naked fakir', as Churchill famously described him.[4] Early observers warned that Gandhi was a new kind of opponent, and that it was precisely his eccentricity that would immunize Gandhi against the standard workings of power: 'Persons in power should be very careful how they deal with a man who cares nothing for sensual pleasure, nothing for riches, nothing for comfort or praise or promotion, but is simply determined to do what he believes to be right. He is a dangerous and uncomfortable enemy – because his body, which you can always conquer, gives you so little purchase upon his soul.'[5]

As early as 1906, while serving as a volunteer stretcher bearer with the forces of the colonial government during the Zulu Rebellion in Natal, Gandhi had fashioned his unique approach to public service by taking his *brahmacharya* vow, which required him to live a life marked by desirelessness – a life of chastity, poverty, non-violence and truth – as a precondition for effective, 'disinterested' public work. Gandhi's vision of the activist renouncer was informed by his meditations on the *Bhagavad Gita*, which on his reading cultivated a desireless, disinterested form of action that was not preoccupied with its outcome. Such selfless action, lived in the furnace of public life, was just as valid a path towards self-realization as ascetic withdrawal. It was Gandhi's ascetic activism, with its concomitant symbolism as expressed in his outer appearance, the cult of the spinning wheel and his experiments in communal living, which enabled him to restore the dignity of rural life in India and to develop a deep relationship with the Indian public. As a renouncer by choice, a *sanyasi*, Gandhi appealed to and mobilized millions of impoverished Indians, renouncers by necessity, in his struggle for *swaraj*, self-rule. Accordingly, Gandhi was praised as a 'man among men' rather than as an otherworldly saint. He was referred to as *bapu*, 'father', mainly because of what were perceived to be his human virtues: worldly wisdom, courage, love and especially a warm sense of humour; he was revered because of his closeness to life, not as an ideal remote from reality. Members of the Anglicized middle classes in India, however, frequently failed to understand him and found him a barbarian, a visionary and a dreamer.

For some, then, Gandhi was the saintly, selfless leader, committed to poverty and non-violence, who brought down an empire; for others, he was a religious eccentric, who complicated and delayed, at a high cost, the inevitable by spiritualizing the political processes leading to India's independence. The dramatic range of interpretations has not narrowed with time. Gandhi's unique place in India's imagination regularly implicates him even in contemporary political disputes, with some wanting to preserve and others to 'debunk' his legacy in order to further their own political agendas. Gandhi posed and continues to pose a challenge to interpreters primarily because of his self-understanding and the actions that it inspired. He had no intention to live a life that conformed to standards and expectations defined by others; he did not live, as it were, in the eyes of others. Even in the preface to his autobiography, he made it clear that it was not his intention to contribute to a genre that was 'peculiar to the West'. Rather, instead of writing a 'real' autobiography, Gandhi was going to narrate his 'experiments in the spiritual field', which were foundational for his public work.

These experiments did not line up in a continuum; rather, they were spiritual trials, which were valuable for the lessons that they taught, and the lessons, in turn, served as stepping stones towards action and were to be reviewed in light of the consequences of such action. There was no finality to the relative truths of these lessons, and they were to be abandoned, if lived experience proved them inadequate. John Bunyan's classic *The Pilgrim's Progress* (1678), which Gandhi knew and admired, may have been an inspiration as he placed questions of spiritual progress, of gradual self-realization, at the centre of his reflections, giving his own life a certain revelatory quality. For Gandhi, the quest for truth – a path that was 'strait and narrow and sharp as the razor's edge' – eclipses in importance the appearance of consistency. When new insights had been gained, he never hesitated to contradict views he previously held to be true, advising his audience that if there were inconsistencies between any two writings of his, they 'would do well to choose the later of the two on the same subject'.

Gandhi's approach to his 'experiments with truth' is instructive in that it reveals how he came to understand himself and his work: 'But I worship God as Truth, only I have not yet found Him, but I am seeking after Him. I am prepared to sacrifice the things dearest to me in pursuit of this quest. Even if the sacrifice demanded be my very life, I hope I may be prepared to give it.'[6] To Gandhi, truth meant above all 'truthfulness': the determination to make one's life a true reflection of one's beliefs and commitments. Narayan Desai, who spent the first two decades of his life in Gandhi's *ashrams* at Sabarmati and Sevagram, noted that it was his 'crystal clear transparency' that made Gandhi unique: 'There was no discord or deviation between his thought, word and deed.'[7]

The concern with truthfulness leads to a concern with the concrete, minute details of everyday life. If I am committed to justice, for example, and I want to be true to this commitment, I must examine every aspect of my life in order to establish how much my way of being in the world entails, and relies on, injustice: the food I consume, the clothes I wear, the products I use – how much 'injustice' is implied in the social practices that sustain me? Are the clothes I wear priced cheaply because the methods of production are exploitative? And if I cannot be sure, am I not obliged to ensure that I know how my life is sustained, and the moral cost of it? And if I find that there are aspects of my way of life that are not in congruence with the truth I cherish, am I not compelled to change my life *at once* in order to make it a more perfect manifestation of this truth? Truth, for Gandhi, was therefore an existential concern. It required introspection in order to identify and clarify the truth that should govern life, as well as the willingness to surrender to truth, to change one's life accordingly and to accept and suffer the consequences.

Truthfulness comes with its own power – it empowers people – and Gandhi placed it at the very centre of his public service, trying to harness it for his campaigns. He called it *satyagraha*, the 'force born of truth', and considered it the infallible antidote to injustice and evil. Evil, Gandhi noted, 'cannot by itself flourish in this world. It can do so only if it is allied with some good.'[8] People are tricked into tolerating and promoting evil among them, because they are made to fear the consequences of doing otherwise, or they fool themselves into believing that their desires will be satisfied through their complicity. Therefore, if I am serious about defeating evil, my first step must be to courageously withdraw myself from it – to examine my life in every detail, to establish how my way of life has 'allied' with it, and to eliminate it from my own habits, my own actions, my own thoughts and feelings. If everyone does this, evil will be starved of the life-support that it feeds on, and over time it will evaporate.

The site of the quest for truth is the here and now, the mundane fabric of everyday life. As Uday Singh Mehta noted, for Gandhi, it was the everyday, even in its most banal form, that supplied 'the very material through which one gives ethical substance to one's life'.[9] The power of *satyagraha* was available to everyone, everywhere, always. Here and now, I can examine my life, and I can withdraw whatever tacit or explicit support I may give to the concrete injustice surrounding me. My 'conversion' will surely attract the attention of those who have vested interests in perpetuating injustice, but at the same time it may inspire others to follow my example. This quest for truth does not require the 'elevated gravity of the political' (Mehta), which as Gandhi observed, always had 'larger purposes'. Gandhi was suspicious of the abstraction and teleology implicit in modern politics, which assumed that purposeful change required collective organization; and that transformative political action was to be predicated on the ability to determine the likelihood of desired outcomes. In this sense, Gandhi was a profoundly anti-political thinker and activist. He did not share the founding orientations of modern politics, in which violence is accepted now in order to enjoy peace in some future; in which injustice is tolerated now in order to create justice for everyone in some future, and in which we will change *only* if everyone else does so, too. For Gandhi, modern politics amounted to an infinite deferral. This, in fact, is the reason why he so often *appeared* to accept the terms in which social life was given: change was never preconditioned upon a 'political' transformation of these terms, which would require collective action, political organization, that is, time and resources. Change *can* take root from within any given terms, at any time, and it starts with my examining how my life sustains those terms, and changing accordingly. I must not wait for politics to resolve the problem for me in some indefinite future.

Gandhi pursued his spiritual quest with vigilance, intensity and energy – attributes that were easily mistaken for political purposefulness. Yet, those who abandoned their former lives in order to follow him, to take part in his campaigns and become *satyagrahis*, and to live with him in his *ashrams*, did so because in terms of the sacrifices he was willing to make in his quest for truth, he was prepared to go further than most. Those who met Gandhi personally would often later recall the encounter as one of the greatest spiritual experiences of their lives, for Gandhi appeared to have shown them, by example, a path towards a better version of themselves. Agnes M. Phillips, who met Gandhi in South Africa, recognized in Gandhi a 'master', a teacher, whose 'simplicity and integrity were very manifest. ... He made one think of the deeper things of life and religion without any apparent effort on his part. ... His influence was such that it was impossible to do or even to think meanly.' Henry S. L. Polak wrote that, on his first visit to Gandhi, he felt that he was 'in the presence of a moral giant, whose pellucid soul is a clear, still lake, in which one sees Truth clearly mirrored'. Karel Hujer, who met Gandhi in 1935, found his first sight of Gandhi 'the most inspiring moment of [his] life', because in Gandhi's presence, he 'realised that boundless spiritual beauty which lifts the soul above this world'. Asaf Ali noted Gandhi's 'penetrating appeal to what is noble in human nature', an appeal that was always also a personal appeal, bringing listeners, through their attraction to him, to recognize what is noble in themselves. And, in turn, as his listeners came to discover the higher, more noble dimensions of their souls, they would commit themselves to act upon their discovery: 'I remember when we left his presence, how overcome we were at the thought of what we had promised to do!'[10]

What the accounts of these eyewitnesses suggest is that the encounter with Gandhi presented them with the vision of a more devoted, more deliberate life that *they could live*. Already Gopal Krishna Gokhale had observed in Gandhi the 'marvelous spiritual power to turn ordinary men into heroes and martyrs'.[11] Through their encounters with Gandhi, men and women discovered hitherto unknown possibilities in themselves, and often they felt empowered to act upon those possibilities.

In the many personal relationships that he maintained – at peak times, Gandhi would write approximately sixty letters per day – and even by proxy, Gandhi served the role of a *basanos*, a touchstone. In Greek antiquity, the word *basanos* referred to a dark-coloured slate on which pure gold, when rubbed, left a coloured mark, helping merchants and moneychangers assess the value of the many coins circulating throughout the Aegean world. The term was also used, however, as a metaphor for a tool, instrument or process that could reveal the truth behind appearances. The metaphor is used, for example, in some of the Platonic dialogues, and in one of them, the *Laches*, one of Socrates' interlocutors implies that being drawn into a conversation with Socrates was like being rubbed against a touchstone (187E–188B), making it impossible to hide the truth of one's life. Personal recollections of conversations with Gandhi frequently reveal a similar touchstone effect, as, for example, when he persuades a very young Kamalnayan Bajaj to admit that his silk, gold-embroidered cap was *less* beautiful than Gandhi's white, plain cotton cap that he wore with his *dhoti*. Bajaj had to admit that he and his pride had been 'caught' by Gandhi, and he felt embarrassed, but through Gandhi's reassurance the embarrassment was turned into an invitation for self-improvement.[12]

While some resented the embarrassment of the encounter and blamed Gandhi, others were willing to search for the cause of the embarrassment in themselves, and thus to consider the possibility of a better, truer notion of themselves. Gandhi's touchstone effect placed the individual members of his audience in a liminal situation. They were 'caught' between the hope that they may be able to sustain this truer notion of themselves, and the fear that they may fail. 'Sustaining' means here that they succeed in allowing their heightened sense of who they could be permeate their being and their actions – that they reach out to that nobler version of themselves that they saw, dimly, reflected in Gandhi. 'Failing' means that they do not recognize how they are implicated in the liminality of the touchstone encounter – that the insights gained, the hope and the fear, are externalized by locating them with the agent of the touchstone effect. Gandhi, they may say, has moved them not because of the truth he helped them discover about themselves, but because of a peculiar quality that he possessed that separated him from them. 'Integrity' was, and continues to be, a label often used to denote this quality. The attribution of 'integrity' is a short circuit of the touchstone liminality: it allows us to freeze in admiration where we should seek self-improvement in accordance with what we have seen.

It is to Gandhi's immense credit that he made it so very difficult to objectify him through attribution, both during his lifetime and posthumously – after all, he succeeded in mobilizing millions for his *satyagraha* campaigns. The people who followed him did not freeze in admiration but, on the contrary, were empowered to act and to make sacrifices that even to them seemed impossible without his inspiration. Even his critics acknowledge that 'as a man, he [was] most remarkable for making every day, perhaps every minute, a matter of reaching forward, for never settling in any one place in his long, intricate spiritual journey', making it hard to nail him down in terms of descriptive attributes.[13] Perhaps as an apophatic figure, he embodied an integrity of a higher order, turning his life into a mirror for us to see ourselves, forcing us to examine our lives as we respond to him.

Recommended reading

The one hundred volumes of Gandhi's *Collected Works* are available online, for example at https://www.gandhiheritageportal.org/. His autobiography, written in 1925, was published separately as *An Autobiography. Or the Story of My Experiments with Truth* (Harmondsworth: Penguin, 1982, and many other editions). Judith M. Brown edited a useful collection of key writings entitled *Mahatma*

Gandhi: The Essential Writings (Oxford: Oxford University Press [Oxford World's Classic], 2008), which covers all aspects of his life and work including his self-understanding, the search for God, the creation of moral societies, the struggle for *swaraj* and the nonviolence of *satyagraha*. The most recent biography is Ramachandra Guha's two-volume work *Gandhi Before India* (London: Allen Lane, 2013) and *Gandhi: The Years That Changed the World 1914–1948* (London: Allen Lane, 2018). Veena R. Howard's *Gandhi's Ascetic Activism: Renunciation and Social Action* (Albany: SUNY Press, 2013) provides a comprehensive analysis of Gandhi's unique style of spiritual and political activism.

Notes

1 Joseph J. Doke, *M. K. Gandhi: An Indian Patriot in South Africa* (London: The London Indian Chronicle, 1909), 7.

2 John H. Holmes, 'Who Is the Greatest Man in the World Today?' in Charles Chatfield (ed.), *The Americanization of Gandhi: Images of the Mahatma* (New York and London: Garland Publishing, 1976), 599–621, the quote is from p. 620. On Gandhi's reception in the United States, see Lloyd I. Rudolph, 'Gandhi in the Mind of America', in Lloyd I. Rudolph and Susanne Hoeber Rudolph, *Postmodern Gandhi and Other Essays: Gandhi in the World and at Home* (New Delhi: Oxford University Press, 2011), 92–139.

3 Quoted in Claude Markovits, *The Un-Gandhian Gandhi: The Life and Afterlife of the Mahatma* (London: Anthem Press, 2004), 17–19. For a discussion see Ruth Harris, 'Rolland, Gandhi and Madeleine Slade: Spiritual Politics, France and the Wider World', *French History* 27 (4) (December 2013): 579–99.

4 Quoted in Geoffrey Ashe, *Gandhi: A Study in Revolution* (London: Heinemann, 1968), xi.

5 Gilbert Murray, 'The Soul As It Is, and How to Deal with It', *Hibbert Journal* 16 (2) (1917–18): 191–205. The quote is from p. 201.

6 M. K. Gandhi, *An Autobiography. Or the Story of My Experiments with Truth* (Harmondsworth: Penguin, 1982), 15.

7 Narayan Desai, *My Gandhi* (Ahmedabad: Navjivan Publishing House, 1999), Kindle, loc 162.

8 John Strohmeier (ed.), *The Bhagavad Gita, According to Gandhi* (Berkeley: North Atlantic Books, 2009), 4.

9 Uday Singh Mehta, 'Gandhi on Democracy, Politics and the Ethics of Everyday Life', *Modern Intellectual History*, 7 (2) (2010): 355–71, p. 358.

10 There are numerous printed accounts of meetings with Gandhi. The ones used here are from the two collections edited by Chandrashanker Shukla, *Gandhiji as We Know Him* (Bombay: Vora, 1945) and *Reminiscences of Gandhiji* (Bombay: Vora, 1951).

11 Quoted in Thomas Weber, *Gandhi as Disciple and Mentor* (Cambridge: Cambridge University Press, 2004), 50.

12 Bajaj, in Shukla, *Reminiscences of Gandhiji* , 26–7. Evoking the figure of Socrates in the context of Gandhian ethics is not accidental, because Gandhi translated Plato's *Apology* into Gujarati in 1908, at a time when he was developing *satyagraha* as a concept and practice. Socrates, for Gandhi, was a soldier of truth, 'a great satyagrahi.' See Phiroze Vasunia, 'Gandhi and Socrates', *African Studies* 72 (2) (2015): 175–85.

13 Jad Adams, *Gandhi: Naked Ambition* (London: Quercus, 2010), 283.

13

Tolstoy and the Tolstoyans

Facing life as a whole

Charlotte Alston

In the last thirty years of his life (1880–1910) Tolstoy published a series of tracts, short stories and a novel that expounded his Christian anarchist philosophy, based on the principle of non-resistance to evil by violence. He rejected the state, condemned private property and money, and advocated living by one's own physical labour. He also came to believe in abstinence from tobacco and alcohol, vegetarianism and complete chastity. At least partly because of his existing stature as a novelist, these tracts were rapidly translated and widely published. While Tolstoy's contemporaries in the literary world were (on the whole) horrified at his turn away from literature, his later writings had a remarkable impact on groups and individuals who were disillusioned with modern industrial society and with the politics of the time.

Tolstoy asked his readers to live honestly, and not to hide from the difficult questions that their conscience asked them. If they did not believe in war, they should not fight. If they wanted to help the poor, they should not exploit them by relying on and profiting from their labour.

Not to lie means not to fear the truth, not to invent excuses to hide from myself the conclusions of reason and conscience, and not to accept such excuses when they are invented by others; not to fear to differ from all those around me or to be left alone with reason and conscience, and not to fear the position to which truth will lead me, believing firmly that whatever truth and conscience will lead me to, however strange it may be, cannot be worse than what is based on falsehood.[1]

Having realized the truth of one's situation, Tolstoy argued, it was impossible to go on living as one had before. His polemics inspired readers in Russia, but also across Europe and America to change their lives, abandon their careers and try to put their newfound principles into practice. The experiences and the debates Tolstoy's followers engaged in shed light on the demands and the limits of integrity; the consequences of compromise; and the obstacles that behaving with complete integrity put in the way of interacting with others and converting them to the cause.

The profound responses that some of Tolstoy's readers had to his work occupied an important place within the Tolstoyan movement: they were consciously described as 'conversion' or 'enlightenment' experiences, and they provided copy for Tolstoyan newspapers and inspirational examples for others to draw on. Some readers mention elements of personal crisis or vulnerability prior to their reading of Tolstoy; others make it clear that they were already engaged in some kind of spiritual quest. Some maintain that they had already reached the same conclusions as Tolstoy and that he confirmed them. But the most common are accounts in which the individual is sailing along quite happily in his or her life until a reading of Tolstoy reveals a new understanding of life. The emphasis in the majority is firmly on the impact of reading the text; on what Isabella Mayo described as the 'revelation' that is brought about 'when one's inner consciousness instantly affirms a new truth presented to one'.[2] Tolstoyan conversions were usually sudden; there was little or no social pressure to convert (in fact the opposite was often true), and the advocate of the new philosophy (Tolstoy) was only remotely involved in the process. Although there were elements of the mystical about the language used in some of the accounts (the individual being filled with inner light, or rising to a loftier plane), these were rational, active conversions based on the reading of one or more texts. Frederik Van Eeden described this as a moral event. 'We live', he wrote, 'in a state of somnambulism. We may be said to know but not yet to feel or to realize the injustice of our position. A slight shock to our mind is sometimes able to wake us up and open our eyes to the disagreement between our confessed morals and our actual mode of living ... The pushing force comes from the men of faith and of force of character. The mind may be prepared intellectually, but it wants ethical incitement to change its potential energy into active movement.'[3]

Many of the commentaries make clear the importance of Tolstoy's confessional style, the lack of dogma and preaching, and the sense, instead, that the author was sharing an experience with his readers, and inviting their participation. Tolstoy was after all a novelist, and adept at moving or persuading his readers. Anton Chekhov, for example, recalled that Tolstoy's philosophy 'took possession' of him for six or seven years. It was not Tolstoy's general ideas or propositions that affected him so profoundly, he concluded, but the author's 'manner of expressing it, his reasonableness, and probably a sort of hypnotism'.[4] If the language was reasonable, however, the solutions Tolstoy offered were uncompromising. One unifying and very important element of the Tolstoyan 'conversion' experience is that Tolstoy's polemics seem to have answered the contradiction that many of his readers, whether businessmen, aristocrats, shopkeepers, soldiers or active members of the socialist movement felt in their lives. Tolstoy asked his readers to be honest with themselves and with others: to follow their own conscience and reason, and not to carry on behaving in the ways that conventional society demanded. He did not allow for any compromise between their ideals and their actions; he resolved all doubts.

The Tolstoyan philosophy also seemed to offer a robust and complete world view, and required that followers bring every aspect of their lives into accord with their beliefs: action on a single issue was not enough. Tolstoyism engaged with a very broad range of reformist causes, from pacifism to temperance to dress reform to diet. The work of small societies engaged in particular spheres of reform was all very well, John Kenworthy argued. But all these people, 'humanitarians, socialists, vegetarians, anti-vivisectionists, teetotallers, land-reformers, and all such seekers of human welfare' needed to be aware that their efforts were 'but a detail of the whole work of social regeneration; and that we cannot rightly understand and direct our own little piece of effort, unless we know it and pursue it, as part of the great whole'.[5] In 1900, when Percy Redfern established the Manchester Tolstoy Society, he explained the rationale as follows:

> Now I can temporarily associate with different groups – vegetarians, socialists, land reformers, 'rationalists', theosophists, Wesleyans and so forth. If I had some definite bias towards any particular material reform that might content me. But I want to face life as a whole. That we cannot do in mixed societies in which we must not introduce controversial subjects foreign to the particular aims of that society. So in addition to working occasionally with particular bodies one seeks society with others who also wish to face life as a whole. Hence a Tolstoy socy [sic].[6]

Underlying all these different areas of reform in which Tolstoyans were interested was the principle of non-resistance. Tolstoy, and sincere Tolstoyans, understood this to mean that they would not use force, or coercion, under any circumstances or in any sphere of their life. The commitment to complete non-resistance was one of the first struggles to confront Tolstoy's followers when they accepted his philosophy. It was faced head on in everyday life, social interaction and commercial transactions. While in England in 1899, Johannes Van der Veer chose to miss a train to Gloucester when the feeling struck him that, if he were truly non-resistant, it was wrong to rush for a place and deny others the chance of a seat. Non-resistance also remained a central point of discussion in lectures, meetings and the pages of Tolstoyan newspapers well into the 1900s. Was it really wrong to act to restrain someone who intended to kill you, your wife or your child? Was the motive not more important than the action? Couldn't force sometimes be motivated by love for one's fellow men? Tolstoyans struggled sincerely with these issues themselves, and they debated them with those on the fringes and outside their movement.

Also at issue was the difference, or similarity, between physical force and moral force. Most Tolstoyans passionately believed in the need to convert public opinion, not only by example but by persistently speaking the truth about the state of society. But the question of verbal coercion or persuasion was not so clear-cut for everyone. Jane Addams felt that Tolstoy distinguished too firmly between physical force and moral force. Shouldn't they also avoid forcing their views on to others, or condemning them because they disagree? Non-resistance for Addams meant 'selecting the good in the neighbourhood and refraining from railing at the bad'. In fact, she maintained that the anticipation of conflict between oneself and society, 'the expectation of opposition and martyrdom, the holding oneself in readiness for it, was in itself a sort of resistance and worked evil or at best was merely negative'.[7] Likewise Jane Holah believed that non-resistance was not merely about physical force, it was 'an attitude of mind in which we devote our whole attention to the development of good'.[8]

The Tolstoyan refusal to participate in any political, governmental or legal process also divided them from other reformers: from anti-vivisectionists because they could not condone legislative solutions; from pacifists because they saw no use in arbitration or lobbying for disarmament. It divided them from members of the socialist and even the cooperative movement, because they disapproved of organization or political representation. Christian socialist John Bruce Wallace despaired at what he regarded as a gross parody of Tolstoy's teachings, which were in his view hardly appropriate in England. By abstaining from the political process, the British Tolstoyans were wasting talent and energy that might reform the system from within, and were handing over power to reactionary forces. John Kenworthy, Arthur St. John, Vladimir Chertkov and Eliza Pickard were all drawn into this debate and responded with a vigorous defence of the non-resistant, Tolstoyan position – for them involvement in any political process, or in an unjust capitalist society, was an impossibility.

In their interactions with each other and the outside world, Tolstoyans also faced threats to the integrity of their principles and their practices. Their publishing enterprises were a case in point. *Posrednik*, the principal Tolstoyan publishing house in Russia, benefited enormously from the involvement of Ivan Sytin, a commercial publisher with extensive trade connections and access to a network of salesmen who distributed books in the countryside. Sytin welcomed the opportunity to apply his business expertise to a project that he considered had moral worth, but he never entirely distanced himself from his commercial operations, some of which involved the publication of precisely the kind of material the Tolstoyans sought to combat. Other leading Tolstoyans involved in this enterprise were very hostile to this aspect of Sytin's work, and they eventually dispensed with his services (and the quality of their publications and distribution suffered as a result). Likewise, Arthur Fifield, the manager of the English Tolstoyan publishing house the Free Age Press, sought to steer a course between managing an ethical business, and managing a successful business. The Tolstoyan opposition to copyright was a particular problem – it made newspaper editors and publishers extremely reluctant to take their material.

> Of course I know 'no copyright' is the ideal, just as giving the books away without any charge is the ideal, getting the paper made for nothing, composing, printing, binding, distributing, and living without financial relations are also the ideal. And as we compromise on these points, knowing it is compromise, yet yielding because the development of the general consciousness has not yet reached the point where those who feed, clothe, house, make paper, print for us, cease to impose their wills on us – so the events of the last few months have shewn me that the human consciousness has also not reached the point where the imposition of our will on newspaper editors, translators, booksellers, can be effected without bad results, both to the 'writers' (whether Tolstoy himself or not), those willed upon, and the spread of the ideas.[9]

Likewise, the Tolstoyans who established communal agricultural enterprises faced challenges to their principles, and challenges in putting them into practice. Since following the dictates of one's own conscience was such an important feature of the Tolstoyan world view, Tolstoyan communities often embraced a broad range of beliefs and practices. Yelena Shershenyova described life at the New Jerusalem commune, founded north of Moscow in 1923, as follows:

> Vanya Zuyev tempered his body by sleeping in winter on the balcony, eating raw vegetables and seeds, and using absolutely no cooked food. He thought that was more healthful and convenient. Seryozha Alekseyev did not cut his hair; and once he suddenly decided to go around completely without clothes, believing the natural state would strengthen chastity and cultivate a healthy view of sexual difference. A few of us – Kostya Blagoveshchensky, Seryozha Alekseyev and Vanya

Zuyev, Petya Shershenyov, Zhenya Antonovich, and for a while I, too – did not use milk, wishing to have no part in cattle raising, and consequently in the killing of young bulls and old cows that were good for nothing but their meat. Except for me, all the others just mentioned would not wear leather boots for the same reason, that is, because they wanted to be consistent vegetarians all the way. Nobody made fun of anybody else; we respected each other's views.[10]

But the questions of beliefs, occupations and organization were not always so easily solved. The diverse range of views in the British Tolstoyan movement on marriage and sex caused numerous disputes and controversies. Some hard workers resented others who they felt were doing less to get these enterprises on to a self-sufficient footing. And the question of organization itself was fundamentally problematic. Was it possible to work hard and organize while also living the 'right life' spiritually, and retaining independence of conscience and action? Self-sufficiency required organization. A commitment to complete non-resistance required that there be no organization. Tolstoyan colonists either entered into communal projects with little clarity about how the society they wished to create ought to operate, or they worked this out in detail but thereby compromised the ideal.

The ultimate tests came from external threats that required colonists to protect themselves and abandon the principle of non-resistance, or to observe it, and watch their projects fail. At Whiteway colony in Gloucestershire, colonists watched dispiritedly in 1899 as Samuel Bracher led away their cows, in an attempt to reclaim some of the money he had put into the colony; and in the years to come they struggled to remain non-resistant in the face of the destruction of their crops by their neighbours' livestock. The Christian Commonwealth's demise began when some of its members petitioned for the colony to be put into receivership so that they might claim their share of the value of the land. Torn between abandoning the principle of non-resistance by opposing the troublemakers in court, or allowing the colony to be broken up and effectively destroyed, the colonists opted to defend the case. Ralph Albertson believed that if 'they had taken away our horses or money or any property we should not have prosecuted them'. But this was an attempt to destroy the community completely. 'It was a situation that could not be met by anything in our philosophy. If we were to live we had to fight. It was the end of our dream of strictly obeying the Sermon on the Mount.'[11] The decision to contest the case poisoned the atmosphere at the Commonwealth and alienated many of the colony's prominent sympathizers. The International Brotherhood at Blaricum in the Netherlands collapsed in an incident of actual violence, in which numerous colonists were involved. When Brotherhood residents ripped up the rails of the steam tram that ran past the colony as an expression of sympathy with striking railwaymen, their neighbours (fishermen and farmers who needed to transport their goods to market) attacked the colony, even launching a firebomb at Lodewijk van Mierop, who demonstratively sat reading his Bible. The ensuing debate about what measures to take to defend the colony inevitably led to its demise.

The Tolstoyan movement drove some of its members into bankruptcy, and seriously affected their mental health. Johannes Van der Veer eventually came to believe that 'a consistent application of the Tolstoyan doctrine must lead to one of the following consequences: perishing in miserable wretchedness, growing mad or making away with oneself'.[12] Tolstoy's instruction to reject all material well-being and to always put others before oneself was, he concluded, contrary to human nature. And what was the use of propagating a theory that demanded the impossible? He joined the Dutch Social Democratic Party, convinced that socialism, which 'has in view the happiness of all men', was 'a sound view, with which the future lies, and that of the Tolstoyans a sentimental view, which will necessarily die out in the near future'. Aylmer Maude agreed that it was impossible to live the Tolstoyan philosophy. 'We should use our prophets as we use our mines', he concluded, 'seeking and valuing the veins of rich ore, and wasting as little time as possible on the sand and earth [i.e. the impractical conclusions] we find on our search.' Peter Kropotkin disagreed. He wrote to Maude that Tolstoy's greatness lay 'precisely in having come to the conclusions concerning life which he came to. Of compromises between a high ethics and philistinism we have only too many. Every philistine household and every 6/- novel is a commentary upon them. The question is, must these compromises go on unaffected, till mankind becomes all through a race of double-tongued sophists, and we go towards that, or must we get hold of an ideal, and see whether there are not means to bring that ideal into life'.[13]

There were, nevertheless, many individuals who continued to quietly apply their principles as best they could in their own lives and in their interactions with others, rather than through grand schemes. G. D. Lawrie, a retired railway official at Carlisle, wrote in 1913 that 'Tolstoy is still foremost in my estimation as a teacher of the true life. His advice in practical affairs of life is always right I think.'[14] Florence Worland and her husband Charles Daniel continued their publishing enterprises well into the 1920s, catering for new and 'cranky' reform interests – penal reform, dietary reform, reform in education – while also retaining their focus on Tolstoy, and maintaining contact with the other Tolstoyans that remained. Reflecting on her experience, Worland contended that 'Tolstoy ruined not those who took him seriously, but those who did not take him seriously enough! ... Only those in whom there was no guile went through the Tolstoyan "movement" and came out the other side in full possession of sanity and integrity, albeit not "Tolstoyans"'.[15]

Recommended reading

Rosamund Bartlett's *Tolstoy: A Russian Life* (London: Profile Books, 2010) is a recent biography that sets Tolstoy's life and thought in context, and explores his legacy. Inessa Medzhibovskaya, *Tolstoy and the Religious Culture of his Time: A Biography of a Long Conversion* (Plymouth: Lexington Books, 2009) is another excellent recent study that contextualizes Tolstoy's religious thought. Aylmer Maude's *Life of Tolstoy* in two volumes (Oxford: Oxford University Press, 1929–30) is a classic study by a sometime member of the Tolstoyan movement, which contains many insights and asides about Tolstoy's followers. For a study of the Tolstoyan movement internationally, and the ways in which Tolstoy's ideas were interpreted in different contexts, see Charlotte Alston, *Tolstoy and His Disciples: the History of a Radical International Movement* (London: I.B. Tauris, 2014). The memoir accounts collected and translated in William Edgerton's *Memoirs of Peasant Tolstoyans in Soviet Russia* (Bloomington and Indianapolis: Indiana University Press, 1993) give further insight into the motivations and daily struggles of Russian Tolstoyans in the 1920s.

Notes

1. Leo Tolstoy, *What Then Must We Do?* Tolstoy Centenary Edition (Oxford: Oxford University Press, 1934), 304–5.
2. Isabella Mayo to Vladimir Chertkov, RGALI, 13 July 1905, f. 522, op. 2, ed. khr. 613.
3. Frederik Van Eeden, *Happy Humanity* (New York: Doubleday, Page and Company, 1912), 89.
4. Anton Chekhov to A. S. Suvorin, 27 March 1894, in Louis S. Friedland (ed.), *Letters on the Short Story, the Drama, and other Literary Topics by Anton Chekhov* (London: Bles, 1924), 208–9.
5. John Kenworthy, 'Men and the Animals', *The New Order* (March 1899), 43.
6. Percy Redfern to Tolstoy, 4 August 1901, GMT, TS 235/54.
7. Jane Addams to Aylmer Maude, 30 July 1896, in Mary Lynn McCreen Bryan (ed.), *The Jane Addams Papers* (Microfilm) (Ann Arbor: University Microfilms International, 1985–6), Reel 3.
8. Jane Holah, 'Tolstoy and the Churches', *The Open Road* 2 (1) (January 1908): 56.
9. Arthur Fifield to Vladimir Chertkov, 13 December 1900, RGALI f. 552, op. 2, ed. khr. 967.
10. Yelena Shershenyova, 'The New Jerusalem Tolstoy Commune', in William Edgerton (ed.), *Memoirs of Peasant Tolstoyans in Soviet Russia* (Bloomington and Indianapolis: Indiana University Press, 1993).
11. Ralph Albertson, 'The Christian Commonwealth in Georgia', *Georgia Historical Quarterly* 29 (3) (September 1945):140–1.
12. J. K. Vanderveer, 'Tolstoyan Asceticism', *The Social Democrat* 5 (6) (15 June 1901): 177–80, and 5:7 (July 1901): 200–3.
13. P. Kropotkin to Aylmer Maude, 18 November 1910, MS1380/1183, Brotherton Library, Leeds.
14. G. D. Lawrie to Aylmer Maude, 13 October 1913, MS1380/1182, Brotherton Library, Leeds.
15. Florence Worland, 'Meetings and Partings III', *Focus* 1 (3) (March 1926): 161.

14

Simone Weil

Against being true to yourself

D. K. Levy

Simone Weil was a French writer and thinker active in the first half of the twentieth century. She was born into an affluent life in Paris in 1909. While working for the Free French in London on a manifesto for re-conceiving government in post-war France, her unyielding mode of living overcame her always-fragile health. She died aged 34, in 1943, in England.

Very early, she demonstrated a strident, uncompromising compassion when as a child she gave up sugar in solidarity with French soldiers in the First World War. While still a schoolgirl, she declared her solidarity with the Communist Left. Uncompromising in her student persona, she was brilliant and high-achieving while receiving the best education France could offer in languages, classics and philosophy. For the few years of her working life she taught philosophy in French secondary schools, before pursuing interventions in the affairs of her time such as the labour movement and the Spanish Civil War. She left France in 1942, about two years after its fall to the Germans.

Weil was not celebrated in her lifetime, though the force of her intellect was known in part through essays she published in magazines, often pseudonymously. Her celebrity came posthumously when notes on Christian spirituality she wrote towards the end of her life were published as *Gravity and Grace*. Her writings influenced those within the church such as Pope Paul VI and the former archbishop of Canterbury, Rowan Williams, as well as those outside the church such as T. S. Eliot and Albert Camus. Interest in her spiritual writings has remained constant. Her philosophical writing retains a modest following among intellectuals and philosophers, notably through the work of Iris Murdoch.

Weil's early fame came from her writings on spirituality, so much so that some have called her a saint or a mystic – though she did not think of herself this way. When the whole of her writings are considered, especially her essays rather than her notebooks, it is clear that she is first and foremost a thinker formed by her training in philosophy. The compassion and strongly held opinions evident early in her life showed themselves later in the political motives that moved most of what she did – rather than thought – in her short life. As an activist, initially her interests lay in the labour movement as well as pacifism. Her pacifism was soon attenuated by her recognition of the political weakness of the labour movement in the face of the might of government, industry and society. Violence, she then thought, could be righteous in defence of human dignity, for example, against the threat of fascism. However, her experience of combatants' conduct in the Spanish Civil War drove her to conclude that, on the contrary, force could never be righteous. She thought that legitimating someone as the permissible object of force inexorably nurtured tribalism, making murder seem natural. Force or overwhelming might disturb those who use it as much as those who suffer it, an insight she set out in her essay on the *Iliad*. In all her thought, Weil worked with the philosopher's method of patient contrasts and a seriousness born of her belief that clarification was politically urgent.

Weil's view of force is one example of how her developed ideas repudiate commonplace ideas in Western culture, including its counter-culture. She denied the importance of political rights; of justice by due process; of state or private ownership; of the private sphere of life; and that legitimacy could be conferred by a collective, public will. Instead, she elevated as fundamental to human moral and political being the response to the afflicted; the inestimable significance of a human being; the needs of the soul as the basis for government; meaningful labour; and good and evil.

One of her more arresting, if opaque, ideas concerns the impersonal reality of people. Weil affirmed the reality of people against the various ways in which their reality is denied. Science, we might say, seeks to deflate humans to bags of minerals and water with a flicker of electrical activity and habits of behaviour. Economists and political theorists seek to smooth away our differences using idealizations and demographers' generalizations to consider us as types or populations. Opposing this, one might guess that Weil therefore affirmed the individual *personality* of each person as the basis for his or her reality. She did not. The reality of a person, what is sacred about them, Weil maintained, is not an individual's personality; nothing about their hopes, dreams, values or the events of their life.[1] What we respond to above all else in someone's presence is what is *impersonal*, for this must be the first aspect of our awareness of them, if we can respond to them in any way that is characteristically *interpersonal*. And we can and do respond interpersonally – in a way distinct from our response to objects – to persons about whom we know nothing at all. As she writes, we avoid a lamppost on the street differently from how we avoid a person, without knowing anything of their personality or individuality. We move around an empty room differently from how we move in one that contains a stranger.[2] Indeed, the importance of the impersonal, what makes it sacred, is that our response to it does not depend on the personal. In this sense, the impersonal is *invulnerable* to the vicissitudes or distortions or loss of personality. No matter what happens to someone's person or personality, the impersonal is unchanged – indeed, cannot be changed. This, for example, is why it is the perfect object for the perfect love of God, or the imperfect love of which we are capable.

From these observations and reasoning, Weil derives her conception of the impersonal, which has many applications. The impersonal includes truth, love, beauty and mathematics, while the personal includes desire, imagination, perspective and material substance that constitutes us as natural beings. The impersonal is supernatural in a sense that echoes Plato and (the form of) the good. This suggestive sketch of one of her ideas is one to which we will advert below as one light under which we can illuminate integrity by casting doubt on a commonplace understanding of integrity.

Turning to the extent to which Weil illustrated integrity in the course of her short life, we can use an illuminating distinction in the idea of integrity that is not peculiar to Weil. On one side of the distinction, Weil appears undistinguished as an exemplar of integrity. On the other side, she exemplified much integrity.

The distinction appears as between integrity *within* a system and integrity *contra* or against a system. Integrity we can here understand in the familiar way as exhibited when someone resists pressure to compromise something towards which we seek fidelity; such as love, truth, beauty, an ideal or a religious creed. By 'system' is meant a moral or ethical system in the familiar sense suggested by the expressions 'Judaeo-Christian ethics' or 'Western values' that consists in shared ideas of virtue, vice, principle and values that contribute to judgements of right conduct.

Integrity *within* a system is exemplified by resisting the pressure to yield to vice or another form of conduct that is not right. It is within the system, because the refusal to yield to the pressure is made because what is pressed is acknowledged to be vice. The integrity shown does not call into question the ethical system or the vice whose intelligibility as vice depends on that system. Integrity within a system is then roughly synonymous with firm adherence to a code – that is, the system – or with being incorruptible. Refusing a bribe is a good example of integrity within a system. Refusing to tell lies for management though it would further one's career is another.

Integrity *contra* a system is characterized, I suggest, by resistance to the pressure to yield to norms or normative conceptions other than one's own or those one believes to be correct. A straightforward form of this kind of pressure is when norms are presented as virtue, as a better ethical system – or constituents of a better ethical system. Imagine a doctor put under pressure to kill a terminally ill patient in order to save others. This 'least bad' option is urged on her as the right action, the best action, the action with highest value or the most rational. She exemplifies her integrity by being unwilling to kill a patient, rejecting any decision-making according to these terms, and in so doing rejects the conceptions of virtue (or vice) pressed on her. She does not yield because she is incorruptible, as described earlier, for what is pressed on her does not appear to her just as vice, but as an unsupportable perspective. Instead, she is rejecting any characterization of any medical situation as one in which there are reasons for killing for instrumental gains because, as she sees it, there never are or could be such reasons.

Another form of this pressure is when the norms are pressed on someone not under the guise of virtue, but as norms whose (normative) basis otherwise compels deference. For example, the norms may be presented as the norms of the majority ('this is just how *we* think'), the sane ('are you crazy?'), the wise, the prudent or the happy. Again, someone who does not yield to the pressure exemplifies integrity in refusing to accept the norms proffered as compelling. Unlike the case of the doctor, this kind of refusal is terribly isolating. The doctor resists but in doing so contests solely that ethical system; while this latter variation contests much more (maybe everything) and is thus much more isolating. Apposite examples are Socrates, Epicurus, Father Zossima from the *Brothers Karamazov* or the popular idea of a saint (maybe Jesus, too). Many of these examples are now familiar and their appearance as revolutionary or strange or shocking is difficult to conjure. J. M. Coetzee's novel *Elizabeth Costello* is a rare example of literature that successfully presents the attenuated intelligibility of remote world views, laying our own world view alongside a fictional author who likens our treatment of animals to the Nazis' treatment of the Jews.[3]

Returning to Simone Weil, there is little reason to think she exemplified integrity within a system. One reason is that she was not *in* a system except perhaps as a schoolteacher and that for not more than a few years. So she was probably not much tested within a system. Second, she proved impractical in realizing plans. While she had many courageous ideas, they often did not come to pass. Though she joined a fighting unit in the Spanish Civil War, she saw no combat and was evacuated after being burned in a cooking accident. When life in occupied France became desperate, she sought refuge first in Vichy, before eventually sailing for New York to enable her parents' departure. In her last role, she accepted work in London for the Free French government under Charles de Gaulle, though he was an individual who exemplified most of what she had set her life against.

Weil was not afraid of controversy. She was more than once let go at the end of a year teaching secondary school because she did not respect the social order of small towns. She scandalized towns, for example, by offering free lessons in Greek and philosophy for men of the labouring class. She used her spare wages to enable this because she thought that education (especially linguistic) was a basic human need. This is a first example of considerable integrity contra the system that one can attribute to her. Another example was her decision to undertake automotive factory work, doing menial piecework for a year. In part, this was to share in the labour of the labourers whose cause she had championed at the same safe remove enjoyed by other activists. She sought the slavery of factory work despite her education, her background, her opportunities and the expectations of those up and down the social classes. These are two examples that suggest her rejection of prevailing norms. To these might be added her rejection of pacifism while *also* repudiating the righteousness of arms; her refusal to join the Roman Catholic Church; her earnest and official proposal that French society and government should be reordered around the idea that justice is seeing that no harm comes to citizens in respect of the needs of the soul.

These examples could be expanded or augmented, though it is unclear whether they offer a basis for general insights into integrity because Simone Weil was such a singular person from an arguably singular time. She was at her most revolutionary and integral in her ideas, which will give us a refined understanding of integrity.

Weil never wrote about integrity as such. So any application of her ideas to integrity is speculative and an elaboration. Nonetheless, her idea of the impersonal is illuminating, for it may be that her notion of an impersonal good offers a reason for rejecting familiar – possibly all – conceptions of moral integrity.

The familiar conceptions of integrity are of a piece with the earlier idea of integrity as incorruptibility. Combining this with the idea that integrity is exemplified in life when one is tested by the pressure to compromise, we get a picture of integrity as moral rectitude plus courage under pressure – that is, what people mean when they speak of keeping the faith under the pressure to change. Or, most generally, integrity is having the courage of one's convictions, whatever these may be as long as they are one's own. As Polonius intoned, stating what many think a commonplace, above all else, 'to thine own self be true'.[4]

Consider a method for clarifying integrity by reflecting on the conditions in which integrity is lost. To begin, we should recall that while integrity is typically shorthand for *moral* integrity, it also makes sense to speak of physical or mental integrity. When one or more of these is lost, what remains is some variation on a supplicant, wanton or sycophant.

One way in which physical integrity might be lost is by torture. I do not mean by injury, but by what is achieved by compromising someone's physical integrity by establishing a physical dominion through pain. The result is a suppression of physical control or volition characterized by involuntary motions such as spasms, uncontrolled bowel movements or immobility. One becomes a mere animal.

Something similar can be achieved by compromising someone's mental integrity. Again torture is one route to disrupting the dominion someone ordinarily holds over her own thoughts. Isolation is one method, but other disruptions of the senses or sleep will serve to detach someone from their mind. Characteristic of compromised mental integrity is the suppression of the moment of discerning hesitation in which illusions or delusions are repelled. Instead, control in the mind is lost. That is, the volition of the mind on which depends the act of (reflective) judgement is suppressed. The mind, now operating involuntarily, thus now incapable of judgement, does not distinguish perception from reality. One becomes mad.

Following the same structure, we can conceive the loss of moral integrity as achieved by (dis)ruptures achieved through the application of power – for example, by inducing fear or by temptation. When someone's moral integrity is lost, unmediated impulses or desires rule. Means–end reasoning, perhaps attenuated, remains, but is no longer oriented to a greater good. With moral integrity compromised, the effort needed to attend to the good is suppressed. Then any course of action seems licit. One is no longer a moral subject.

(Restoration of moral integrity just is awakening someone's attention to a greater good, the good.)

So far the structural parallels in the losses of integrity sketched should be evident. One might ask how we should understand the good which no longer commands a subject's attention after her moral integrity is compromised. Is this the personal good of one's convictions, values or commitments; or is it an impersonal good? By an impersonal good, following Weil, I mean to echo Plato's (form of) the good (*to agathon*). It is also I think the impersonal good of God that Job, in his blamelessness and integrity, will not deny in the Book of Job. It is not Job's good, nor Job's commitment, nor even his credo Job defends. Job's unwillingness to compromise is not defending himself, but God. It is in this sense that good can be impersonal.

If it is the personal good that is lost when someone's moral integrity is compromised, then a problem looms. Can this personal good be properly distinguished from the sense in which anything I do intentionally is something I pursue because I see some good in doing so? (If I did not see some good in it, then I could not explain my doing it – even Satan pursues evil as if it were his 'good'.) That is, it will prove difficult to make a sound distinction between personal good in the sense of prudence and personal moral good. Both provide the same kind of explanation of why I do something in terms of what I allow is my goal, commitment, value, etc. If the distinction cannot be made, then we need an explanation of why compromising one's moral integrity is not the same as changing what one allows is one's personal good. And if the explanation needed is wanting, then one could never lose one's moral integrity. Every seeming loss would be another change in one's personal good. Moral integrity would then be idle.

The problem sketched seems to show that there must be a requirement on moral integrity such that it cannot be courage of *any* conviction. Polonius is wrong. Moral integrity worth the candle applies solely to *some* convictions, namely the truly good ones. To put the lesson another way, just as we can only love what is truly lovable, we can only have moral integrity in relation to what is truly good.[5] That is tantamount to saying that such good must be impersonal.

Weil would likely agree that a personal good could be not be the object of moral integrity. However, for Weil, conceiving good impersonally suggests another difficulty for a familiar conception of integrity. For rather than the courage to hold fast to one's convictions, moral integrity in relation to an impersonal good will be more akin to humility. Since the good is impersonal, it is disowned or unowned. Its appeal is more like obedience to authority, rather than following from choice. One follows in humility – not by advocacy or assertion of one's commitment.

Indeed, for Weil, an attachment to *personal integrity* is holding on to what makes one subject to 'gravity' – her name for the natural forces applying to matter and psyche which constitute one's material substance – and thus vulnerable to pressures on integrity. Instead, solely by vacating the personal – renouncing our subject-hood and capacity to say 'I', a process she calls 'decreation' – do we become oriented to the impersonal good (for some, this will be God). Thus oriented (by grace), integrity is no longer vulnerable, because we have no need of personal or moral integrity.

In short, in the light of Weil's ideas, if moral integrity is fidelity to an impersonal good, then achieving such fidelity neutralizes any relation to courage, conviction or uncompromising integrity. Thus, at most moral integrity is part of becoming good, not being good, contrary to a commonplace view of integrity.

Recommended reading

The anthology of Simone Weil's work edited by Siân Miles (Siân Miles (ed.), *Simone Weil: An Anthology* [London: Virago, 1986; republished London: Penguin, 2005]) gives an accessible and comprehensive overview of Simone Weil's writing, including judicious extracts from the treasures in her notebooks. Her essay in that collection 'Human Personality' is often acclaimed as the finest expression of her later thinking. In the same collection, '*The Iliad*, or The Poem of Force' is interesting both for its reflections on the Greek classic and the way those reflections function as a medium for Weil's thinking about the human condition in times of war. Those interested in the details of her life should read the biography by Weil's friend Simone Pétrement (Simone Pétrement, *Simone Weil: A Life*, trans. Raymond Rosenthal [New York: Schocken Books, 1989]).

Notes

1 S. Weil, 'Human Personality', in S. Miles (ed.), *Simone Weil: An Anthology* (London: Virago, 1986) and elsewhere; translation of 'La Personne Et Le Sacré', in *Écrits de Londres et dernières lettres* (Paris: Éditions Gallimard, 1957).
2 S. Weil, '*The Iliad*, or The Poem of Force', in S. Miles (ed.), *Simone Weil: An Anthology* (London: Virago, 1986) and elsewhere; translation of 'L'Iliade ou le poème de la force' originally published in *Cahiers du Sud*, in Marseilles, December 1940/January 1941.
3 J. M. Coetzee, *Elizabeth Costello* (London: Secker, 2003).
4 *Hamlet*, Act 1, Scene 3.
5 This is the apparent logical grammar of integrity.

15

Guan Yu

'Righteousness that is not righteousness' in the *Romance of The Three Kingdoms*

Bryan W. Van Norden

Romance of The Three Kingdoms is one of the Four Great Novels of traditional Chinese literature, and it continues to be a source of fascination and inspiration. The first television miniseries based on the novel was seen by over one billion people, and 53 per cent of those who saw it watched every one of its eighty-four episodes.[1] The novel is inspired by historical events of the third century CE, when the Han dynasty disintegrated into three rival states vying for supremacy. *Three Kingdoms* is fascinating in part because of its storyline, which features clever strategies, intrigue, fierce loyalty and betrayal. But perhaps what draws readers is to the story more than anything else are the unforgettable characters.

On a superficial level, we can read the characters as simple archetypes. LIU Bei, leader of the state of Shu Han, is the model of a virtuous ruler. His sworn blood brothers ZHANG Fei and Lord GUAN (Guan Yu) are paradigms of courage and steadfast loyalty. ZHUGE Liang is Liu Bei's brilliant master strategist. CAO Cao, ruler of the rival state of Wei, is the villain of the story: treacherous and cruel.

However, as literary critic Andrew Plaks points out, *Three Kingdoms* is actually an ironic re-envisioning of its characters, in which the careful reader sees 'the author probing beneath the heroic surface toward the underlying issues'.[2] Liu Bei does show the classic Confucian virtues of benevolence and loyalty, and he agrees to the reigning emperor's request to protect him against Cao Cao. However, Liu also clearly harbours ambitions of becoming emperor himself, which will require that this same emperor be deposed. In a famous scene, Cao Cao suggests to Liu Bei that, of all the people alive, only the two of them are talented and ambitious enough to unify China. Caught off guard, Liu is so startled by the comment that he drops his chopsticks. He claims that he was alarmed by a sudden crack of thunder, but in reality Cao has exposed the fact that he and Liu are more similar than Liu would like to admit. In fact, we might be tempted to admire Cao Cao for his honesty about who he is, in contrast with Liu Bei, who is, as the old saying goes, 'Confucian on the outside but realpolitik on the inside'.

The ruler of the third kingdom is Sun Quan of Wu. The simplistic reading is that he is weak-willed and easily manipulated. But doesn't his uncertainty simply reflect the fact that – unlike Cao Cao and Liu Bei – he lacks the monomaniacal ambition to rule all of China, and only wants himself and his people to survive? Perceptive readers of *Three Kingdoms* might wonder whether, if the other rulers were like Sun Quan, China might have avoided the three and a half centuries of internecine conflict that followed the fall of the Han dynasty.

Liu Bei's followers are similarly complex. The brilliance of Zhuge Liang is evident – at military strategy, diplomatic negotiations and even magic. However, he is also a tragic figure. One of his abilities is to read the future through astrology. As a result, he knows that, no matter how many times he helps Liu Bei succeed, their cause will ultimately fail. (No spoiler here: every Chinese person who reads or watches any version of *Three Kingdoms* already knows that Liu Bei fails to establish a permanent kingdom, just like any American watching a film about the US Civil War knows that Lincoln doesn't get to see the second act of *Our American Cousin*.) Despite recognizing the futility of what he is attempting, Zhuge perseveres, motivated by his beliefs that he has an obligation to use his talents for the greater good, and that Liu Bei is the best of a group of imperfect leaders. Chinese readers will no doubt be reminded of the comment by Kongzi (Confucius) that 'the gentleman takes office in order to do what is righteous, even though he knows that the Way will not be realized' (*Analects* 18.7).[3]

Zhang Fei and Lord Guan continue to be two of the most popular characters from this story, and even today they often appear together as door gods (*menshen*) in Daoist temples. *Three Kingdoms* portrays Zhang Fei as a skilful and courageous warrior. It also portrays him as impetuous and a drunk. Lord Guan has no such failings – at least none that are so conspicuous. Equally famous for his bravery and talent as a fighter, Lord Guan is still revered as a paragon of loyalty and integrity. But like the other main characters of *Three Kingdoms*, he is more complicated than this.

There are several Chinese words that pick out something like integrity, each with a slightly different nuance. However, the most central term is *yi* 义, conventionally translated as 'righteousness'. Righteousness is the disposition to do what is ethically appropriate, especially when one is tempted by things like wealth or lust. As Kongzi explained, a good person, 'when seeing profit, focuses on righteousness' (*Analects* 14.12). Kongzi's later follower Mengzi argued that the characteristic motivation for righteousness is an ethically informed sense of shame. His examples of what triggers this kind of shame include cheating in a ritual hunt, and begging for goods like meat and alcohol (which were not staples of the average person's diet in ancient China). However, Confucians emphasize that we should only feel shame about the right things: many people mistakenly look down on things that are actually not shameful, like shabby clothes. In addition, having any governmental position in a virtuous administration is a genuine honour, but serving in even the highest position in a corrupt government is shameful. (This is a good illustration of the perennial relevance of Confucian ideas.) Confucians also agree that courage is not a distinct virtue, but is simply unwavering righteousness. Kongzi said, 'To lack courage is to see what is righteous and not do it' (*Analects* 2.24).

In many ways, Lord Guan seems to be the epitome of righteousness. This is illustrated in one of the most famous stories in *Three Kingdoms*. After a ferocious battle in which he became separated from his blood brothers Liu Bei and Zhang Fei, Lord Guan was surrounded and massively outnumbered by the army of Cao Cao. Cao could have pressed his advantage and killed Lord Guan, but, instead, he negotiated Guan's surrender, hoping that he could win the illustrious warrior over to his side. Lord Guan was inclined to fight to the death, but Cao's negotiator pointed out that this would actually be doing a disservice to Liu Bei. Liu's wives were in Guan's retinue, so Guan's death would leave them unprotected. In addition, the negotiator reminded him that, as long as he stayed alive, Guan had a chance of being reunited with Liu again. Lord Guan agreed to the surrender on three conditions: First, he would not officially surrender to Cao Cao, but to the Han emperor (who was currently under the 'protection' of Cao); second, Liu Bei's wife and concubine would be safe and treated with respect; and third, Guan would be permitted to leave and rejoin Liu Bei, should his whereabouts be determined. (It was still uncertain at this point whether Liu Bei had survived the battle and, if so, where he had fled to.)

On the journey back to the capital, Cao Cao tried to engineer a compromising situation by making Lord Guan and Liu Bei's wives share one room: 'But Lord Guan never entered the chamber; he remained at attention outside the door, holding a candle that burned through the night until dawn. His eyes showed no trace of fatigue.'[4] Once in the capital, Cao Cao tried to win Lord Guan over with gifts, hosting him at multiple banquets each week. Cao also gave Guan gold, silver and silks – which Guan promptly turned over to Liu Bei's wives for safekeeping – and ten beautiful women, whom Guan sent to wait on Liu Bei's wives. The only gift that made Guan happy was Red Hare, a horse famous for its speed. When Cao Cao asked Lord Guan why he seemed unmoved by gold and beautiful women but bowed in thanks when given a horse, Guan replied, 'It is a gift that will enable me to reach my brother in a single day should his whereabouts become known' (83). He went on to explain that he and Liu Bei 'are sworn to die for each other. Bound by that oath, I cannot remain here' (84). Lord Guan eventually learns that Liu Bei and Zhang Fei are alive. With the exception of Red Hare, he leaves behind all the gifts that Cao Cao has given him, and escapes with Liu Bei's wives. After making a last attempt to persuade him to return, Cao Cao orders his soldiers not to pursue Lord Guan; however, in order to escape from Cao Cao's territory, Lord Guan has to kill Cao Cao's generals who are guarding five key passes.

Lord Guan's character – as manifested in such things as his respectful behaviour towards Liu Bei's wives, and his refusal to keep most of the gifts Cao Cao tried to win him over with – appears to be righteous. However, this same disposition leads to the defeat of Liu Bei. Cao Cao attempted to defeat the allied armies of Sun Quan and Liu Bei in the famous battle at Red Cliff. Zhuge Liang organized a brilliant ambush that routed Cao Cao's army, sending him fleeing for his life. Cao Cao's retreating army is continually whittled down by further ambushes, but he desperately orders his soldiers on: 'The troops, starved and exhausted, trudged ahead, trampling over the bodies of the many who had fallen. The dead were beyond numbering, and the sound of howls and cries on the trail did not cease' (277). On the Huarong Trail, thinking that they had finally escaped their pursuers, Cao Cao despairs to discover that his path is blocked by Lord Guan and his soldiers.

All appears lost, but one of Cao Cao's advisers suggests, 'In times past, Your Excellency showed him great kindness; now, on your personal appeal to him, we might be spared.' Cao Cao advances by himself towards Lord Guan and reminds him of the kindness Cao had shown him before. At first, Lord Guan explains, 'I cannot set aside public duty for personal considerations.' But Cao continues, 'You still recall, do you not, how you slew my commanders at five passes when you left my service? A man worthy of the name gives the greatest weight to good faith and righteousness' (278).[5] The narrator explains that, because he felt that he had an obligation to repay the kindnesses shown by Cao Cao, and because Lord Guan's 'sense of righteousness was solid as a mountain', he was moved to let Cao and his remaining troops escape.

Cao Cao soon rebuilds his army's strength and poses a threat again. However, Zhuge Liang organizes a tripodal balance of power, in which each of the three kingdoms is afraid to attack one of the others.[6] When Liu Bei and Zhuge Liang are needed in the western part of their territories, they leave Lord Guan in charge of their territory in the east. Before leaving, Zhuge gives Lord Guan eight words of advice: 'North – repel Cao Cao; east – conciliate Sun Quan' (316).

Sun Quan soon sends an emissary to Lord Guan, who proposes that they cement their alliance by marrying Sun's son to Guan's daughter. However, Lord Guan angrily refuses, screaming that he would never have his 'tiger-lass married off to a mongrel' like Sun Quan's son (323). It is not clear why Lord Guan thinks his daughter is too good to marry the son of a duke, but he later provides a rationalization: 'I gave my allegiance to Imperial Uncle

Liu in the peach garden when we swore to uphold the house of Han. What would I be doing in the ranks of traitors in revolt such as you?' (339–340) In other words, he, Liu Bei and Zhang Fei took an oath to defend the Han state, so they must oppose those like Cao Cao and Sun Quan who seek to overturn it. His effort at solidifying their alliance rejected by Lord Guan, Sun Quan, instead, forms an alliance with Cao Cao. After this, Lord Guan is defeated and captured by Sun Quan, who gives him a chance to apologize, but Lord Guan responds with nothing but abuse, railing at Quan as a 'Green-eyed scamp! Red-whiskered rodent!' (340). Sun Quan, with genuine regret, has Lord Guan beheaded. Liu Bei then attacks Sun Quan to avenge the death of his blood brother, with disastrous results.

So far, it seems it was Lord Guan's righteousness that eventually undermined Liu Bei's quest. But is this really true? Philosophers who study the virtues are careful to distinguish between a virtue and its semblances. A semblance of a virtue is a disposition that superficially appears to be the virtue, but lacks some crucial aspect. For example, rashness is the name of a semblance of courage. A rash person does some things that seem courageous, like exposing himself to great risk in combat. But the truly courageous person risks his life and well-being in the pursuit of genuine goods, like loyalty to one's friends or relief of the oppressed. In contrast, a rash person might take risks because he wants to impress other people or simply because he lacks the wisdom to recognize what is dangerous. Consequently, Confucians agree that real courage is simply persevering in the pursuit of righteousness. Mengzi approvingly quotes another Confucian who said: 'If I examine myself and am not upright, although I am opposed by a common fellow coarsely clad, would I not be in fear? If I examine myself and am upright, although I am opposed by thousands and tens of thousands, I shall go forward' (*Mengzi* 2A2).[7]

The distinction between rashness and courage suggests that at least part of what distinguishes genuine virtues from their semblances is that the former are combined with other virtues. Most later Confucians follow Mengzi in identifying four primary virtues: benevolence, righteousness, wisdom and propriety. Liu Bei is the character in *Three Kingdoms* who most manifests benevolence (love for others), Zhuge Liang is the paradigm of wisdom and Lord Guan of righteousness. But Liu Bei's benevolence is sometimes marred by a lack of wisdom. When Lord Guan is killed, Liu Bei's love for his blood brother leads him to attack Sun Quan, even though Zhuge Liang warns him that he must simply accept that Lord Guan died through his own foolishness and that the war Liu plans will lead to defeat. But Zhuge's wisdom is also of limited value because it is insufficiently informed by benevolence. Liu Bei, on his deathbed, tempts Zhuge with the possibility of his assuming the kingship, instead of Liu Bei's son. Zhuge refuses, in part because he knows that this offer is just a test of his loyalty. However, Zhuge also realizes that he is simply too coldly analytic to inspire the passionate devotion that led people to willingly follow Liu Bei through years of struggle. Liu Bei's son is mediocre, yes, but just the memory of his father's compassion will lead people to follow him.

What about Lord Guan? In his case, his righteousness is limited by his paucity of wisdom and propriety. If Lord Guan were wiser, he would realize that he must not let Cao Cao survive at Huarong Trail. His first instinct, that public duty must trump personal considerations in that situation, is correct.[8] Lord Guan is similarly lacking in propriety. Propriety is the virtue manifested in showing decorum and deference in interactions with others. Liu Bei illustrates propriety in his efforts to acquire the services of Zhuge Liang. Liu Bei goes to ask for Zhuge Liang's help three times, and is turned away the first two times. Liu understands that Zhuge is both reluctant to sign on to what appears to be an impossible struggle and needs to know that Liu values his services highly enough that he will actually listen to his advice. Only after Liu has proven his willingness to defer to a wise adviser does Zhuge agree to serve him. However, Lord Guan and Zhang Fei are outraged by Zhuge's behaviour, and find it inexplicable why Liu Bei defers to him. This inability to see the appropriateness of deference and decorum is part of what leads Lord Guan to casually call Sun Quan, whose support is so crucial, a 'rodent' and his son a 'mongrel'.

Lord Guan fails to show deference and humility in a more subtle way. He claims that he rejects the proposed marriage alliance because Sun Quan and his followers are nothing but 'traitors in revolt' against the Han dynasty. But, of course, Sun Quan has done nothing fundamentally different from what Liu Bei has done. In fact, by the time Lord Guan was captured by Sun Quan, Liu Bei had already declared himself King of Hanzhong, and he would later declare himself emperor. Sun Quan, in contrast, would not declare himself King of Wu until after the last emperor of the Han was deposed by Cao Cao. One has to wonder whether Lord Guan actually rejected the offer of marrying his daughter to Sun Quan's son because he had a more 'eligible' groom in mind: Liu Bei's son Liu Shan. This marriage would have made Lord Guan the father-in-law of the future emperor of Shu Han. If Lord Guan had manifested the virtue of propriety to a greater extent, he would have had the humility to agree to the marriage between his daughter and Sun Quan's son, thereby preserving the tripodal balance of power.

The great twentieth-century Chinese intellectual Hu Shih quipped that *Romance of The Three Kingdoms* is too fictional to be good history and too historical to be good fiction. He also complained that the author had failed to maintain the consistency of the characters. However, it may rather be that, as the literary critic C. T. Hsia has argued, the characters are admirably realistic precisely because they are, like real people, multifaceted and flawed.[9] Plaks argues that we see in Lord Guan 'the overemphasis of a perceived sense of honor often leading to unwanted consequences'.[10] To his insightful reading of *Three Kingdoms* as an ironic critique of the heroic ideal, we might add that the strengths and weaknesses of its characters can be particularly well understood from the perspective of virtue ethics. In particular, *Three Kingdoms* teaches us a lesson about the limitations of individual virtues when they are not supported by other virtues that are sufficiently developed. Lord Guan's righteousness increasingly seems like a mere semblance of a virtue to the extent that it becomes detached from wisdom and propriety.

Ethical traditions that emphasize the virtues are always aware of the danger of confusing a semblance with a genuine virtue. Mengzi, writing almost a millennium before Lord Guan lived, warned that 'the propriety that is not propriety, the righteousness that is not righteousness – the great person will not practice these' (*Mengzi* 4B6). But avoiding semblances is not easy. A semblance confuses people about true virtue because it 'seems but is not' (*Mengzi* 7B37).[11] Consequently, the possessors of a semblance (like Lord Guan) get both external and internal reinforcement: 'The multitude delight in them; they regard themselves as right' (*Mengzi* 7B37). The key to avoiding this trap is to maintain vivid self-awareness. For example,

Liu Bei may not want to admit to others that he hopes to dethrone (or take advantage of Cao Cao's dethroning) the reigning emperor, but he has at least admitted it to himself, which is why he drops the chopsticks when Cao Cao confronts him about it. In contrast, Lord Guan seems to believe the rationalization that his daughter is too good to marry into the family of Sun Quan. Even when facing death after his defeat he cannot admit his mistake. Thus, Lord Guan illustrates the importance of the deceptively simple advice from that other Confucian classic, the *Greater Learning*: 'Let there be no self-deception.'[12]

I dedicate this essay to my friend, the late Jiyuan Yu, who was taken from us far too soon. 'For whom should I show excessive grief if not for this man?'

Recommended reading

Moss Roberts has produced the standard translations of *Three Kingdoms*, including a complete, four-volume translation, with extremely useful endnotes (Luo Guanzhong, *Three Kingdoms: A Historical Novel*, 4 vols. [Beijing: Foreign Languages Press, 2008; reprint]), and an abridged one-volume version (Luo Guanzhong, *Three Kingdoms: A Historical Novel*, abridged ed. [Berkeley: University of California Press, 1999]). The televised Chinese miniseries based on the novel is available on youtube.com with English subtitles: Wang Fulin, *Sanguo yanyi* [*Romance of The Three Kingdoms*], China Central Television, 1995.

Two of the greatest studies of the classic Chinese novels, each with a chapter on *Three Kingdoms,* are C. T. Hsia, *The Classic Chinese Novel: A Critical Introduction* (Hong Kong: Chinese University Press, 2016; reprint), and Andrew Plaks, *The Four Masterworks of the Ming Novel* (Princeton: Princeton University Press, 1987). A collection of secondary essays discussing *Three Kingdoms* from a variety of perspectives is Kimberley Besio and Constantine Tung (eds), *'Three Kingdoms' and Chinese Culture* (Albany: State University of New York Press, 2007). The *Analects* of Confucius and the *Mengzi* are found in translation in Philip J. Ivanhoe and Bryan W. Van Norden (eds), *Readings in Classical Chinese Philosophy*, 2nd ed. (Indianapolis: Hackett Publishing, 2005).

Notes

1 Junhao Hong, 'From *Three Kingdoms* the Novel to *Three Kingdoms* the Television Series', in Kimberly Besio and Constantine Tung (eds), *Three Kingdoms and Chinese Culture* (Albany: State University of New York Press, 2007), 127.

2 Andrew Plaks, *The Four Masterworks of the Ming Novel* (Princeton: Princeton University Press, 1987), 408.

3 This and further translations from the *Analects* are taken, slightly modified, from Philip J. Ivanhoe and Bryan W. Van Norden (eds), *Readings in Classical Chinese Philosophy*, 2nd ed. (Indianapolis: Hackett Publishing, 2005), 53. Translations from the *Mengzi* are taken from the same volume.

4 LUO Guanzhong, *Three Kingdoms: A Historical Novel*, trans. Moss Roberts, abridged ed. (Berkeley: University of California Press, 1999), 81.

5 I have slightly modified Roberts' translation, which has 'honor' instead of 'righteousness' for *yi*.

6 It is said that *Three Kingdoms* was Mao Zedong's favourite book, and it is hard not to see parallels between Zhuge Liang's strategy and Mao's decision to re-establish diplomatic relations with the United States so that he could play the United States and the Soviet Union off against each other. Of course, Kissinger and Nixon would have insisted that *they* are the Zhuge Liang and the Liu Bei in this story.

7 On Mengzi's account of courage, see Van Norden, 'Mencius on Courage', in *The Philosophy of Religion*, vol. 21 of *Midwest Studies in Philosophy* (Notre Dame: University of Notre Dame Press, 1997), 237–56.

8 The brilliant comparativist Jiyuan Yu would agree with my appeal to the virtues in understanding the novel, but would object that my simple resolutions of the ethical dilemmas confronting Liu Bei and Lord Guan fail to do justice to the irresolvable complexity of actual human life: 'It is appropriate for Guan to refuse to stay in the camp of Cao and return to Liu; and it is also appropriate for him to spare Cao Cao by repaying his previous kindness.' Yu adds that the 'success of *Three Kingdoms* may indicate that Confucianism, in its refusal to establish universal moral principles that can be used to guide all actions and in its focus on the character and virtues of a moral agent, grasped the true complexity of human ethical life'. (Jiyuan Yu, 'The Notion of Appropriateness [*Yi*] in *Three Kingdoms*', in Besio and Tung, *'Three Kingdoms' and Chinese Culture*, 39.)

9 C. T. Hsia, *The Classic Chinese Novel: A Critical Introduction* (Hong Kong: Chinese University Press, 2016; reprint), 34–5, 40–1.
10 Plaks, *Four Masterworks of the Ming Novel*, 487.
11 This passage is discussed by Winnie Sung, 'The Village Worthies', this volume.
12 Justin Tiwald and Bryan W. Van Norden (eds), *Readings in Later Chinese Philosophy* (Indianapolis: Hackett Publishing, 2014), 191.

16

Gerrard Winstanley

Radicalism and the struggle for integrity during the English Revolution

David Loewenstein

Leader of the experimental agrarian communist group known as the Diggers, Gerrard Winstanley (1609–76) provides a striking illustration of radicalism and the struggle for integrity during the English Revolution (c. 1640 to 1660). This period of great religious upheaval, social turmoil and political experimentation posed significant challenges to an activist and visionary writer committed to effecting dramatic social change. How did one maintain a sense of integrity, a commitment to one's radical social and religious principles, in a period of such disruption, instability and conflict as the English Revolution? This, after all, was not only a time of revolutionary change; it was also an unsettled period when social and religious radicals, including Winstanley, encountered fierce resistance to their ideas and activism, including from their more orthodox Puritan contemporaries.

From April 1649 until April 1650, Winstanley led the small and fragile agricultural community of Diggers (or 'True Levellers' as they preferred to call themselves) in Walton-on-Thames and Cobham, Surrey. This experiment in communal living and work was designed to act out his daring radical social vision: the land should be nothing less than 'a common treasury for all' humankind. That social vision, however, tested the limits of radicalism during the English Revolution. The Digger experiment was ultimately unsustainable and collapsed. Nevertheless, Winstanley's writings probed with great acuity the plight of the common people, the causes of class conflict, and the interconnected forces of oppressive power – economic, legal, political and religious – that continued to trouble the English Revolution and the experimental republic established in 1649. The ambiguities and limitations of the English Revolution, in turn, tested Winstanley's integrity as a social and religious radical.

Social activism and integrity

In the summer of 1649, while the Digger experiment was underway, Winstanley published one of his memorable aphoristic assertions underscoring the importance of making practical demonstrations of one's convictions: 'For action is the life of all, and if thou dost not act, thou dost nothing'. Consequently, in April of that year he had acted as a 'True Leveller', taking his spade and breaking the ground on St George's Hill, Surrey, 'thereby declaring freedome to the Creation'. Without collective action – the practical as well as symbolically charged action of digging and planting the commons – 'words and writings were all nothing' and Digger integrity as a radical social movement meant little.[1] In fact, 'words and writings' meant a great deal, for they allowed Winstanley to articulate in vividly written texts the daring and humane radical ideas of the Diggers. These works continue to move readers today. How did Winstanley reach this commitment to social activism that enabled him to lead the fragile Digger experiment while continuing to write visionary works challenging the political and religious institutions of revolutionary England?

During the early 1640s Winstanley would have been exposed to the ferment of political debate and radical ideas in Civil War London, though there is no evidence he became radicalized while living there. The social instabilities generated by the Civil War years, however, contributed significantly to Winstanley's radical social and political perspectives: the later 1640s, when he was struggling with poverty and beginning to write, were years of severe economic depression, political uncertainty and social dislocation of the lower classes. Harvest failures from 1646 to 1649 accentuated the social and economic crisis immediately following the Civil War by causing high food prices, near famine, heavy taxation and escalating poverty – a sense of social turmoil expressed in Winstanley's writings. While working as a hired farm labourer in the Surrey countryside, Winstanley converted to communism during the unsettled period of December 1648 to January 1649, an experience that had a profound impact on his subsequent writings and political activities. By starting to dig and plant the common land on St George's Hill, Walton, on 1 April 1649, Winstanley, William Everard (initially a joint-leader) and a small group of followers were engaging in practical georgic and communal activities. Yet the Diggers were also doing more than this: they were engaging in provocative social and symbolic acts aimed at challenging the powers of the earth and their subtle Antichristian practices. Digging was a means of 'declaring freedome to the Creation', and setting the earth 'free from intanglements of Lords and Landlords', so that 'it shall become a common Treasury to all' (CW 2:80), meaning that all creation would belong to all of humanity, not to the powerful few. Prophetic words and symbolic actions consequently interacted in Winstanley's career as a communist visionary writer and thus were essential to his identity and integrity as a Digger.

In *The New Law of Righteousness* (26 January 1648/9), Winstanley first records a visionary trance at the end of 1648 that resulted in his conversion to communism, that crucial event in his career coinciding with the climactic events of the English Revolution. With his preface dated a few days before King Charles I was executed, Winstanley hoped that the cataclysmic political events of the Revolution would finally bring about significant social change. The problem was that the sense of exhilaration generated by the traumatic events of December 1648 to February 1649 was qualified by disappointment among radicals. The Rump Parliament turned out to be a cautious regime with little revolutionary enthusiasm. Winstanley's substantial pamphlet warned about the ongoing politics of economic enthralment, class divisions and ecclesiastical bondage. The 'particular propriety of *Mine and Thine*' (CW 1:482) remained a terrible curse, fuelling class conflict as the rich and gentry hardened their hearts against the poor, 'treading them like mire in the street' (*CW* 1:531; echoing 2 Sam. 22:43). The Digger experiment would begin two months later, but Winstanley was already calling for 'righteous actions' (*CW* 1:1:531) in response to the socioeconomic conditions that kept the poor in a state of misery. Indeed, in *The New Law of Righteousness*, Winstanley introduces his visionary communist notion of making 'the earth a common treasury' (as it had been at the beginning) (*CW* 1:482), a theme that remains pervasive in his writings until his last published work, *The Law of Freedom*.

The first Digger manifesto combines Winstanley's radical social vision and his revolutionary mythmaking. Although a collaborative work, *A Declaration to the Powers of England* (20 April 1649) clearly shows the mark of Winstanley's own creative vision as it opens by revising, in terms of Digger communism and language, the myth of Genesis itself:

> In the beginning of time, the great Creator Reason, made the Earth to be a common Treasury, to preserve Beasts, Birds, Fishes, and Man, the Lord that was to govern this Creation; for Man had Domination given to him, over the Beasts, Birds, and Fishes; but not one word was spoken in the beginning, that one branch of mankind should rule over another. (*CW* 1:4)

Winstanley does not hesitate to reinterpret the Bible freely to express his vision of agrarian communism and to challenge a social system that reinforces the suffering of the poor. According to Winstanley, our relation to the treasures of the earth must be completely rethought and reimagined. As Winstanley creatively reinterprets the Bible, he expresses in original ways the notion that humankind's relation to the earth fundamentally defines social, political, religious and individual freedoms. By 'buying and selling' the earth and locking up its treasures (thereby making them unavailable to all, especially the poor), the covetous among humankind create the conditions for multiple and interconnected forms of tyranny, including economic, political, ecclesiastical and social bondage.

Committed to a programme of righteous, collective action as a means of restoring economic equality, the Diggers became the unique movement of the rural poor during the English Revolution.

By attempting to cultivate unused waste and common land, they sought to eradicate the tyranny of particular interest and private property. In the Digger writings, the notion that the poor and the meek would inherit the earth (see Matthew 5:5) was a daring revolutionary vision that deeply challenged orthodox assumptions about class, social hierarchy, property and power in seventeenth-century England. Winstanley's experimental agricultural community, however, was vulnerable. By April 1650 the Diggers had been driven off the land by local landlords and their henchmen after suffering repeated harassment and vicious assaults (including the burning of their houses and goods).

Attempting to sustain the integrity of Digger radicalism, given the collapse of the Digger communal experiment, remained a challenge for Winstanley. Although that experiment had failed by the spring of 1650, he nevertheless published his final and most ambitious revolutionary tract in 1652, a blueprint for a communist utopia first conceived during his Digger years and addressed to Oliver Cromwell, the most powerful man in England: 'You have power,' he writes to the Lord General, 'I have no power'. *The Law of Freedom in a Platform* is characterized by an uneasy mixture of radical social idealism and more sober political realism reflecting the disappointment of Digger defeat, as well as the frustrating political, social and economic realities that have enabled kingly power to remain 'in power still in the hands of those who have no more right to the Earth than ourselves' (CW 2:288, 285). Winstanley elaborates his vision of social reform, civic activism and labour, and true righteousness in a communist society free of the Antichristian practice of 'buying and selling' the earth and individual property-ownership; he offers many practical recommendations for governing his free, carefully organized commonwealth and for preventing the creeping in of lordly oppression and covetousness. Yet his utopian platform also expresses his anxiety about the spirit of darkness overspreading the land. Under the new republic little had changed for the commoners of England, even though they played an instrumental role in parliament's struggle against the king. Despite complaints from the poor about hardships caused by enclosure and about the destruction of common rights by acquisitive landlords, the Rump Parliament had done little to relieve their burdens and suffering. As the defeated Digger dares to remind its godly leader, the troubling ambiguities of the Commonwealth remain. Winstanley argues that a man must either be 'a free and true Commonwealth's man, or a monarchical tyrannical Royalist'; instead, the gentry and political leaders of the republic have too often taken an ambiguous 'middle path between these two' positions (CW 2:291). The disappointment of Digger defeat, then, did not stop Winstanley from attempting to expose forms of kingly power which had cast a long shadow over the English Commonwealth.

Religion was another focus of acute struggle when it came to Winstanley's identity and integrity as a radical visionary. His writing and activism occurred during a period of intense religious ferment when Puritanism had fragmented and sectarianism was flourishing. Repelled by the practices and teachings of a professional ministry, Winstanley developed heterodox religious views, as well as a strong belief in complete liberty of conscience. His religious outlook became extremely unorthodox by 1648 and was increasingly tied to his political and social radicalism, and he soon found himself called 'a blasphemer, and a man of errors' (CW 1:567). Mainstream Puritans were fiercely intolerant of the heretical positions held by Winstanley and other religious radicals.

Yet Winstanley's religious views and practices had not always been heterodox. As a younger man, he worshipped in a parish church, subscribed to orthodox Puritan beliefs about humankind's innate sinfulness, and lived in fear of a distant, terrifying God. Rather than following his own inner convictions and the Spirit within him, Winstanley describes how he knew only what he received

> by tradition from the mouths & pen of others: I worshipped a God, but I neither knew who he was, nor where he was, so that I lived in the darke, being blinded by the imagination of my flesh, and by the imagination of such as stand up to teach the people to know the Lord, and yet have no knowledge of the Lord themselves, but as they have received by hearsay, from their books, and other mens words. (CW 1:313-14)

Suffering under the coercive power of the established church, the younger Winstanley was intimidated and kept in awe by the learned ministers, rituals and teachings of orthodox religion; he feared hell and damnation, endured the harshness of predestinarian theology and lived in a state of spiritual helplessness, anxiety and enslavement as he 'lay dead in sin' (CW 1:23). In that state of spiritual confusion, Winstanley himself had known little 'of the Spirit's inward workings' (CW 1:99). In his heterodox writings, he laments his own past religious conformity and passiveness, as well as his subjection to the established clergy, causing him to exist in a spiritual state that seemed alien to his true self: 'I was a blind Professour to a strict goer to Church ... and a hearer of Sermons, and never questioned what they spake, but believed as the learned Clergy (the Church) believed' (CW 1:567).

At some point in his past – Winstanley does not tell us precisely when during the upheavals of the 1640s[2] – he began to doubt seriously the orthodox doctrines and practices of the professional clergy and became fiercely anti-formalist in religion. The 1640s, with the outbreak of civil war and the collapse of censorship and church government, were years of millenarian speculation, religious flux and choice when other radical religious writers also underwent considerable change. Sometime between 1643 and 1648 Winstanley underwent a period of acute religious struggle and depression. 'Tossed with many troubles within his own spirit' (CW 1:343), his heterodox religious positions began to develop significantly; they were very likely deepened by his second financial collapse and by a spiritual crisis in late 1647 and early 1648. The winter of 1647–8, just before he began publishing his first visionary pamphlets, was a period of severe economic hardship for the lower classes and personal trial for Winstanley, and seems to have been a moment of great spiritual revelation for him. While experiencing a powerful visionary trance (occurring in the equally trying winter of 1648–9), he heard a voice urging him to '*Worke together. Eat bread together*; declare this all abroad', resulting in his conversion to communism and prompting him to undertake the Digger experiment.[3] In addition, the mid-1640s and the momentous political events of the end of the decade constituted a period of extensive radical Puritan challenges to mainstream godly power and to a compulsory national church; this was also a period of intense religious questioning. From one perspective, 'the old World' of religion – including its theological orthodoxies, religious forms and church ordinances – seemed to be 'running up like parchment in the fire, and wearing away' (CW 2:5).

Adhering to his inner spiritual convictions was crucial to Winstanley's integrity as both a religious and social radical. As a visionary writer maintaining a fierce independence in relation to religious authorities, he no longer depended upon 'other mens words' and teachings (CW 1:314), nor upon forms of external ecclesiastical authority. His heterodox writings thus present him responding to divine impulses and drawing upon the inspiration and teaching of the Spirit in order to challenge the religious and social orthodoxies of his age with prophetic fervour. Antinomian in his radical spiritual impulses and in his profound scepticism about human religious institutions, Winstanley, much like the apostolic Quakers of the English Revolution, presents his texts as 'Written in the Light of inward experience' (CW 1:97), so that he follows above all authorities (even the Bible) the indwelling Spirit.[4] Paradoxically this radical religious stance, with its emphasis on individual inspiration, reinforced Winstanley's commitment to collective labour, since he envisaged dramatic spiritual renewal and social transformation occurring simultaneously.

One of the most provocative ways Winstanley asserts his radical spiritual convictions in his writings is by rejecting the terrifying God of orthodox Puritanism and changing the very name of God: '*I am made to change the name from God to Reason; because I have been held under darknesse by that word as I see many people are*' (CW 1:414). In this way, Winstanley challenges professional, learned ministers who keep the common people subservient and poor, stress their sinfulness and helplessness, and hold '*forth God and Christ to be at a distance from men*' (CW 1:412). From Winstanley's heterodox perspective, God is no external God but the mighty Spirit Reason that dwells within all creatures and a dynamic, pantheistic force infusing the creation with new life: 'For the Spirit is not confined to your Universities', Winstanley tells the orthodox clergy, 'but it spreads from East to West, and enlightens sons and daughters in all parts' (CW 1:410). This power of righteousness and restoration is crucially an internalized spiritual force since the more orthodox belief of 'Jesus Christ at a distance from thee, will never save thee; but a Christ within is thy Saviour' (CW 1:420).

To what degree did Winstanley maintain his integrity as a heterodox thinker and writer later in life? The answer to this question has generated debate since we possess no written expressions of Winstanley's radical religious convictions beyond the visionary and communist writings he published between 1648 and 1652. Indeed, in 1660 Winstanley was attacked by an ex-Ranter for 'a most shameful retreat from *Georges-hill*, with a spirit of pretended universality, to become a real Tithe-gatherer of propriety' (Laurence

Clarkson, *The Lost Sheep Found*, 23). Did Winstanley abandon his integrity as an agrarian communist and religious radical and eventually become more respectable? Since Winstanley had voiced in print his own sharp criticisms of immoderate Ranter behaviour and idleness (CW 2:167, 235-40), we need not accept this view of Winstanley's 'retreat' from radicalism at face value. Still, in 1659 and then again in 1666, Winstanley served as a waywarden of Cobham parish and then as church warden in 1667 and 1668, and he appears to have risen to the ranks of the gentry (see CW 1:18-19).[5] Yet, in considering the shape of his religious career, we need to be wary about demanding too much consistency in an age of enormous religious flux.

Moreover, in assessing Winstanley's long-term religious integrity, it may be significant that, at the end of his life, he abandoned the established church, attended Quaker meetings in London, and married a second wife who was a committed Quaker. In religious terms, the Winstanley who had followed 'the Light of inward experience' during his years of greatest spiritual radicalism and communist experimentation chose to align himself, in his last years, with a sectarian community that likewise sought inspiration from the inner light and refused, despite periods of harsh persecution during England's Restoration, to conform to the established Church.[6] Winstanley's involvement with the Quakers at some point after 1670, however, did not stimulate him to produce more heterodox writings. Yet during the last years of his life, Winstanley seems to have asserted a dimension of religious nonconformity and maintained, albeit more quietly, his integrity as a religious radical. Most importantly, however, Winstanley's integrity as a religious radical during some of the most traumatic years of the English Revolution contributed to his daring social activism, his visionary heterodox writings and his penetrating analysis of class conflict and oppressive power.

Recommended reading

The standard scholarly edition of Winstanley's writings is now *The Complete Works of Gerrard Winstanley*, ed. Thomas N. Corns, Ann Hughes and David Loewenstein, 2 vols. (Oxford: Oxford University Press, 2009). For a fine detailed account of Winstanley and the Diggers in historical context, see John Gurney, *Brave Community: The Digger Movement in the English Revolution* (Manchester:

Manchester University Press, 2007). For a good biographical study, one that places Winstanley's life and writings in the context of the radical ferment of the English Revolution, see John Gurney, *Gerrard Winstanley: The Digger's Life and Legacy* (London: Pluto Press, 2013). An important collection of essays evaluating Winstanley's career and the originality of his writings is Andrew Bradstock (ed.), *Winstanley and the Diggers, 1649–1999* (London: Frank Cass, 2000). For the classic account of Winstanley and the Diggers in relation to radical movements and beliefs of the English Revolution, see Christopher Hill, *The World Turned Upside Down: Radical Ideas During the English Revolution* (Harmondsworth: Penguin, 1975), especially chapter 7.

Notes

1 *A Watch-Word to the City of London, and the Armie* (1649), *The Complete Works of Gerrard Winstanley*, ed. Thomas N. Corns, Ann Hughes and David Loewenstein, 2 vols. (Oxford: Oxford University, 2009), 2:80; further references to Winstanley's works are cited within my text preceded by *CW*.

2 For what is known about Winstanley's early religious life and contexts, see *CW* 1:6–7, 14–15; J. D. Alsop, 'A High Road to Radicalism? Gerrard Winstanley's Youth', *The Seventeenth Century* 9 (1994): 11–24; John Gurney, *Gerrard Winstanley: The Digger's Life and Legacy* (London: Pluto Press, 2013), ch. 2; John Gurney, *Brave Community: The Digger Movement in the English Revolution* (Manchester: Manchester University Press, 2007), ch. 3.

3 Winstanley's trance is first mentioned in *The New Law of Righteousness*, *CW* 1:513; see also 2:14–15.

4 For Winstanley's assertion that the Quakers were perfecting the work of the Diggers, see *CW* 1:17.

5 J. D. Alsop, 'Gerrard Winstanley: Religion and Respectability', *The Historical Journal* 28 (3) (1985): 705–9.

6 Compare James Alsop, 'Gerrard Winstanley's Later Life', *Past and Present* 82 (1) (1979): 81, who stresses differences between Winstanley and the Quakers and who concludes that Winstanley's adoption of Quakerism does not confirm any radical religious conviction at the end of his life. See also Gurney, *Brave Community*, 221.

17

Amadou Bamba

Integrity and the struggle for spiritual cultivation

Alexus McLeod

Amadou Bamba, founder of the Murid[1] *tariqa* (school) of Islamic Sufism, lived the simple life of a Sufi ascetic. Sufism is not a distinct religion, but rather a particular strain of thought or emphasis within Islam, focused on the inner cultivation of the spirit, the control and elimination of the *nafs* (ego) and complete submission to and realization in God – this way of practice is referred to as *tasawwuf* (from which the word 'Sufi' derives) in Islam. Bamba is well-known as both a sheikh and founder of the Muridiyya and as a key figure in the story of French colonialism in West Africa and the history of Senegal. These are connected: 'Know that the true Sufi is an erudite person who puts rigorously his knowledge into practice,' runs one of Bamba's poems,

> so as to become free of any impurity and to have his heart filled with deep and wise thoughts, turning his back on worldly advantages arising from his fellow creatures and making resolutely his way toward his creator, he holds as equals gold coins and clod of earth. He resembles, by his forbearance, the

ground on which any sorts of refuse are thrown but which produces in return only good things.²

Bamba's legacy as a whole (including, and particularly, his non-violent struggle against the ills of colonialism) can be understood in terms of a deep integrity, a commitment to what he saw as divinely ordained principles for living and an understanding of suffering and struggle as divine gifts, aiding the person of dedication and faith in overcoming the ego and achieving true understanding of God and the cosmos.

Bamba's commitment to the principles he saw within Sufism and Islam more generally led him to a position on the French colonial enterprise different from that of other figures associated with anti-colonial movements in Africa and throughout the world. His position has sometimes been called 'accommodationist', but a fairer description of Bamba's position would be that his commitment to what he saw as the vital and necessary principles of inner cultivation and Islamic mysticism led him to view the French colonial project as both a useful trial, in key with the Sufi conception of the gift of suffering, and an opportunity to develop a particular type of spiritual discipline. Indeed, it was principally Bamba's integrity that led both to conflict with the French and to the creation of a new order, and ultimately to his accommodation with the colonial order. His primary aim was the development of the community in terms of spiritual knowledge, and he came to see the structure of French colonialism as similar to any other form of political domination, foreign or local; and as such, it was an opportunity to develop the kind of mind necessary for true understanding of and devotion to God. Bamba wrote that he was 'neither a friend nor an enemy to the French',³ and he rejected the idea of waging *jihad* against the colonial regime in terms of physical conflict to avoid religious repression.

The concept of *jihad* in Islamic thought is complex, but is crucially grounded in the idea of struggle against that which takes one away from God, from understanding of, and devotion to, God. This can have a number of meanings. The Muslim has a duty to struggle against anything that undermines the possibility of such devotion and understanding. In cases in which external forces aim to destroy this possibility, one has a duty to resist through physical struggle. Such physical struggle, however, can only go so far as to end the oppression in question. That is, warfare in this sense is limited to defensive action. However, it is not only (or even primarily) external forces that may endanger the possibility of devotion to and understanding of God. Most often, what stands in the way are features of our own mind and character – our ego (*nafs*), delusion, desires and attachments. And these things are much more difficult to resist than are offensive outside forces. For this reason, Sufis often make a distinction between the 'greater *jihad*' of struggle against the negative forces of one's own mind and character, and the 'lesser *jihad*' of physical struggle against oppressors. This distinction is maintained in a saying (*hadith*) of Muhammad claiming that the struggle against one's desires and delusion is the greater struggle.[4]

Amadou Bamba's commitment to this principle, and to the idea that suffering should be understood as a test from God to discern a person's commitment and to undermine a person's *nafs* (ego), led him away from the violent resistance against French rule that became commonplace during the nineteenth century. Such violence was often then, as today, claimed to be based on Islamic principles of defence of the community. Amadou Bamba rejected this reasoning. Part of this was due to his rejection of the association of religion and political power. Bamba found the common links between religious leaders and the representatives of the state problematic, as they led to the undermining of faith and spiritual commitment. It is difficult, if not impossible, according to many Sufis, to avoid the corruption and proliferation of ego-based concern that naturally comes with worldly power. It is in part for this reason that many Sufis reject wealth as well as political power. Bamba's own father had been an adviser to a number of kings of the Wolof people in northern Senegal, and Bamba's experience with this, as well as his familiarity with connections between religion and politics in various groups in his youth, led him to see the problems inherent in both allegiance to and cooperation with political powers as well as resistance to them. In the former case, religion was modified and its integrity undermined in the service of the interests of political rulers. In the latter case, violence often emerged, leading one inevitably away from commitment to the knowledge of and submission to God, as people instead became inflamed by worldly desire. Bamba attributed to this the political violence he witnessed, hypocritically justified in the name of Islam. He said of this: 'I lost the slightest interest I had in worldly and temporal matters when I saw, while living in Kajoor, the bodies of Muhammad Fati and Ale Lo, two persons from a respected Muslim family in Njambur, killed by dammeel for mere political reasons.'[5]

Bamba's rejection of such worldly power was not merely theoretical. After his father's death, he turned down an invitation to meet the Wolof rulers and be established as his father's successor. Despite the knowledge of some that Bamba rejected such trappings as part of his commitment to Islamic and Sufi principles, the expectation was still that one would overlook this in such situations. Traditional and practical considerations dictated that one should court the rulers. The primary reason for this deference was that rulers could benefit religious leaders in terms of wealth and power, which Amadou Bamba found offensive. He wrote of this episode: 'Lean toward the sultans they told me, so that you could benefit from gifts that would solve all your material needs. I responded, I am satisfied with God, I put my trust in him.'[6] This rejection of the rulers led numerous people to consider Bamba mad. But Amadou Bamba's commitment to his ideals would not waver in the face of potential wealth, nor would it be undermined by the political ordeals of his later years.

In his commitment to spiritual cultivation and rejection of worldly power and prestige, Bamba followed the widespread Sufi practices of poverty and asceticism, avoiding lavish food, clothing and other luxuries that had the power to pull the mind from reflection on and devotion to God. Bamba did not push this asceticism to the extreme of self-denial or flagellation, though, as some other groups did. Interestingly (and perhaps ironically) enough, this founder of the Sufi sect most commonly associated today with wealth and business himself rejected wealth and its trappings. His commitment to hard work and social usefulness was not grounded in an instrumental aim for wealth or power, but as with other aspects of his life and character, it was grounded in his view that such effort represented the application of natural human abilities, and thus our commitment to and obedience of God.

The measure of human beings, according to Bamba, was the extent to which they submitted to God and the divine will, not their material possessions or power. But this pursuit of spiritual realization, ascetic though it was, was no solitary endeavour. While Bamba rejected involvement with rulers and those of power, he did not reject the importance of the community. Indeed, the people were central to his conception of spiritual cultivation. Bamba saw work on behalf of the people, with the primary aim of advancing their spiritual state, as a human responsibility. The hard work, social commitment and focus on education that characterized the Sufi *tariqa* he founded was grounded in this responsibility that all of us have to each other's spiritual development.

Amadou Bamba excelled in learning and rose to a position of leadership fairly early, during his thirties in the mid-1880s. He developed a following, and in 1888, founded the village of Touba, imagined as a site for education of the Muridiyya. The location and purpose of the village demonstrate aspects of Bamba's character. He planned the site at a relatively remote location, so as to avoid the attractions of politics, wealth and power associated with the cities and more populated regions. Bamba would here focus on education and spiritual development, teaching his followers that what brought one closer to God was commitment, knowledge and the use of one's natural abilities for obedience to God's will. Wealth and power played little role in this will, according to Bamba.

Amadou Bamba's numerous conflicts with the French colonial government of Senegal demonstrate his commitment to what he saw as the essence of his faith and his Sufi determination to know and draw closer to God. While Bamba at no stage in his life and career took up arms against the colonial power, as did so many other of his contemporaries, he was tried and exiled on two different occasions by the French, leading to two long periods of exile – the first for seven years in Gabon, at the time a distant and rural 'backwater' in Central Africa, far from Bamba's home and people; and the second for five years in Mauritania, closer to home, but again isolated in the desert. In sending Bamba away from Senegal, the French administrators sought to undermine his local influence, with the idea that a religious leader not present to his people would easily be forgotten. During his two exile periods, Bamba continued to study and write, including a number of important works on Islamic principles, as well as collections of poetry.

The periods of exile did not exhaust the hardship imposed on Bamba by the French – he was, for instance, sentenced to house arrest in his home in Senegal for fifteen years. But none of these attempts by the French to undermine Bamba's influence had their intended effect. In fact, they had the opposite effect – Bamba's followers were galvanized by his commitment to God and the community even during his time of exile (having learned of this during his return to Senegal in the period between his exiles), and devotion to him grew exponentially during his time away from Senegal. Indeed, the exiles likely played a large role in the elevation of Amadou Bamba to the level of legend and saint.

Bamba and his community of Muridiyya came under the scrutiny of French colonial administrators in the 1880s, as a result of the spreading of vicious rumour and disinformation by local Wolof rulers who resented and felt threatened by the growing influence of this Sufi holy man. Bamba's shunning of these rulers years before likely contributed to their animosity as well. They convinced the already nervous French that the Muridiyya planned to create their own state and to undermine the authority of the colonial administrators. This led the authorities to arrest Bamba in 1895, after which he was put on trial before a colonial council for subverting the colonial regime and intending to incite rebellion. According to the traditional account, after listening to the charges against him, Bamba's only response in his defence was to recite the chapter *al Ikhlaas* (translated as 'purity' or 'sincerity') from the Quran. Some claim that after this, Bamba remained silent for the rest of the trial and refused to answer questions, while others claim that, though he was uncooperative, he offered short answers to the questions of the prosecutors, and demanded evidence that he had plotted revolt. Needless to say, the council did not appreciate Bamba's defiance, and unanimously decided to send Bamba to exile in Gabon.

Bamba's response to his exile demonstrates further his ability to adhere to the highest principles, rather than allowing himself to be derailed by adversity. While others in similar situations turned to violence or engagement with the state, Amadou Bamba saw his exile as a gift from God. The Sufi view of suffering takes it to be a boon, as it helps to undermine the selfish *nafs* (ego), and in this way to bring one closer to God. The person who suffers, Bamba held, is one who is the true servant of God. 'God tests His servant in the proportion of the strength of his faith,' he said. 'If he remains resolute, He increases the suffering but if, on the contrary, he falters and becomes miserable, He leaves him alone or diminishes the suffering.'[7]

Amadou Bamba received his wish for further suffering. After a brief reprieve of less than a year following his seven-year exile in

Gabon, the French authorities again began to worry about religion-inspired revolts, and again arrested him, after which he was exiled to Mauritania, where he remained for the next five years. During this exile, the relationship between French and the Muridiyya who Bamba had left behind grew to a greater level of trust, and the Murid leader was brought back to Senegal. He did not gain complete freedom, however. Bamba was restricted to house arrest in the village of Ceyeen, a remote site distant from Bamba's home region and the epicentre of the Murid movement. It was a partial concession to the Muridiyya. They would get back their leader, but he would be distant, severely constrained and maintained by the French, presumably to head off any possibility of revolt.

During this period, Bamba made a daring and perhaps surprising move. At the time, the Moor religious leader Ma al-Aynayn was waging a violent struggle against the French in Mauritania and southern Morocco. In light of this, Bamba issued a *fatwa* (religious ruling) declaring violent *jihad* against the French such as that of Ma al-Aynayn unjustified on Islamic grounds. He reasoned that there was no religious suppression under French control (although there was certainly pressure towards Christianization) and, interestingly, that the current weakness of native forces in comparison to the French made it unwise to engage in violent revolt, as the likeliest outcome would be defeat, death and the potential suppression of the religion. Bamba also argued that the example of Muhammad and the early Islamic community suggested that they should allow the French their own concerns, and, instead, focus on the elevation of the soul.

While Bamba's *fatwa* sounded like capitulation and a plea to French authorities for more freedom to some, others understood this position as consistent with the ideals Bamba had always upheld, from his youth and his turn to Sufism through both of his exiles and his house arrest. Bamba's actions in previous years also demonstrated that he was not one to sacrifice his commitment to Islamic and Sufi ideals to ensure material gain or personal benefit. Despite the reasons for his commitment to peaceful coexistence with the French, the colonial administrators saw this as a highly useful position, and their relations with Bamba became less hostile. In addition to the fact that Bamba's followers were now major contributors to the colonial economy, through the application in agriculture of their Murid commitment to hard work, the Muridiyya represented by this time a major force in Senegalese society. Even had they not wanted to, the French would have to treat the case of Amadou Bamba with care. While this influence may have led some to make political demands, Bamba believed that the well-being of his followers was best attained through devotion to God, not through political entanglements that most often led to secularization and the diminishment of devotion through attachment to political power and wealth. The French allowed Bamba to return to his home region (although not his home village) in 1912, and for the next years until his death in 1927, Bamba developed his views on spiritual cultivation and the proper relationship with worldly powers. His relationship with the French warmed significantly, as Bamba encouraged his followers to work with the colonial government when it did not cut against their Islamic principles. In his later years he remained as committed to these principles as ever. When the colonial administration offered him the French Legion of Honor in 1918 in recognition of his encouragement of colonial accommodation, he rejected it. It was not honours or power that motivated Bamba, but his commitment to cultivating closeness to God for both himself and his community.

Amadou Bamba demonstrated integrity through his unwavering commitment to his religious principles even in the face of pressure and temptation to abandon them many times during his life. His faithfulness and his commitment to spiritual development not only for himself but also for the wider community led him to reject the path of resistance to the French colonial project, even while he resisted French attempts to undermine Islamic religious devotion in the region. Bamba remains a revered figure in Senegal, as well as in the wider diaspora across the world. He is celebrated in numerous ways, including parades and days named in his honour. Although Bamba has come to be seen as a symbol of Senegalese identity, it is perhaps ironic that this should be so. Bamba's message was universal – resistant to nationalism, politics or ethnic identity. The very faith that allowed him to act boldly in the face of resistance from both French and native forces led him to proclaim a universal message for the spiritual cultivation of humanity. The fact that Amadou Bamba is little known outside of West Africa is unfortunate. His example is, as his message was, meant for the entire world.

Recommended reading

There is very little work on Amadou Bamba in English. Most studies of his life and movement are written in French, as a result of the small interest in Bamba outside of Senegal and the wider Francophone scholarly community. There are a few excellent works on Bamba in English, however – starting with Cheikh Anta Babou's *Fighting the Greater Jihad: Amadu Bamba and the Founding of the Muridiyya of Senegal* (Athens: Ohio University Press, 2007). A newer work on Bamba is Michelle Kimball's *Shaykh Ahmadou Bamba: A Peacemaker for Our Time* (Selangor: The Other Press Sdn Bhd, 2018). A number of translations of Bamba's works into English have been published, including Abdoul Aziz Mbacke's *Ways Unto Heaven* (Dakar: Majalis, 2009), a translation of Bamba's *Masalik-ul-Jinan*, and Rudolph Ware's *Jihad of the Pen: The Sufi Literature of West Africa* (Cario: American University in Cairo Press, 2018), which includes some of Bamba's poetry, and Sana Camara's *Sheikh Ahmadu Bamba: Selected Poems* (Boston: Brill, 2017).

Notes

1 Translated from Arabic as 'seeker' – generally referring to a novice or beginner on the Sufi spiritual path. Giving the school this name was a sign of the humility that was a central part of Amadou Bamba's Sufism.
2 Quoted in Abdoul Aziz Mbacke, *Ways Unto Heaven* (Senegal: Majalis, 2009), 85.
3 Cheikh Anta Babou, *Fighting the Greater Jihad: Amadu Bamba and the Founding of the Muridiyya of Senegal* (Athens: Ohio University Press, 2007), 154.
4 Though this *hadith* is disputed by some historic Islamic scholars as having a weak or unestablished chain of transmission, it is extremely influential in Sufi schools, and thus foundational to Amadou Bamba's project.
5 *Fighting the Greater Jihad*, 56. 'Dammeel' is a word of the Wolof language, translating to 'ruler' or 'king'.
6 *Fighting the Greater Jihad*, 60.
7 *Fighting the Greater Jihad*, 134.

18

Abai Kunanbayev

Integrity and the law in nineteenth-century Kazakh society

Tenlik Dalayeva

Kazakhs led a nomadic life in medieval and modern times. They followed a unique system of moral guidelines, a set of legal norms or customary law known as *adat*. When the Kazakh steppe was incorporated into the Russian Empire in the eighteenth and nineteenth centuries, at first the law of the Russian Empire coexisted with the Kazakhs' *adat* norms, and then it gradually came to dominate in the whole Kazakh territory. The difficulty was that many of the criminal laws and the system of power relations of the Kazakh nomads did not coincide with the way that law was understood in the Russian Empire. For example, in a case where damage was caused by cattle, Kazakhs preferred to seek out the perpetrators so that the aggrieved party could obtain compensation, rather than punishing the offender under Russian law. The clash between the two systems made apparent the incompatibility of these two societies' ideas about integrity and the way it was embodied in law.

Ibrahim Kunanbayev (Abai) was a famous Kazakh poet and educator of the second half of the nineteenth century.[1] He had experience as a regional governor, or *volost* ruler. This experience allowed him to directly observe the changes that had occurred in the moral norms of everyday life of the Kazakh population as a result of the spread of capitalist relations in the Russian Empire. Abai wrote many works, but as Kazakh nomads had a tradition of oral transmission, they were not collected or preserved during his lifetime. Many of Abai's works that were written offhand are lost to us forever. The *Book of Words* (Kazakh: қара сөздері, *Qara sözderi*) is one of the most famous works that survives. In it, Abai recorded his attitude to his own time, and all the changes that took place in the Kazakh steppe.

This portrait explores the clash of ideas about integrity in Kazakh and Russian law. It looks at how Abai negotiated this clash, and how his position as someone who was respected (on both sides) for his personal integrity helped him to do so. Of course, there is also the question of the integrity of the accounts we have of Abai's thoughts, given the problems of oral transmission and the fact that much is lost to us. The chapter is based on materials held in the Central State Archive of the Republic of Kazakhstan, and in the museum of Abai.

Abai Kunanbayev's views and his status as a figure of integrity were shaped by both time and place. He was born into the Kazakh tribal aristocracy. Abai's grandfather, Oskenbai, was a famous warrior *(batyr)*, and his father, Kunanbay Oskenbayuly, was a senior sultan, having received that post thanks to his influence among the tribesmen. His father prepared him for a career in local government. Abai received his primary education in two culturally very different systems. At the age of nine he was sent to the madrasah of Imam Ahmed Riza, a Muslim theological school in Semipalatinsk. Sometime later, he voluntarily began to study in a Russian parish school in the same city. At the behest of his father, Abai returned home and at the age of fifteen he became involved in the proceedings of contentious cases. Abai soon became known among the people as a fair *biy* (a judge elected by the people), showing his knowledge and impartiality in contrast with the local Kazakh aristocrats. Abai's intellectual formation was also influenced by his friendship with Russian political exiles such as E. P. Michaelis, S. S. Gross and N. I. Dolgopolov. He began to read the classics of Russian literature: Pushkin, Lermontov, Nekrasov,

Tolstoy, Turgenev, Saltykov, Dostoevsky, Belinsky, Dobrolyubov and Pisarev. He translated some of their works into Kazakh. Throughout his life Abai recorded his reflections on the transformation in the life of the Kazakh people in poetry. In the last decades of his life he turned to prose. He placed no importance on preserving his poetry, however. He would write a poem on a piece of paper and give it to another person. He did not keep them himself. Between 1885 and 1890 some of Abai's poems were printed in a Kazakh newspaper, by his friend Kokbai Dzhanatayev. After his death, more effort was made to preserve Abai's legacy – first by his family and then by scholars. Abai's nephew, Kakitai Kunanbayev, helped to collect materials for his obituary, and in 1909 published the first collection of the *Poems of the Kazakh poet Ibrahim Kunanbayev* with his own money in St. Petersburg. Mukhtar Auezov wrote the first scholarly biography in 1924, and went on to compile four volumes of biography and write two novels about Abai in the decades that followed. The epic novel *Abai's Way* made Abai's name well known among other nationalities in the Soviet Union. In the 1940s and 1950s the historian Alkei Margulan engaged in a further search for archival documents and manuscripts relating to Abai: in the archives of St. Petersburg, Moscow, Ufa, Omsk and Orenburg. Writers, literary critics and linguists have now produced many works about Abai and his creative legacy. Philosophers and cultural theorists have explored his ethical, aesthetic and sociological views. In 1995, the people of the Republic of Kazakhstan celebrated Abai's 150th anniversary. This was the biggest event in the first years of the independence of the state, and was attended by delegations from twenty-five countries, represented by heads of state and prime ministers. It brought Abai to the attention of the world.

Although Kazakh tribes began to be affiliated to the Russian Empire in 1731, it was not until the introduction of the 'Statute on Siberian Kazakhs' in 1822 that the Russian imperial administration began to use law as an instrument of power and control over the nomadic Kazakh people. Dissemination of the laws of the Russian Empire occurred gradually. Administrative divisions modelled on those of the Russian Empire were instituted, and Kazakh aristocrats were brought into positions in local government in this new imperial administrative system. At first, high-level legal and administrative systems coexisted with the customary law of the Kazakhs, which remained the primary regulator of daily life.

Customary law (*adat*) was important to the Kazakhs in the nineteenth century because of their nomadic way of life. The laws of the Russian Empire contained rules for the life of the settled population. The legal and judicial norms of the empire were not consistent with the mentality of the Kazakh people, and this caused a clash of ideas about honesty and integrity. When Senator Fedor Engel was appointed to observe and report on the Bukeyev horde in August 1827, he noted that the 'Kirghiz are afraid of the Russian court, and not without reason, as the rites of our proceedings are directly opposite to their manners, customs and concepts. Further, Kazakhs are forced to come to the city for judicial trials and in this sometimes long absence from their houses and households they go bankrupt.'[2]

According to Kazakh norms, all litigations were conducted in oral form in the presence of representatives of the opposing sides. The purpose of the *biy* was not only to identify the perpetrator and punish the guilty, but also to preserve harmony between tribal groups who would afterwards once more have to share pastures. A *biy* was a mediator in disputes, whose goal was to find the most mutually beneficial solution for both sides. In the eighteenth century, *biys* whose solutions were fair became famous, first in their own clan and then in the whole tribal community. *Biys* were not appointed as such; their recognition came from fellow Kazakhs.

The main purpose of the Russian imperial court proceedings was to determine the degree of guilt and punish the guilty from the point of view of the law. Justice in court decisions according to Russian legal norms involved punishing the guilty, but was not concerned with compensation for damages to the injured party. Kazakhs did not have such a punishment as detention, or prison. They did have two forms of punishment in the form of a fine: *Ayyp* – a fine or compensation for minor crimes; and *Kuhn* – a payment for more serious crimes. With the gradual strengthening of the influence of the Russian Empire in the Kazakh steppe, the Russian administration sought to further regulate the legal norms of the Kazakhs.

In a decree of 22 June 1854 concerning the extension of the laws of the Russian Empire to the Siberian Kazakhs, it was stipulated that 'the title of *biys* is to remain for all those who now enjoy it, but for the future it can only be granted to sultans, or village elders who have served at least six years'.[3] The status of a *biy* would no longer depend on the degree of knowledge of the norms of *adat*, but, rather, on new rules imposed by the government of the Russian Empire. However, there were precedents in the interior provinces of the Russian Empire for using local customs to solve local cases. *Volost* courts were 'more focused on the principle of fairness in decision-making, and less formalized' than courts of general jurisdiction, and so it was considered permissible and potentially more efficient to rely on local customary law.[4]

In 1864 the Russian Empire introduced judicial reforms. On the eve of the implementation of these reforms, the West Siberian governor general A. O. Dyugamel asked court counsellor Yatsenko to gather opinions from the sultans and *biys* concerning the judicial changes. In response, the Kazakhs asked to preserve the *biy* courts and congresses, and offered to elect *biys* for three years. *Biys* would be 'elected Kazakhs of good morals who are at least 25 years old and not older than 70 years, are not defiled by the court or the public verdict, are not under investigation or under trial, and are known for their honesty'.[5] When all of the Kazakh steppe came under the jurisdiction of the Russian Empire in the summer of 1865, administrative and territorial reforms were also introduced. In 1867–68, the steppe was divided into *oblasts, uezds, volosts* and administrative *auls* (villages). Kazakhs were represented in local government at the level of the *volost* and the *aul*. Those who served as *volost* rulers had responsibility for the distribution of agrarian land, the analysis of land disputes and the imposition of taxes. Proceedings on contentious issues remained in the hands of *biys*, but *biys* had now to be approved by the *volost* ruler. This was a compromise between local tradition and imperial innovation. Below the level of the *uezd* chief, the Russian administration actually had relatively little control; this was compounded by the mobile lifestyle of the Kazakhs, and the resulting poor communication. The delivery of mail was carried out through the use of horses and camels.

Every three years there were elections for *volost* rulers, *aul* elders and *biys*. Because these local government positions gave access to administrative resources, and allowed Kazakh tribes to manage the pastures of the *volost* and the *auls* at their discretion, and in their own favour, these elections saw a struggle between factions, particularly over election to the position of *volost* ruler. In the struggle to control these elected positions, corruption as a sociocultural phenomenon was becoming the norm in the life of Kazakhs.

Abai first became known among Kazakhs as a *biy*. He first held an administrative position at age twenty, when he became a deputy for his brother, Kudaiberdy Kunanbayev, the *volost* ruler in the Kuchuk Tobyktinsk *volost*. Kudaiberdy Kunanbayev died in 1866, three months before the end of his term, and Abai served as *volost* ruler until the next election was held. In 1872 he engaged in a more serious struggle for power, when he stood for election as *volost* ruler in the Kyzyl-Molina *volost* against the son of the famous and wealthy Orazbay. Abai won the election, but he gave the post of *volost* ruler away to his younger brother Iskak. According to Abai's son Turagul, although Abai recognized that the position of *volost* ruler was now the only one in which it was possible to provide more equitable economic conditions for the Kazakh *auls*, he was reluctant to stand for election, and did not seek positions in the *volost* administration, or nominate himself for election. He became a *volost* ruler only at the call of his countrymen, who had hoped for his fair decisions in the emerging conflicts between family and tribal groups. In his decisions Abai combined the norms of Kazakh customary law (*adat*) and the norms of the Russian legislation for the steppe population.

In the period 1875–1878 Abai acted as *volost* ruler in Konyr-Kokshe. A report of 21 June 1885 stated that Semipalatinsk's *uezd* chief believed that in the Konyr-Kokshe *volost* 'almost no ruler could safely serve and govern for three years. Almost all of them have been subjected to the court intrigues of rich or influential Kazakhs who wanted to rule or who were at enmity with the chosen ruler.' As a result, the people of Konyr-Kokshe were offered the chance to elect an outsider as *volost* ruler, 'namely Ibrahim Kunanbayev, who was known ... as a man who was very instructive, intelligent and honest'. The people unanimously chose Kunanbayev. 'For almost the whole duration of Abai Kunanbayev's administration (2.5 years) the *volost* was characterized by order. Before this, there had been daily pillages and frequent murders.'[6]

The following incident testifies further to Abai's character. In May 1898 the Semipalatinsk *uezd* chief organized the elections for the ruler of the Mukursk *volost* for the period 1899–1902. There was a long-standing dispute over the boundary line between the Mukursk and Chingiz *volosts*, and Abai as a *biy* was invited to mediate in these disputes. There Abai was attacked by the Mukursk *volost's* ruler and his entourage. This case was the subject of investigation by the Prosecutor's Office in the District Court, but as a result of bribing of representatives of the local administration, the case was stopped under the pretext of lack of evidence. In search of justice to protect his civil dignity and to expose the lawlessness of the local authorities, Abai sent an appellate review to the Governing Senate of the Russian Empire. Here, Abai showed a clear knowledge of the working and provisions of Russian law.

The thirty-page appellate review was written by Abai in the Russian language. This handwritten original document is now in the Central Historical Archive in St. Petersburg. This case showed the Kazakhs that knowledge and competent application of laws, and possession of the Russian language, could protect them from the tyranny of their countrymen who occupied positions at the local level. Through his actions Abai demonstrated to the Kazakh people the tools and direction of their fight for their rights against the local effects of the colonial administration. He advocated appealing to the higher imperial power that had imposed its rule upon them, in order to overcome the local corruption that the imposition of that same system had generated.

A report of 25 August 1903 by *uezd* chief I. S. Navrotskiy to the Semipalatinsk military governor Galkin stated that 'the service of Kunanbayev was marked by executive and intelligent energy, devotion to the government and lack of bigotry'.[7] Navrotskiy noted that Kunanbayev had repeatedly been chosen as a leading *biy* in Semipalatinsk and neighbouring *uezds*. 'He lives quietly and calmly. He is extremely careful in matters that are not personally related to him, that is, he never assumes the leadership of parties, either in his own or in other neighbouring volosts, although the leaders of the parties turn to him for advice.'[8] Despite these characteristics and the fact that Abai did not openly criticize the government of the Empire, he was placed under surveillance by the Russian government, which feared him because of his influence on the Kazakh population. His integrity, and his reputation for integrity, were the very things that elicited the suspicion of the Russian government. He positioned himself as a mediator between the Russian system of power and Kazakh society, observing the interaction between them, and seeking opportunities for peaceful integration of Kazakhs in the Russian space on the basis of the existing legal norms of the empire.

Due to his understanding of Russian culture, his reading of Russian classics and knowledge of the laws of the Russian Empire,

Abai saw opportunities for integration and further development of the Kazakh people at the beginning of the twentieth century. In his *Book of Words*, Abai wrote honestly about what he saw as the weaknesses of the Kazakhs, which prevented them from developing in the economic and political sense. In this text Abai reflected his attitude to his own time, and to all the changes that took place in the Kazakh steppe. He also began to think more about the purpose of man and the meaning of life, about good and evil, and about justice and injustice. *Adam Bol!* (Be a Human!) was the *leitmotif* of his work. Abai felt the only way to change things for the Kazakhs was through enlightenment.

> Watching my people sink deeper and deeper into discord, I have come to the conclusion that the *volost* chiefs should be elected from among men who have had at least some Russian education, however little. If there are none, or only persons whom people do not wish to nominate, then let the *volost* chiefs be appointed by the *uezd* authorities and the military governor. This would be beneficial in several ways. First of all, ambitious Kazakhs would have their children educated; secondly, the *volost* chiefs would no longer be dependent on the whims of local magnates, but take their orders from the higher authorities. To avoid the inevitable objections and denunciations, an appointee should not be subjected to any local control and verification.[9]

According to Abai, the main defects of the *biy's* court at the end of the nineteenth century were that firstly, it was subject to bribery, and therefore the *biy's* court could not resolve any case fairly and secondly, *biys*, trying to cash in, consciously created red tape, rather than solving cases. *Biys* multiplied disputes, rather than reducing them.

> I would have respected a *volost* chief and a *biy*, but on our steppe there is neither divine nor human justice. Power bought by servility or with money is not worth much.
> ... I wish I could find a clever man to honour. Yet there is none ready to use his intelligence to serve the cause of conscience and justice, while one and all will be quick to guile and perfidy.[10]

Abai also set great store by knowledge, and science. For some, he believed the greatest pleasure was derived from wealth and the multiplication of livestock. For others, pleasure was associated with power. For a third group, pleasure was associated with cognitive activity. For Abai, the latter was the supreme pleasure inherent in a moral and sensible people.

The most difficult thing is to instill humanity, loving kindness, in them. For Allah is the way of truth, and sincerity and truthfulness are the enemies of evil. Will a friend accept an invitation sent through an adversary? Truth cannot be attained unless the soul has a love of it. Human knowledge is gained by means of love of truth, through a thirst to discover the nature and essence of things for one's self. This is not, of course divine omniscience: human curiosity and a striving for knowledge give learning only commensurate with man's reason.

But, above all, one should come to love Allah. It is known that Knowledge is one of the attributes of the Most High, and therefore a love of Knowledge is a sign of humanity and integrity. Those who pursue it for gain and for base, selfish aims can never attain the heights of Knowledge.[11]

In his later years Abai tried to promote knowledge, science and education through his work, but sharing his thoughts and works with the people at large was difficult. His inner circle adopted his ideas, and many of his followers became members of the *Alash* national movement at the beginning of the twentieth century, promoting Kazakh autonomy.

As the Kazakh steppe was incorporated into the Russian Empire in the nineteenth century, the introduction of Russian legal and social structures generated a clash in moral norms, and in the relations of people to each other and to power. The clash between the two systems compromised the operation of legal and moral norms in Kazakhstan, and introduced new possibilities for corruption. The search for ways to preserve honesty as a necessary standard for protecting the interests of the common man became the goal for figures of integrity. While Abai understood the traditions of the Kazakh people, and was respected by the Kazakh nomadic communities as someone who applied their customary law with fairness and authority, he believed that it was essential for Kazakhs to understand and utilize the legal and moral norms of the Russian Empire. In order to overcome the corruption that had been introduced by the clash in these two systems, Abai believed Kazakhs needed to learn to understand and appeal to the imperial system that had imposed these difficulties in the first place. Abai's experiences as a *biy* and as *volost* ruler in these changing times caused him to reflect on the nature of integrity and humanity, in works that were passed down and reconstructed by the Kazakh community and by historians in the century after his death.

Recommended reading

It is best to begin acquaintance with Abai from reading his works: *Abai Kunanbayev, Selected Poems* (Moscow: Progress Publishers, 1970); *Abai Kunanbayev, Book of Words* (Semey: Abai International Club, 2003). Mukhtar Auezov wrote the epic novel *Abai zholy* (The Path of Abai) in four volumes. An abbreviated version was published in English: Mukhtar Auezov, *Abai* (Abridged) (Moscow: Progress Publishers, 1975).

In her article 'We Are Children of Alash ...', *The Central Asian Survey* 18 (1) (1999): 5–36, Gulnar Kendirbaeva gives an idea of how Kazakh intellectuals were looking for a solution to the problems of national and cultural survival of the Kazakh people in the early twentieth century. Understanding the cultural struggles of the Kazakhs in this period will help to better understand the personality of Abai, who preceded the Kazakh intelligentsia and was the poet of the transitional cultural period. The article by Sydykov E. B., Kurmanbayev Y. A. Dopolneniye 'k obrazu: Abay – volostnoy upravitel' (Addition to the image: Abai – district governor) *Doklady Natsional'noy Akademii Nauk Respubliki Kazakhstan* (Reports of the National Academy of Sciences of the Republic of Kazakhstan) 2 (2013): 89–91 is devoted to the activities of Abai at the post of volost governor. Readers may also be interested in an article by Naomi Caffee, 'How Tatiana's Voice Rang Across the Steppe: Russian Literature in the Life and Legend of Abai', *Journal of Eurasian Studies* 9 (1) (2018): 12–19.

Notes

1 Abai was a nickname given to him by his grandmother Zere and mother Ulzhan. It means literally 'prudent, cautious, circumspect, thoughtful'.

2 Rossiiskii Gosudrarstvennii Istorichestkii Arkhiv [RGIA] f. 1291. op. 82. del.1 l.129. In the Russian Empire, Kazakhs were mistakenly referred to as Kirghiz, and this name is therefore found in archival documents of the nineteenth century. In this chapter the correct name, Kazakhs, will be used.

3 Tsentral'nii Gosudarstvennii Arkhiv Respubliki Kazakhstan [TsGA RK] f. I-345. op.1. del. 1738. l. 1.).

4 A. A. Sorokin, 'Krest'yanskiy volostnoy sud Rossiyskoy imperii v otsenkakh obshchestvennosti kontsa XIX v', *Bulletin of Tomsk State University* 417 (2017): 147–8.

5 TsGA RK, f. I-345. op. 1. del. 807. l. 14 ob.).

6 S. Baizhanov (ed.), *Abai zhane arkhiv* (Almaty: Gylym, 1995), 32.

7 Ibid., 133.

8 Ibid., 133–4.

9 Abai Kunanbayev, *Book of Words* (Semey: Abai International Club, 2003), 84.

10 Ibid., 119.

11 Ibid., 152.

19

Amrita Sher-Gil

Identity and integrity as a mixed-race woman artist in colonial India

Nalini Bhushan

Amrita Sher-Gil was born in Budapest, Hungary, in 1913, the daughter of a Sikh painter-philosopher from Lahore, India and a singer mother, a Hungarian Jew. Her artistic sensibility was forged in the aristocratic and artistic-intellectual circles of Hungary and India in which her family moved; she herself trained at Paris' Ecole des Beux Arts. She enjoyed the freedom afforded by the bohemian sensibilities of her peers, absorbing the writings of Dostoevsky and the poet-philosopher Baudelaire, as well as mastering the then-current painterly techniques of Gauguin, Matisse and Cezanne. While in Paris, she won the top prize at the Grand Salon, and became one of its youngest Associates. After settling in Shimla – then the summer capital of the British government in India – Sher-Gil won the 1937 gold medal from the Bombay Art Society for her painting *Group of Three Girls* (1935).[1]

Sher-Gil's interest in visually capturing the interior spaces of women was ignited at a traditional Indian wedding, when she was just twelve years old. The marriage was between a child bride of thirteen and her husband-to-be, aged fifty. In the midst of the wedding festivities the young Amrita noticed the sense of weariness, in a girl practically her own age, a sorrowfully quiet acceptance and a palpable powerlessness. It evoked in Amrita a deep and lasting empathy for the predicament of women who – so unlike her own relatively privileged situation – lived in an environment without the psychological freedom, social support structure or the economic resources to choose their own life path. This empathetic sensibility revealed itself with great clarity in Sher-Gil's art, with her deeply intimate portrayals of women, many of whom were quite different from her in social and economic circumstance. The visceral connection with the young girl, though initially forged in the quite specific context of a traditional Indian experience, enabled her to paint via an imaginative extrapolation from her own quite particular situation to the emotional interiors of women in situations and contexts very different from her own, culturally, racially, geographically, politically and economically. Her portrayal of the many different women she encountered in Europe and India, including especially her self-portraits as a biracial woman, would end up being some of her most interesting, powerful and evocative works.

Amrita Sher-Gil died suddenly in 1941, at the age of twenty-eight. Her body of work – arising from her singular situation and life, at the intersection of the live social, political, economic and personal fissures of the first half of the twentieth century – had a profound impact on painting, and provides particularly illuminating material for reflecting on the competing forms of, and tensions within, integrity.

Integrity might be thought of as a kind of *self*-integration, from which one creates a stable character capable of consistent action and speech. The achievement of this form of integrity is more admirable the more fractured may be the different aspects of the particular self. With her multiply inflected identities – Sikh and Jewish, Indian and European, economically privileged and yet female in a presumptively patriarchal world – Sher-Gil's life provides ample scope to manifest (or not) this sort of integrity.

But integrity, particularly when we turn to artistic integrity, may also be thought of as a kind of authenticity. This may be authenticity in self-expression (being true to oneself or one's experience), or authenticity in capturing-creating the artistic object (rather than romanticizing it, being sentimental or forcing it into false categories). Concern with such artistic integrity was particularly high in a European culture actively engaging with non-European culture, thereby making itself vulnerable to accusations of *kitsch*. This notion of integrity as authenticity took on a particular form in the context of colonialization. In British India, artists and art critics argued that authentically Indian art involved the appropriate depiction of Indian tradition. This required that artists with integrity depict subject matter – the country, the history and, women in particular – in ways that reflected their status as emblems of Indian valour, religiosity, domesticity, spirituality or suitably idealized female beauty.

Sher-Gil's example has something to teach us in her successful sidestepping of this then-dominant notion of authenticity as a reactive integrity that resorted to idealized tradition with her choice to embrace, instead, a different political authenticity; and, in her union of this with integrity as self-integration. To illustrate this, we will first look at two self-portraits as exercises in self-integration: 'Self-Portrait as Tahitian' (1934) and 'Two Girls' (1939). Next, we will examine the ways in which her portraits of women are authentically Indian, without being idealized prototypes of tradition. We will then consider Sher-Gil's cosmopolitan modernism as a form of political integrity.

In *Self-Portrait as Tahitian* (Oil on Canvas, 1934; see Figure 19.1), Sher-Gil is nude from the waist up; she seems to represent herself as an exotic other (Tahitian), and appears framed in the gaze of a shadowy, voyeuristic figure. Sher-Gil's own identity in the painting is thus at first glance decidedly ambiguous, as is her relation to power and to the gaze of the voyeur and to us as viewers. It is also impossible to ignore the influence of the famous European artist Gauguin in both the style and content of this work.

Self-Portrait as Tahitian is arresting and illuminating in a number of ways. Consider, immediately, its title. What might it mean, in the context of self-integrity, for Sher-Gil to portray herself as something she is clearly *not*, namely, Tahitian? Here is a quick surface interpretation: the self-portrait reflects her desire to exoticize *herself*, much as Gauguin in his portrayals of his Tahitian subjects exoticized *them* to a Western public. Using this genre of interpretation, Sher-Gil might be taken to be portraying herself as a pure, simple, innocent and primitive other, much different from her

FIGURE 19.1 Amrita Sher-Gil, *Self-Portrait as Tahitian* (1934).

actual sophisticated modern multilayered self. On this analysis, we have a failure of self-integration, and worse, a self-representation that is in the end inauthentic in what it represents.

This is a possible reading. But notice immediately that it is complicated by the fact that Sher-Gil, in fact, *is* a racial hybrid (by her own lights and by those who saw her through the lens of race). In real life she is not as she appears. This bit of context helps to push back against the notion that *Self-Portrait as Tahitian* is an instance of an artist exoticizing herself through imaginative but ultimately failed self-portrait. Rather, a more powerful, and ultimately more convincing interpretation comes to mind: that in *Self-Portrait as Tahitian* Amrita is revealing the non-European facet of herself (the Tahitian being at the time the aesthetic non-European prototype *par excellence*). In this connection, it may be instructive to compare the aesthetics of Gauguin's own well-known depictions of Tahitians with Sher-Gil's version, in part by situating the two in their respective biographies (and geographies). Gauguin's own self-persona was that of a cosmopolitan who belonged nowhere, an aesthete in exile, without any roots; in addition, Gauguin was, in fact, an outsider to the people and culture he chose to portray. Sher-Gil, in contrast, is a multiply rooted cosmopolitan in her own self-representation (in letters and as revealed in her self-portraits); a hybrid of insider/outsider with regard to many peoples and cultures. Given these multiple situational differences, the evocation of the artist Sher-Gil painting a Tahitian woman (who happens in this case to be herself) has an aesthetic power that is simply not evoked by Gauguin's Tahitian paintings.

This brings us to an aspect of this work that has an additional and complicating link to contemporary feminist art projects.[2] Sher-Gil, we said, is revealing an aspect of herself in *Self-Portrait as Tahitian*, namely, that of being non-European. But, of course, she is not literally part-Tahitian. So the analysis is in need of complication. We might productively view Sher-Gil in this work as *performing* rather than revealing identity. For understood literally, as revealing her Tahitian aspect, the self-portrait is straightforwardly fictional. But if, instead, we understand it as a performance, we come to understand something different about what Sher-Gil is doing in this painting and about identity more generally – namely that, far from being constituted by something quite determinate, to be revealed or concealed, our identities are multidimensional and fluid, shifting now from one set of qualities deemed salient, and now to another. They are all real; but we can choose to perform one aspect rather than another depending upon the context.

On this reading, not only does *Self-Portrait as Tahitian* have an aesthetic power that Gauguin's own works lack; it has also an integrity understood as self-integration.

While *Two Girls* (Oil on Canvas, 1939, see Figure 19.2) is not obviously a self-portrait – in that it depicts two girls standing side by side – it becomes infinitely more interesting when viewed, as least from one perspective, *as* a self-portrait. Dalmia says of this

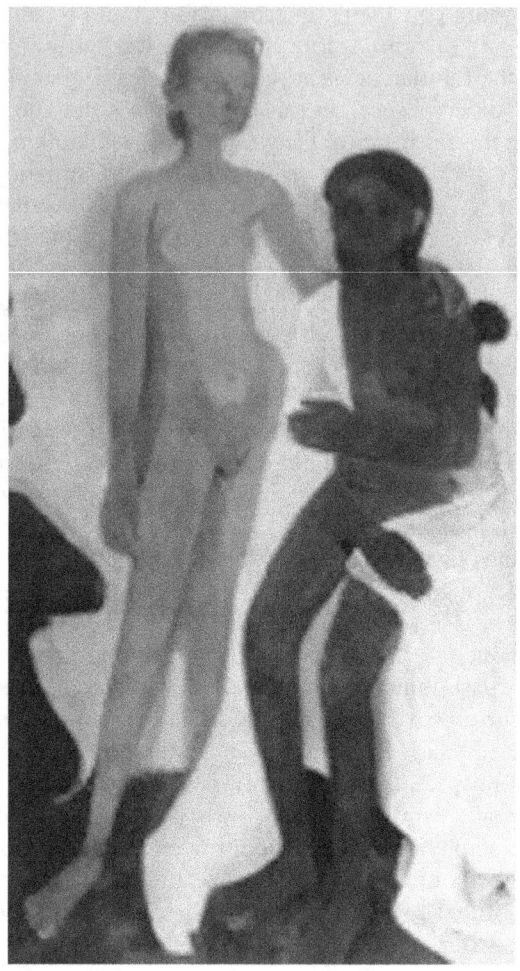

FIGURE 19.2 Amrita Sher-Gil, *Two Girls* (1939).

painting: 'The juxtaposition of the fair and the dark girl, clearly experiencing a mutual attraction, reflected at the bare minimum of two aspects of Amrita's own personality, the international and the Indian, of which she was constantly aware. They coexisted in this painting without erasure and without apology.'[3]

Dalmia's analysis of *Two Girls* is psychological, seeing in the two girls a reflection of two aspects to Sher-Gil's own personality. This analysis fits with the idea of identity as performance proposed with respect to *Self-Portrait as Tahitian*. In this painting, as well, we might see Sher-Gil as *performing* identity, identity in difference, but, crucially, 'without erasure and without apology'. Dalmia's phrase constitutes an intriguing piece of commentary. Why might there be an instinct for erasure, a need to apologize in the first place? Having two aspects to one's personality, understood psychologically, is not sufficient to warrant the comment. So there is more that remains to be unpacked. Now, as highlighted above, it was a sociological fact about India at that time that mixedness was a fraught racial position for anyone to inhabit. Dalmia's interpretation of *Two Girls* is on the right track in that it puts Sher-Gil in a position of active and creative interrogation with different parts of herself. It is reasonable to posit a difference in and attraction between two aspects of personality and one that the painting explores. But one needs to go two steps further. There is the fact of Sher-Gil's mixed racial heritage. In addition, Sher-Gil was at ease sexually with both men and women, and quite open about it, an attitude that was rarely publicly expressed by any individual in the Indian context, particularly in that period.

We might then see the hybrid 'performance' of self-identity in *Two Girls* as multifaceted: simultaneously psychological, social and sexual. While this interpretation is, in part, imaginative narrative reconstruction, it suggests specific ways in which identity is both complicated and freeing for an artist like Amrita Sher-Gil. Race, gender and sexuality function in her work as markers of otherness, but (and here's that paradox) markers with which she is intimately associated and which she intimately embodies.

These self-portraits, *Self-Portrait as Tahitian* and *Two Girls*, may therefore be viewed together as the successful integration of fragments of a self through a creative act of will and, in this respect, reflect Sher-Gil's integrity as an artist and as an individual.

It is instructive to think about Sher-Gil's paintings of women against the backdrop of Western art history, where women have historically been portrayed as objects to be seen, and where the women portrayed gaze out of the canvas in a way that reveals an acute awareness of the fact that they are objects of the (male) gaze.

Some of the most moving of Sher-Gil's paintings are her portraits of women.[4] Each of these painterly occasions presents to the outsider a world – a woman's world – that draws the viewer inextricably into *its* interior, and into *their* interiors. And yet, each of these works keeps the viewer at a distance, whether the occasion is a wedding preparation, one of rest or of simple companionship, whether the works are of Parisian or Indian women, whether they are erotic or mundane; and each of them conveys woman as stillness, of quiet impenetrable depth rather than transparent surface. One is left with the following paradoxical feeling: that at the same time that one is immediately drawn to the visual beauty and painterly quality of Sher-Gil's female subjects (the surface), one is struck by how little is revealed about them (the depth). There is a distinct absence of gaze in the demeanour of her subjects; if they look anywhere at all, even if it is out from the canvas, it seems to be inward, embodying a subjectivity that is Other, one that is not directly representable in the painting but which is evoked by it via the body. Strikingly, then, Sher-Gil's female subjects convey their feelings not by gaze but by the orientation of their bodies.

In this aspect, we find that while Sher-Gil's *style* appears to fit the Western genre of representational art, it is, in fact, much closer to the Indian aesthetic *rasa* sensibility in being primarily evocative. In the end, the works are not about the particular women they depict, but about arousing in the viewer one of the basic human emotions (or *bhava*) of great interest to Sher-Gil – that of sorrow or pathos. This, in turn, puts the viewer in a position to rise above mundane human emotion, to experience and taste the painting's *karuna rasa* or aesthetic beauty (understood as an importantly impersonal and, in this way, universal, aesthetic quality).[5]

Sher-Gil's focus was on rural India as the site of experiences and sensibilities of actual communities rather than the imagined nation of India-in-the-making. And while primitivism per se has come under intense scrutiny in a decolonial world, Mitter has argued convincingly that 'primitivism as a form of critical modernity offered rich and different possibilities to Indian artists'.[6] For instance, Mitter views 'ruralism' as one form of creative response in the Indian context to modernity. Sher-Gil's work, then, is not simply or easily characterizable as a derivative primitivism modelled after a Western artist.

Even when the viewer can tell that some of Sher-Gil's images are, indeed, romanticized, even if not idealized, this knowledge does not get in the way of the viewer connecting with what she takes to be a vital, visceral reality – a world that is, in fact, inhabited by women. Here Sher-Gil's status as alternately insider and outsider is an advantage: she is sufficiently 'outside' to have that critical distance and ability to see what insiders do not (for instance, her observation at twelve of the plight of the child bride, mentioned at the outset) but sufficiently 'inside' for the experiences to actually, not merely imaginatively, resonate in her both psychologically and aesthetically. In this sense, Sher-Gil's focus on women as the subjects of her paintings is an aspect of her integrity in the artistic domain.

Freedom was a theme that operated self-consciously but also as a powerful undercurrent in colonial India on a number of fronts: politically, socially, psychologically and aesthetically. Often these were interrelated, as for instance, when Mahatma Gandhi (*Hind Swaraj*, 1910) quite explicitly laid out the route to political freedom as via self-mastery or psychological freedom. The notion of Nation was palpable for many of the leading Indian artists of the time as well; indeed, one's artistic identity was inevitably bound up with one's national identity. The truly free art, then, was one that expressed or embodied the spirit of a people hitherto devalued, with 'the authentically Indian' taken as a sensibility sharply distinct from the Western colonial sensibility.

For artists in India during this period the context of nation building served to throw up an almost impossible challenge: to be creative, a mark of the greatest of artists, which involves the artistic freedom to take and use whatever techniques one willed; and, simultaneously, to be authentic (which, in this case meant to be authentically *Indian*). Ravi Varma of the Bombay Art School and Abanindranath Tagore of the Calcutta Art School are two notable artists who seemingly rose to the challenge, navigating the difficult aesthetic chestnut of the authentic versus the creative in very different ways.[7] Both artists worked with techniques from outside of India, in the process transforming the aesthetic style and presentation of traditionally Indian subject matter. Varma, for instance, turned to European masters for aesthetic inspiration and to a popular Indian audience for aesthetic appreciation; in so doing he secured his position as India's pre-eminent artist. His somewhat younger contemporary, Tagore, in contrast, explicitly turned to Asia for aesthetic inspiration and against the European colonizer, appropriating his techniques from Japanese masters, and turned to the Indian cultural elite for aesthetic appreciation. The heady mix of aesthetic and political ferment in the drive to independence perhaps rendered it inevitable that Varma eventually came to be regarded as merely a cheap imitator of European art while Tagore's star reached its zenith when he was anointed the national artist of India as his *Bharat Mata* came to symbolize the modern image of Mother India.

The idea of Nation was inseparable from the artistic identity of these two most successful of Indian artists during the colonial period. What is striking about Sher-Gil is the absence of this commitment to Nation. While the land that is India – its geography, its peoples, their poverty, their suffering – permeates her work, her attitude to India *qua Nation* was scathing and dismissive. This criticism of Nation was shared by notable others. Nobel Laureate Rabindranath Tagore[8] (uncle of the artist Abanindranath Tagore), for instance, argued passionately against the view taken by the Indian nationalists of his day, such as Gandhi, accusing them of constructing an abstract and imagined India out of touch with reality, and of projecting onto a real India a homogeneity (in the name of unity, captured in the national slogan of the day, *Bande Mataram,* or, Hail to the Motherland) that belied the palpable reality of its religious, economic, social and artistic diversity.[9]

Sher-Gil expressed her own dissatisfaction with the kind of nationalism that was alive and well in the visual arts in colonial India. For instance, she argued that the Bengal School, as represented by Abanindranath Tagore, although it claimed to be the hub of the renaissance in Indian painting was, in fact, the opposite, a route to aesthetic stagnation, as it clung too tightly and reverently to a venerated past. She was similarly critical of the academic artists of the Bombay School for clinging, again, too tightly and too reverently, to Western art. She herself saw a way out of that seemingly impossible challenge for the contemporary Indian artist in colonial India, the dilemma of the authentic versus the creative. It was '... to see the art of India ... produce something vital *connected with the soil*, yet essentially Indian'.[10] Sher-Gil wanted artists in India to pierce through the veil of an imagined abstract India to an actual land with its teeming millions, its actual art and life experiences and to capture those Indian lives and sensibilities. She looked to the possibility of an artistic authenticity that was disconnected from an authenticity tied to nation building and to national pride.

In this aspiration and in her work as an artist she exhibited a cosmopolitan consciousness that was qualitatively different from the cosmopolitanism of both artists A. Tagore and Varma. In particular, she saw no conflict between thinking of herself as an Indian artist in the public sphere and her self-professed radical aesthetic individualism. As she put it, 'I am an individualist, evolving a new technique, which, though not necessarily Indian in the traditional sense of the word, will yet be fundamentally Indian in spirit. With the eternal significance of form and colour I interpret India.'[11] Sher-Gil was way ahead of her time in both articulating and embodying in her work a form of cosmopolitanism that involved individual love for country without nationalism, crossing with aesthetic ease the boundaries between the local and the global, the European and the Indian, the colonizer and the colonized, between the privileged and the underprivileged, between male and female, and between female and female. In a climate that valued above all else a political and moral nationalism as an integral, and primary, aspect of an artistic identity, Sher-Gil distanced herself from that notion of integrity in a way that other artists of her time could not, expressing, instead, a distinctive political integrity as a cosmopolitan Indian.

Recommended reading

Readers looking for more essays on Amrita Sher-Gil should consult Yashodhara Dalmia's excellent edited anthology, *Amrita Sher-Gil: Art and Life* (Oxford, India: Oxford University Press, 2014). This anthology is an invaluable collection of essays that includes one by Sher-Gil, 'Evolution of My Art' (cited in the essay above), as well as essays by prominent art critics from the past and the present. Geeta Kapur's collection of essays, *When Was Modernism* (India: Tulika Books, 2000) has a chapter 'Body as Gesture: Women Artists at Work' that includes a discussion of Amrita Sher-Gil. Additionally, Sonal Khullar has an important chapter on Sher-Gil's work, 'An Art of the Soil', in her monograph *Worldly Affiliations: Artistic Practice, National Identity, and Modernism in India, 1930-1990* (Oakland: University of California Press, 2015).

Notes

1 Sher-Gil had already won awards outside of India winning the top prize at the Grand Salon while she was an art student in Paris, and becoming one of its youngest Associates.

2 The North American artist Cindy Sherman's self-portraits come to mind in this connection. Sherman herself considers photographs to be a mask, but the viewer is struck more by the performative and freeing aspects of her work rather than the elusive dimension of her self-portrayals.

3 Yashodhara Dalmia, *Amrita Sher-Gil: A Life* (New Delhi: Penguin Books, 2006), 199.

4 Take, for instance, *Sleep* (1932); *The Professional Model* (1933); *Group of Three Girls* (1935); *Bride's Toilet* (1937); *Child Wife* (1939); and *Woman on Charpoy* (1940). All are accessible online. The first two were painted in France, the last four in India. Her women in India are always clothed; Sher-Gil's own self-portraits, however, are of her both clothed and nude.

5 I think it is no accident that Sher-Gil was drawn, as were many other Indian painters, to Western aesthetic formalism. It fits much more with the Indian aesthetic *Rasa* theory than either representationalism or emotivism in its emphasis on the impersonal and the disinterested quality of the experience of *rasa*.

6 Partha Mitter, *The Triumph of Modernism: India's Artists and the Avante-Garde 1922-47* (London: Reaktion Books Ltd., 2007), 33.

7 See my 'The Development of a Cosmopolitan Aesthetic in Colonial India', in Monique Roelefs (ed.), *Contemporary Aesthetics*, Special issue: *Race and Aesthetics* (2010); reprinted as 'An Indian in Paris: Cosmopolitan Aesthetics in Colonial India', and in Nalini Bhushan and Jay L. Garfield (eds), *Indian Philosophy in English: From Renaissance to Independence* (Oxford: Oxford University Press, 2011).

8 See his 'Nationalism in India' (1917). Reprinted in Bhushan and Garfield, *Indian Philosophy in English*.

9 See his 'Creative Unity' (1922). Reprinted in *The Collected Works of Rabindranath Tagore*, ed. Sisir Kumar Das.

10 Vivan Sundaram, *Amrita Sher-Gil* (Bombay, n.d.), 142, emphasis added.

11 Amrita Sher-Gil, 'Evolution of My Art', *The Usha*, Amrita Sher-Gil special issue, 111 (2) (1942a): 101; Amrita Sher-Gil, 'Indian Art Today', *The Usha*, Amrita Sher-Gil special issue, 111 (2), Lahore.

20

Friedrich Christoph Dahlmann and Georg Waitz

Two models of scholarly integrity

Herman Paul

Although 'scholarly integrity' is a phrase of twentieth-century origin, reflection on what constitutes good scholarly conduct is as old as scholarly inquiry itself. Some of the most famous scientific controversies – think of Thomas Hobbes' criticism of Robert Boyle's 'air-pump' experiments in the 1660s – were, among other things, debates over standards of proof and methods of research. Without much anachronism, it can be argued that they pertained to what would nowadays be called scholarly integrity (was it wrong to engage in probabilistic reasoning, as Boyle did, or did Hobbes make himself guilty of dogmatism?). Interestingly, as Steven Shapin and Simon Schaffer have argued, the debate ran high because participants did not agree on what counted as proper scholarly conduct. This was partly because, in seventeenth-century England, such conduct was imbued with social and political meaning: deviation from 'philosophy' of the sort represented by Hobbes was, to some extent, a political act.

But integrity could also be contested because scholars disagreed on the relative importance of virtues and skills that they believed to mark a good physicist, biologist or philologist. If scholarly integrity denotes a 'proper order' in the values and virtues guiding scholarly research, as Damian Cox and others have argued,[1] then the history of scholarship offers quite a few examples of scholars quarrelling about integrity. This is to say that scholarly integrity is not a black and white issue, but an area full of grey zones that require careful weighing and balancing of values and virtues. How important is intellectual courage in relation to accuracy, or trustworthiness compared to creativity?

In the nineteenth century, historical studies was generally seen as a very important field of inquiry. Historical study mattered because it provided orientation, most notably in matters of national identity. Although not everyone agreed with E. A. Freeman's famous dictum, 'history is past politics, and politics present history', the motto nicely captures to what extent history was perceived as laying bare the roots of the present and as uncovering patterns of development that politicians, among others, could ignore only at their peril. At the same time, history as practised in especially the German lands had an aura of scientific rigour. It was here that students were trained in archival research and so-called auxiliary sciences (paleography, diplomatics) needed for deciphering and understanding medieval charters. Also, it was German history professors who took a lead in lecturing and writing about historical methodology. Yet the question remained: How did archival research, conducted in accordance with the newest methodological findings, relate to history's task of providing orientation in matters of national identity?

The most illustrious representative of nineteenth-century German historical studies, Leopold von Ranke, did not see much tension between the two. In his harmonious world view, relying on authentic historical documents was a way of allowing the past itself to speak. When Ranke famously stated that 'I wanted, as it were, to extinguish myself, and to let the things speak for themselves, to let the powerful forces appear on their own', the powerful forces that he intended to make visible were national identities as they emerged and matured in the course of history.[2] For Ranke, archival research was therefore simultaneously a mark of *Wissenschaftlichkeit* (scholarly rigour) and an expression of belief in the historical power of national identities.

As this approach rested on contentious metaphysical assumptions (how ontologically real are national identities?) and made rather heavy demands on historians (many archives were not yet well ordered or publicly accessible), it comes as no surprise that Ranke's approach met with resistance. At the University of Berlin (now the Humboldt University), for instance, historian Heinrich Leo chastised Ranke for overrating the value of archival research. Nonetheless, the Rankean paradigm eventually overcame most opposition: its combination of scientific rigour and nationalist commitment turned out to be attractive at a time when 'scholarship' and the 'nation' were generally treated with reverence.

Scholarship and the nation were not fixed entities, though. In nineteenth-century Europe, the amount of archival material available for scholarly inquiry exploded when growing numbers of archives opened their doors to the public and archival 'expeditions' revealed masses of hitherto unknown material. At the same time, German national identity became a political reality when the long-held dream of German unification was realized with the establishment of the German Empire in 1871. Both developments challenged the Rankean synthesis of nationalism and *Wissenschaftlichkeit*. Was it a matter of public duty for state-paid academics to support the Empire, for instance by legitimizing it as a historical inevitability? Or did scholarly integrity require a certain amount of detachment from the politicized public sphere in early imperial Germany?

These were not the only questions dividing German historians in the closing decades of the nineteenth century. In the 1870s, Imperial Chancellor Otto von Bismarck had launched an anti-Catholic campaign known as the *Kulturkampf*, the long-term effects of which made it particularly difficult for Catholic historians to participate on equal footing with Protestant colleagues. Jewish historians suffered even more from exclusion: conversion was virtually a precondition for entrance into the profession. Women, atheists and socialists did not fit the template of a German university professor either. All this brought a degree of contestation to issues of scholarly identity. It was not only ideals of professionalism that elicited controversy; their corresponding mechanisms of inclusion and exclusion evoked resistance too.

Late-nineteenth-century German historical scholarship was therefore a house divided in itself. From a distance, it could seem as if German historians were united in their commitment to archival research, methodological rigour and innovative pedagogical practices such as the history seminar (*historische Übungen*). Yet, at closer inspection, social, political and religious fault lines turned out to generate irresolvable tensions among historians.

That these tensions easily translated themselves to disagreement on what integrity entailed came to the fore in 1886. Within twenty-four hours of each other, Ranke and one of his most influential students, Georg Waitz, breathed their last breaths. Following social custom, the deceased were honoured with obituaries in newspapers and scholarly journals. The image of Waitz presented on this occasion, especially by his students, was that of an impeccable scholar who personally embodied the idea of integrity. Alfred Stern, for instance, praised Waitz for his 'extraordinary critical sense', 'iron diligence' and 'strict conscientiousness'.[3] Others highlighted Waitz's 'industry', 'meticulousness' and 'impartiality'. The image of Waitz emerging from these obituaries is that of a historian who tried at all cost to avoid unproven hypotheses, to abstain from literary ambitions and to be indifferent to recognition beyond academic circles. As Waitz's French pupil Gabriel Monod summarized it: Waitz's devotion to the cause of historical scholarship had 'made him worry less about his reputation than about the progress of science, the absence of all partisanship, of all fanaticism, of all small-minded vanity'.[4]

The first remarkable thing about this image is the prominent role of virtue language. Waitz was not remembered because of scholarly breakthroughs, but because of character traits that he had embodied and tried to cultivate in his students. What seemed to matter was, in other words, not Waitz's published work, but his 'scholarly self'. Typical of this self was, in the second place, its asceticism. The virtues attributed to Waitz were ascetic in the sense that they contributed to self-restraint and self-control for the sake of scholarly advancement. The Waitz-style historian was not a brilliant stylist or flamboyant political commentator, but someone who tried to 'extinguish' himself, as Ranke had put it. This reference to Ranke, finally, is fitting because the character traits ascribed to Waitz were virtues that Waitz himself had regarded as typical of the Rankean tradition. If Waitz was presented as an embodiment of 'criticism', 'precision' and 'penetration', these were virtues that Waitz had claimed to have inherited from Ranke.

Others, however, discriminated between Ranke and Waitz, arguing that Waitz lacked Ranke's breadth of vision. Heinrich von

Sybel, most notably, claimed that Ranke had been a scholar, artist and political commentator at once, whereas Waitz had excelled only in the first of these capacities. This implied that the kind of historian represented by Waitz was one-sided in comparison to Ranke. By wilfully sacrificing artistic aspiration and political commitment, the ascetic historian became a specialist who pursued 'scholarship' at the expense of the 'nation', thereby destroying Ranke's synthesis and exploiting his legacy in a rather reductionist manner.[5] Unsurprisingly, this attack did not go unanswered. Loyal students rushed to Waitz's defence, arguing that it was one thing to please the general public with well-written history books, but quite another to push the boundaries of knowledge and set new standards for future generations of scholars. In their view, Waitz's asceticism was not a limitation, but a virtue *par excellence*.

Clearly, there was more at stake here than Waitz's personal merits. Partly, the controversy was a struggle for power in a field with limited career opportunities. More importantly, however, the dispute fought out in Waitz's obituaries was a debate about the marks of a good historian, focused on the importance of aesthetic talent and political commitment in comparison to research skill. The clash between Sybel and Waitz's students revolved around the question of the causes historians should serve: scholarship only or scholarship for the benefit of German culture and politics?

If Waitz embodied an *ascetic* type of integrity, the *synthetic* type advocated by Sybel was often associated with Waitz's former colleague Friedrich Christoph Dahlmann. Despite an age difference of twenty-eight years, Dahlmann and Waitz had much in common. Both had been known for their sense of duty, lack of sentimentality and other supposedly North German character traits. Both had taught at Kiel and Göttingen and been members of the Frankfurt Parliament of 1848–49. Their names even appeared together on the *Quellenkunde der Deutschen Geschichte*, a huge bibliographical survey better known as 'Dahlmann–Waitz', after its first two editors. Nonetheless, in the closing decades of the nineteenth century, Dahlmann came to be seen as embodying a type of integrity quite different from Waitz's.

This was not how things had looked like half a century before. In 1837, Dahlmann had become famous almost overnight as the leader of the so-called Göttingen Seven: a small group of professors who had risked their chairs by criticizing the Hanoverian king

Ernest Augustus for dissolving the parliament and suspending the constitution. Although this act of civil courage had been interpreted differently along the political spectrum, many admirers of Dahlmann and his colleagues emphasized their unswerving commitment to the law of their country, whatever the costs in terms of career, reputation and personal freedom (Dahlmann had been dismissed from his chair and exiled from the Kingdom of Hanover). If this was integrity, it resembled the ascetic type in so far as it was characterized by a focus on a single good that was worth sacrificing others.

Increasingly, however, Dahlmann came to be remembered not only for his civic virtues, but also as a model of scholarly integrity. Characteristic of this model was a refusal to accept what one might call a compartmentalization of the self, caused by a differentiation of society. Whereas Waitz's name symbolized a sharp distinction between the 'scholarly self' and the 'political self', not to mention the 'religious self' and the 'familial self', Dahlmann came to be regarded as an uncompromised personality whose life and work had been 'one', in the sense that his professional virtues and vices could not be separated from his private ones.[6]

The model of integrity associated with Dahlmann resembled Waitz's in so far as it weighed and balanced different demands made upon historians. Both searched for a 'proper order' among values and virtues. The two were opposed, however, in their basic orientation. While the ascetic model kept non-scholarly commitments at bay, Dahlmann's model aimed to synthesize the demands of research, education, politics and public service. This synthetic model, as we might call it, did not downplay the importance of such virtues as criticism, precision and penetration. All admirers cited Dahlmann's three-volume history of Denmark as proof of how thoroughly its author had appropriated these modern epistemic virtues. The point, however, was that these were not the only virtues that mattered, given that a historical researcher usually also was a teacher, citizen and public intellectual.

Whereas Waitz's ascetic model was embraced especially by historians engaged in source editing, Dahlmann's synthetic model found most resonance among the overlapping categories of loyal students such as Hermann Baumgarten and politically engaged historians such as Heinrich von Treitschke and Conrad Varrentrapp. The latter in particular appropriated Dahlmann as a forerunner of the so-called Prussian School of History, which gradually developed into a major alternative to the Waitz school. Although these Prussian historians did not necessarily share all of Dahlmann's political views, they appreciated his characteristic 'position between scholarship and the state', as Treitschke called it.[7] Accordingly, they granted Dahlmann and his legacy just as important a place in their genealogies of the discipline as Waitz's students did with Ranke.

The extent to which Dahlmann's model came to serve as an alternative to Waitz's is apparent from the fact that it was appropriated even outside the two groups just mentioned – Dahlmann's former students and the Prussian School of History. Scholars as diverse as Johannes Janssen, a staunch Catholic apologist, and Ludwig Weiland, a former student of Waitz with ambitions reaching beyond source criticism, wrote sympathetically about the man whose name increasingly came to serve as a symbol of protest against the hegemony of Waitz-style professionalism. Inevitably, this juxtaposition of Waitz and Dahlmann contributed to a certain schematization that emphasized the differences between the men more than their similarities. To some extent, indeed, the proper names of Waitz and Dahlmann became generic names or labels for distinct scholarly personae. They came to serve as coordinates on imaginary maps of the historical discipline, corresponding to distinct conceptions of scholarly integrity.

This, then, implies that late-nineteenth-century German historians worked with more than one view of integrity. Although few of them doubted the need for accuracy and precision, the issue that divided them was how important these virtues were in relation to other, overlapping or competing virtues. What was contested, in other words, was not the virtues as such, but their relative weight. If scholarly integrity consists of a 'proper order' among virtues, different schools of historians subscribed to different conceptions of integrity.

This, finally, helps explain why historians in late-nineteenth-century Germany lent a human face to issues of integrity by personifying them. Models of integrity were associated with individuals, not because they were invented by Waitz or Dahlmann, but because these historians were seen as embodying a 'proper order' of virtues. This is not to say that concerns about integrity were the only reason for historians to commemorate their predecessors. Honouring outstanding scholars was part of the moral economy of nineteenth-century scholarship. Reciprocal loyalty between teachers and students, more specifically, was one of the key assumptions underlying academic teaching and mentoring practices. However, as suggested by the case of Dahlmann in particular, personified models of integrity were not only invoked by historians with social obligations to the deceased. Waitz and Dahlmann served as *exempla* also because they showed in concrete detail how virtues could be lived out.

Against this background, it is hardly surprising that lithographs or photographs of Waitz and Dahlmann were eagerly shared among historians, as were anecdotes of the sort told by a Belgian visitor to Waitz's seminar in Göttingen: 'Once, when one of the class made a new observation, M. Waitz cried out: "I have learned something myself on a subject I thought I had exhausted!" and drawing his little silver pencil from his pocket, he noted the matter upon the margin of his text'.[8] Such anecdotes served as stories of commitment, as emblems of virtue or as icons of integrity, just as pictures conveyed what a scholar committed to ascetic or synthetic integrity looked like in practice. A history of scholarly integrity therefore amounts to more than a history of abstract virtues and vices. It has to pay attention to 'portraits of integrity', in both a literal and a figurative sense.[9]

Recommended reading

Steven Shapin and Simon Schaffer's study, mentioned in the opening paragraph, is entitled *Leviathan and the Air-Pump: Hobbes, Boyle, and the Experimental Life* (Princeton: Princeton University Press, 1985). A good introduction to Waitz's life and work is provided by Robert L. Benson and Loren J. Weber, 'Georg Waitz (1813–1886)', in *Medieval Scholarship: Biographical Studies on the Formation of a Discipline*, ed. Helen Damico and Joseph B. Zavadil, vol. 1 (New York: Garland, 1995), 63–75. The best available biography of Dahlmann is Wilhelm Bleek, *Friedrich Christoph Dahlmann: Eine Biographie* (Munich: C. H. Beck, 2010). Nineteenth-century debates on the proper order of virtues and the *personae* that embodied them are discussed in Herman Paul, 'The Virtues and Vices of Albert Naudé: Toward a History of Scholarly Personae', *History of Humanities* 1 (2) (2016): 327–38; and 'The Virtues of a Good Historian in Early Imperial Germany: Georg Waitz's Contested Example', *Modern Intellectual History* 15 (3) (2018): 681–709.

Notes

1. Damian Cox, Marguerite la Caze and Michael P. Levine, *Integrity and the Fragile Self* (Aldershot: Ashgate, 2003), 8.
2. Leopold Ranke, *Englische Geschichte vornehmlich im sechszehnten und siebzehnten Jahrhundert*, vol. 2 (Berlin: Duncker & Humblot, 1860), 3.
3. Alfred Stern, 'Georg Waitz', *Die Nation* 3 (1886): 538–40, 538.
4. G. Monod, 'Georges Waitz', *Revue Historique* 31 (1886): 382–90, 384.
5. Heinrich v[on] Sybel, 'Georg Waitz', *Historische Zeitschrift* 56 (1886): 482–7.
6. Conrad Varrentrapp, 'Zur Erinnerung an Friedrich Christoph Dahlmann', *Preussische Jahrbücher* 5 (1885): 485–510, 501.
7. Heinrich von Treitschke, 'F.C. Dahlmann', in *Historische und politische Aufsätze vornehmlich zur neuesten deutschen Geschichte*, 2nd ed. (Leipzig: S. Hirzel, 1865), 359–445, 408.
8. Paul Fredericq, *The Study of History in Germany and France*, trans. Henrietta Leonard (Baltimore, MD: Johns Hopkins University, 1890), 17.
9. Research for this article was funded by the Netherlands Organization for Scientific Research (NWO).

21

Hannah Arendt

Integrity, truth and the political realm

Alexander Beaumont

Margarethe von Trotta's 2012 biopic *Hannah Arendt* ends with an image of a woman reclining on a chaise-lounge, alone, in semi-darkness, a cigarette poised languidly between two fingers.[1] It is a study in stasis, which contrasts sharply with the characterization of the titular character during the rest of the film. For two hours, the viewer has watched Arendt (played by Barbara Sukowa) in ceaseless motion, bustling between her New York City apartment, lecture theatres at the New School for Social Research and seminar rooms full of wide-eyed students who hang on her every word. She travels from the United States of America to Israel numerous times over the course of the film and is just as energetic there; even at rest in the New England countryside, she is represented as possessing an almost implausible vitality. Historical passages in Marburg, during Arendt's undergraduate years, and a later return to Germany to visit her onetime tutor and lover Martin Heidegger construct a portrait of a singularly driven figure, a thinker for whom action is, nonetheless, a cardinal virtue. Her stillness at the end of the film is thus striking. It is something of a truism that great things do not get done when supine; that great people do not become great by lying on their backs. Why, then, should a film that evidently considers its protagonist to be a considerable figure show her recumbent at its conclusion? Taken in isolation, Sukowa's repose in this final moment recalls famous images of inaction such as that in F. Scott Fitzgerald's *The Great Gatsby*, when Nick Carraway enters a glorious jazz-era mansion on Long Island and sees Daisy Buchanan and Jordan Baker completely motionless, as if arranged for the delectation of an invisible camera.[2] In Fitzgerald's novel, inertia signifies superficiality: the easy satisfaction of an unexamined life. In *Hannah Arendt*, however, it is clearly intended to communicate the opposite: the eponymous character's stillness masks a furious act of ratiocination.

Sukowa's representation of Arendt at the end of the film closely resembles the 'almost breathless abstention from external physical movement and activity' represented by the life of solitary contemplation, or what Arendt termed the *vita contemplativa*.[3] Yet if this characterization allows the film to bestow on its subject the greatness it believes her to embody as a thinker, it is still at odds with its insistent representation of her as a doer – or rather, a thinker who acts. In fact, were it not for one final detail, von Trotta's film could easily be accused of concluding pessimistically, since in its final moment it appears to represent Arendt retreating from the life of activity – or *vita activa* – on whose recovery within the Western philosophical tradition she expended so much effort. That detail is easy to miss, since it appears only as the backdrop to the film's closing credits: a night-time shot of the Manhattan skyline, its glittering windows struggling to punctuate a shroud of darkness. The implication of this passage between the solitary, thinking individual and the city in and for which she thinks is sophisticated, yet stark: it is for the sake of a world that contains multitudes, and which seems perpetually under threat, that the intellectual work of any single mind must take place.

The concluding sequence of *Hannah Arendt* thus provides a neat if slightly enigmatic encapsulation of a thinker for whom evil arises as a consequence of a failure to 'think what we are doing' (*Human*, 5), but who simultaneously argued that to do nothing *but* think – that is, to overlook the human capacity to *act* – was to allow the most profound forms of evil of which human beings are capable to be unleashed. Arguably Arendt's greatest insight was that thinking is for naught if it does not take place for the sake of the world we share in common, and for the action that is necessary in order to maintain that common world. In this respect, she presents herself as an unusual candidate for a portrait of integrity. The intellectual integrity of the thinking individual is a common preoccupation among philosophers. What is less common is a philosophical preoccupation with the integrity of the world itself, as a site where 'the capacity of beginning something anew, that is, of acting' (*Human*, 9) is at least as important as the decidedly unworldly process of solitary contemplation. It is in the tension between these two accounts of integrity that Arendt's contribution to any discussion of the term can best be understood.

Insofar as Arendt's commitment to intellectual integrity is concerned, she is unimpeachable. She is, after all, responsible for the *aperçu*: 'There are no dangerous thoughts; thinking itself is dangerous'.[4] Nonetheless, this commitment caused her considerable chagrin during her life, especially during the so-called Eichmann controversy, which provides the focus of von Trotta's biopic and continues to colour Arendt's reputation. In 1961 she travelled to Jerusalem to report on the trial of the Nazi SS Obersturmbannführer Adolf Eichmann for *The New Yorker*. During World War II, Eichmann had overseen the forcible deportation of Jews from around Europe to ghettoes and, ultimately, extermination camps. After the war he fled to Argentina, where he was captured by Israeli Mossad agents, covertly transported to Jerusalem and charged with fifteen crimes, including crimes against humanity. He was found guilty by the Israeli court and hanged in the early hours of 1 June 1962. Arendt had numerous misgivings about the process by which Eichmann was brought to justice, ranging from his non-judicial extradition through to the legal arguments by which his execution was justified. However, while intensely aware of the challenges of trying him, she was emphatic in her condemnation of the man himself. In *Eichmann in Jerusalem* (1963), the book based on her *New Yorker* report, she identifies Eichmann as a 'new type of criminal, who is in actual fact *hostis generis humani*' – that is, an enemy of humankind – but who also 'commits his crimes under circumstances that make it well-nigh impossible for him to know or to feel that he is doing wrong'.[5] The nature of Eichmann's involvement with the Final Solution and the scale of the murder itself clearly rendered him monstrous, but his monstrosity struck Arendt as being of a decidedly mundane sort. He was a 'terribly and terrifyingly normal man' (*Eichmann* 274) who followed orders exactly as the law governing him demanded, even if that law called for the mass extermination of other human beings. Therein lay not just his own crime, but also the essence of Arendt's most (in)famous concept: the banality of evil.

As the politician, diplomat and journalist Günter Gaus noted in a 1964 television interview: '[F]or a portrait of Hannah Arendt, so to speak, a number of questions come out of this book'.[6] One of these, surely, is the question of integrity. The publication of *Eichmann in Jerusalem* resulted in enormous, sustained and lasting animosity towards Arendt. The reasons for this are complex, but they can be divided into two broad categories, the first having to do with the moral implications of her concept of the banality of evil, and the second with what was perceived as her allegation that parts of the European Jewish population were complicit with the murderous regime responsible for the Shoah. The latter in particular – a fundamental misreading of the book, according to Arendt – resulted in personal turmoil. She lost the respect of numerous intellectual peers, as well as many friendships that had been maintained for a good part of her adult life.

Yet, throughout her travails, Arendt remained deeply committed to her understanding of what Eichmann's trial said about the nature of evil in the twentieth century. She also refused to compromise on her right to think and speak for herself, despite attempts to describe her as a traitor to her own people. As she wrote in response to a critical letter from her friend, the philosopher and theologian Gershom Scholem:

> What confuses you is that my argument and my approach are different from what you are used to; in other words, the trouble is that I am independent. By this I mean, on the one hand, that I do not belong to any organization and always speak only for myself, and on the other hand, that I have great confidence in [the philosopher Gotthold] Lessing's *selbstdenken* for which, I think, no ideology, no public opinion, and no 'convictions' can ever be a substitute.[7]

This response by Arendt to her critics furnishes us with a familiar but critically important account of integrity, which she drew from her philosophical training but practised earnestly in her own life: the virtue of thinking for oneself. As she remarked to Gaus: 'What is important to me is to understand', adding, 'I am not particularly agreeable, nor am I very polite; I say what I think' (Remains 3, 14). With these pronouncements, Arendt can easily be located within a long tradition of defenders of academic freedom, who treat the autonomy of the thinking individual as the sine qua non of intellectual integrity. Yet, a commitment to discerning the truth of the matter would seem to have more in common with the *vita contemplativa*, about which she was so wary, than the *vita activa*, whose refurbishment she perceived as forming such a vital part of the fight against evil in the twentieth century. If it is for the sake of the world that thought takes place, does it not behove us to seek worldly influence for our ideas? And is merely to understand the world, as if one were not a part of it but rather examining it like a specimen in a laboratory, not the most detached and unworldly kind of thinking?

This, however, is only one half of the story Arendt has to tell us. The other half lies in an entirely different understanding of integrity, under which it is a characteristic not of the individual but, rather, of the world human beings share in common, and more specifically the world of democratic politics. Arendt sets out this version of integrity most clearly in *The Human Condition* (1958); however, it is perhaps more instructive to look for it in an essay entitled 'Truth and Politics' (1967), where she writes:

> [W]hat I meant to show here is that [the] whole sphere [of political action], its greatness notwithstanding, is limited – that it does not encompass the whole of man's and the world's existence. It is limited by those things which men cannot change at will. And it is only by respecting its own borders that this realm, where we are free to act and to change, can remain intact, preserving its integrity and keeping its promises.[8]

The imperative to maintain the integrity of the political realm lies at the heart of a very significant part of Arendt's thinking. Yet, it seems quite antithetical to the concept of intellectual integrity that we have been discussing so far, which appears to necessitate a commitment to divining – and professing – an account of the truth at all costs. Indeed, one reading of 'Truth and Politics' would conclude that intellectual integrity and the integrity of the political realm are inimical to one another. On the one hand, Arendt asserts that the autonomy of the thinking individual is 'the root of [...] objectivity' and suggests that those who commit themselves to objectivity simultaneously commit themselves to 'intellectual integrity at any price' (Truth 258). Yet, on the other hand, she argues that '[t]ruthfulness has never been counted among the political virtues, because it has little indeed to contribute to that change of the world and of circumstances which is among the most legitimate political activities' (246). Thus, while a commitment to understanding the truth of the matter might represent the pinnacle of intellectual integrity, in the political realm it is of strictly limited value because it bears no capacity for introducing newness and spontaneity into the world. It is, in short, the antithesis of action.

More pointedly, Arendt questions the extent to which truth claims should have a role to play in democratic decision-making, because, while truth may be discerned through a process of *selbstdenken* that demonstrates genuine intellectual integrity, it 'carries within itself an element of coercion', and coercion is injurious to the integrity of the political world (Truth 242). This suggestion raises serious problems for anybody who seeks to influence the political sphere using truth claims – for instance, the medical ethics professor developing a case for state-mandated vaccines, or the meteorologist researching climate change or the reporter investigating new forms of state surveillance. And this is because introducing truth claims into political discourse involves an act of boundary-crossing that compromises the truth-value of one's findings and so inevitably compromises one's intellectual integrity. As Arendt puts it: '[W]hen he enters the political realm and identifies himself with some partial interest and power formation, [the truth-teller] compromises on the only quality that could have made his truth appear plausible, namely, his personal truthfulness, guaranteed by impartiality, integrity, independence' (246).

How do we square this circle? One answer lies in what is arguably the most important term in the Arendtian lexicon: plurality. In *The Human Condition*, Arendt sets out at length the significance of plurality for the common world by pointing out that 'men, not Man, live on the earth and inhabit the world' and arguing that '[w]hile all aspects of the human condition are somehow related to politics, this plurality is specifically *the* condition [...] of all political life' (*Human* 7). Yet it is important that, elsewhere in her writing, she relates the concept of plurality to the individual mind as well. Indeed, it is the plurality of the mind – the 'two-in-one' as she terms it in her final, unfinished and posthumously published book, *The Life of the Mind* (1978) – that makes not just thought but also integrity possible. For Arendt, the distinction between the mind and the world beyond the mind – that is, the place where I am alone with myself and the place where I live in a community with other people – represents a fundamental distinction. And there is no problem as long as, in Arendt's words, 'the thinking ego [...] has no urge to appear in the world of appearances' – in other words, as long as it does not seek to intervene in public life (*Mind*, 197). But where the thinking ego does feel the urge to appear in public, the situation is perilous. Because, while the ego might resemble the world of appearances in its basic plurality – the doubleness that creates the possibility that I can be at variance with myself, and thus lack intellectual integrity – this is not the same kind of plurality as in the world of appearances.

Herein lies what Arendt, in her interview with Gaus, describes as the 'vital tension between philosophy and politics', a tension between 'man as a thinking being and man as an acting being' (Remains 2). Where the individual is a thinking being, she must not in the last instance be at variance with herself: this is what is necessary in order for her to demonstrate intellectual integrity. In other words, while the plurality of her ego provides the possibility for thought, it is something that must be continually overcome in order for judgement to take place. By contrast, where the individual is an acting being, a political creature, she must be wary of imposing upon others the conclusions she has arrived at herself, because the worldly space of appearances – that is, the common world – is only worldly insofar as it remains characterized by a plurality of different thinking minds. Thus, in the world of appearances, unlike in the life of the mind, plurality is something that must be preserved. In the life of the mind, integrity – intellectual integrity – is a virtue; however, as far as political life is concerned, this integrity represents something of a threat, because to treat the political realm as something that cannot be at variance with itself, to subject it to the same expectations that attend the solitary thinker, is to threaten integration: the integration of plurality into singularity, of the many into the mass.

This provides us with a useful way of describing the complex status of integrity in Arendt's writing, and in her life. Integrity – specifically, intellectual integrity – is crucial: it is what indicates that genuine thought has taken place, and to lack it is in the very worst instance to demonstrate the thoughtlessness that was characteristic of Adolf Eichmann. Integration, on the other hand, seems to threaten the annihilation of the plurality of the public world; indeed, it threatens the annihilation of the world itself. Thus, the significance of integrity for the common world is critically different from its significance in the mind of the solitary, thinking individual: for here it is the integrity of the world as a democratic space of appearance that is paramount. Arendt summarizes this position nicely in her interview with Gaus when describing the importance of truth to her thought: 'Do I imagine myself being influential? No. I want to understand' (Remains 3). Herein, as we have seen, lies Arendt's commitment to intellectual integrity. But the limits she places on the influence of her own thought arise out of her respect for the other form of integrity we have been discussing here: that is, the integrity of the public world.

In the wake of the Reichstag fire on 27 February 1933, Arendt had made '*denken ohne Geländer*' – thinking without a banister, that is, without preconceived, universal or transcendental categories – her life's work.[9] Between *Eichmann in Jerusalem* and her death in 1975, she would devote herself to attempting to understand the moral and, more importantly, political implications of *selbstdenken*, insisting that the failure to think on the one hand, and to respect the world as a site of action on the other, had resulted in disaster and could do so again. Considered in this light, the repose in which we leave Arendt at the end of Margarethe von Trotta's film begins to make more sense. It is not a retreat into the *vita contemplativa* that we are witnessing in this moment. It is a pause, a moment of reflection in which the tension between the thinker and the world in and for which she thinks is being negotiated. We may only hope that other thinkers show such a respect for the integrity of the world we hold in common.

Recommended reading

Readers looking for an introductory overview of Arendt's work will find Peter Baehr's anthology *The Portable Hannah Arendt* (London: Penguin, 2003) useful, since it contains substantial excerpts of Arendt's writing across her career (including material, in full or excerpt, discussed in this chapter). Introductions to Arendt's thought abound; among the most insightful, however, continues to be Elisabeth Young-Bruehl's field-defining 1982 book *Hannah Arendt: For Love of the World* (New Haven: Yale University Press, 1982). For a more up-to-date discussion of most salient aspects of Arendt's thought see Patrick Hayden (ed.), *Hannah Arendt: Key Concepts* (Abingdon: Routledge, 2014). Finally, for a fascinating intellectual biography of Arendt as both thinker and human being, see Richard H. King's *Arendt and America* (Chicago: University of Chicago Press, 2015), which places a focus on the oft-neglected republican pedigree of Arendt's thought.

Notes

1 *Hannah Arendt*, directed by Margarethe von Trotta (2012; London: Soda Pictures, 2014), DVD.
2 F. Scott Fitzgerald, *The Great Gatsby* (London: Penguin, 2000).
3 Hannah Arendt, *The Human Condition* (Chicago: University of Chicago Press, 1998), 15.
4 Hannah Arendt, *The Life of the Mind* (San Diego: Harcourt, 1977), 176.
5 Hannah Arendt, *Eichmann in Jerusalem: A Report on the Banality of Evil* (London: Penguin, 2006), 274.
6 Hannah Arendt and Günter Gaus, '"What Remains? The Language Remains": A Conversation with Günter Gaus', in *Essays in Understanding 1930–1954: Formation, Exile, and Totalitarianism* (New York: Schocken Books, 1994), 15.
7 Hannah Arendt, 'A "Daughter of Our People": A Response to Gershom Scholem', in *The Portable Hannah Arendt* (London: Penguin, 2003), 395.
8 Hannah Arendt, 'Truth and Politics', in *Between Past and Future* (London: Penguin, 2006), 259.
9 Arendt uses this phrase, which she takes from the philosopher Friedrich Nietzsche, at numerous points in her writing. For a detailed engagement with the concept, and a book-length exposition of its implications for Western political theory, see Tracy B. Strong's *Politics without Vision: Thinking without a Banister in the Twentieth Century* (Chicago: University of Chicago Press, 2012).

22

Anansi the Spider

Individual trickery and communal integrity

Stephen L. Bishop

Anansi, or Anansi the Spider ('ananse' means 'spider' in the Akan language), is the most well-known folk-tale figure across West Africa. Anansi stories are originally from the Akan people, primarily of Ghana, but also the Ivory Coast, and are often more specifically tied to the Asante people, a subgroup of the Akan. Anansi's influence has spread not only across much of West Africa, but also to the Caribbean (where the name Nancy or Aunt Nancy is more common) as a result of the slave trade and in North America, where he often represents the only widely known African folk-tale character, primarily due to Haley's and McDermott's separate, popular Anansi publications in the early 1970s.[1] Anansi's influence is so strong that a variant of the Akan word 'anansesem' is used in several cultures to describe the entire panoply of folk tales, a rubric inspired by a famous Anansi story, usually called 'How Anansi Obtained the Sky God's Stories' or 'How Anansi Became King of Stories', in which Anansi uses his intelligence and cunning to win all the stories from the Sky God, and thus make them available to mankind.

Anansi is therefore a prominent, even seminal figure in African folk tales. Yet one may well wonder whether he makes for a good example of integrity, for Anansi is a trickster figure, a character whose very nature and symbolism is about lying to, taking advantage of and deceiving others. He therefore seems to represent the antithesis of integrity. Like many trickster figures, however, he is a more complicated character than just a liar or deceiver. In fact, Anansi is an excellent subject of examination in order to tease out the complex ethical questions in not only Akan, but also even more widely encountered African cultural traditions regarding the respect for but limits of personal cleverness, and the centrality of communal integrity. Whereas Anansi often illustrates the advantages of being cleverer than those in one's social circle and being able to use one's wits to come out ahead in a contest, he just as often demonstrates the dangers of taking such trickery too far and violating the ethical norms of community behaviour. More specifically, the admiration for Anansi's individual cleverness can run up against the need for community integrity, and at that point the former often loses out to the latter.

The reason for this ultimate preference of community integrity over individual cleverness is that Akan society (and by extension most sub-Saharan African societies) has a strongly communitarian ethical philosophy. As detailed in Gyekye's *African Philosophical Thought*, the emphasis in indigenous African ethical systems is on what is beneficial to the community, and then, only from that starting point, what is beneficial to the individual. As Gyekye examines in Akan ethics:

> Just as the good is that action or pattern of behaviour which conduces to well-being and social harmony, so the evil [...] is that which is considered detrimental to the well-being of humanity and society. The Akan concept of evil, like that of good, is definable entirely in terms of the needs of society.[2]

Accordingly, 'the Akan individual sees himself as a member of society before he sees himself as an individual'.[3] Gyekye also takes pains to explain that these are not the principles of a revealed religion, of the Word of God translated to mankind, or even of an autocratic leader, but rather arise from a humanist approach to delineating what is most helpful for a given society's health and prosperity.[4] Since this ethical code of conduct is both established and maintained by humans rather than gods, it reinforces the humanistic, communal nature of both its authority and goals. This ethical philosophy does not, however, mean that all individuality is absent. In fact, individuality is not suppressed, criticized or ignored; it is just assumed that it is a natural outgrowth of and supported by the health and well-being of the community of which the individual is a part. If everyone puts communal integrity first, the result will be a social environment where everyone's individual desires and needs will be more easily realized.

This sense of communitarian ethics is perhaps best illustrated, precisely because it is so jarring to most Western audiences, in a non-Anansi, Kenyan folk tale called 'The Giraffe Hunters'.[5] In this tale, a pair of friends agree to take on the dangerous goal of killing a giraffe, with the first friend hiding in a tree with a knife while the second lies in ambush with a bow and arrow in the grass. When the first jumps on the giraffe's neck, the second finds himself unable to shoot the giraffe because he is laughing too hard at the sight of his friend hanging on for dear life as the giraffe swings his head to and fro in an attempt to dislodge him. The first, nonetheless, manages to kill the giraffe on his own with the knife, and then promptly announces that he will not share the meat with his friend since he did not help in the kill as planned. Nonetheless, the second friend ultimately tricks the first by scaring away the latter's wife with a false story about her husband coming home ready to beat her, takes her place, and spirits the meat away as the husband progressively drops it off with 'her'. The second hunter therefore effectively steals the meat he did not help catch, and gets away with it. It appears to be a terrible ethical lesson, and the opposite of integrity. The lesson, however, is that since the two hunters were friends and part of the same community, the first hunter should have still been willing to share the catch with his friend, even though the latter did nothing to actively contribute to the hunt. As perverse as it may seem to more individualistic ethical standards, the first hunter is being criticized and punished for *his* lack of integrity, while his unhelpful friend is rewarded for being clever and pointing out the error of the former's decision to exclude him (one can also assume that the wife's immediate willingness to believe that her husband was coming to beat her is also a criticism of the first hunter's behaviour).

Integrity in this social and philosophical context therefore takes on two different, but concomitant meanings. It is on the one hand a purely ethical principle that is based on what the community determines is best for the community rather than what God wills or a ruler states. Simply put, to do what is in the community's best, productive and healthy interests is therefore to demonstrate ethical social integrity or morality. But on the other hand, integrity is also a simple descriptive state of a well-functioning society when that ethical principle is in force. The principle of acting in the community's best interests and well-being results in a close-knit, mutually supportive society where everyone wins and benefits. This second meaning presents integrity as a practical social integrity or cohesiveness.

The result in traditional oral narrative is that there are two general kinds of Anansi folk tales – those where he is a clever, resourceful character who triumphs over individuals and difficult predicaments that impede his individual flourishing and happiness, and those where he is seeking personal happiness and success *at the expense of* his larger community. He invariably wins in the former cases, thus demonstrating the importance of being a fast thinker, inventive problem solver and/or calm interlocutor. These are, in fact, characteristics that are frequently valourized in other folk tales, even non-Anansi ones, across Africa. But in the latter cases, despite initial success due to his cleverness, Anansi is ultimately exposed not as quick on his feet, creative or composed, but, rather, as lazy, dishonest and, most importantly, acting in a way that is harmful to his fellow community members, and therefore he ends up being unsuccessful in his trickery and consequently suffers punishment. Just as importantly, that punishment usually takes the form of a type of social ostracism or shameful marking, literally setting him outside the bounds of acceptable society, and thereby reinforcing the nature of his lack of *communal* integrity in both senses of the term.

The aforementioned story of how Anansi came to obtain all the stories of the Sky God is a good illustration of Anansi's individual cleverness and trickery being presented as good qualities. The Sky God only agrees to give Anansi the stories if he, a mere spider, can perform three seemingly impossible tasks – capturing and bringing back to the Sky God three formidable creatures: Onini the Python, Osebo the Leopard and Mboro the Hornets. He accomplishes each of these tasks through flattery, traps and lying. For Onini, he claims to be in a dispute about Onini's length with his own wife, who does not agree with Anansi's more generous assessment of it, and finally convinces Onini to let Anansi tie him to a palm branch to get a truly accurate measurement of his impressive size. Once tied up, Onini is easily delivered by Anansi to the Sky God. For Osebo, Anansi digs a pit on the path Osebo takes every day and conceals it with sticks and leaves. When Osebo falls into it and starts complaining loudly, Anansi conveniently arrives, plays innocent, and asks what the problem is. Anansi then feigns pity for him and offers to help rescue him, but he does so using his spider webs as ropes, and is thereby able to ensnare Osebo in the process, making for another easy delivery to the Sky God. As for Mboro, Anansi procures a gourd and some leaves, drenching both them and himself with water to give the impression he is outrunning a rain storm that will arrive soon, and then generously offers Mboro shelter in the gourd, which he promptly stops up with leaves when the offer is accepted, and then delivers this last requirement to the Sky God. Having performed all three seemingly impossible tasks, Anansi consequently receives all the folk tales in the world as a reward. Anansi has thus tricked his way through a series of dishonest statements and actions into a victorious position, but that trickery is to be admired rather than criticized because it has not harmed anyone who is a part of his community since Onini, Osebo and Mboro all represent dangerous, antisocial creatures, while the Sky God himself has not been tricked, and only seen his demands met. In fact, the end result is highly beneficial to his community, as he can now share all these folk tales with them.

   In contrast, a classic example of one type of Anansi's antisocial, anti-communitarian behaviour appears in the folk tale 'How Anansi Got a Narrow Waist'. Anansi, both too lazy to grow his own food and yet too appreciative of the cooking of others to want to pass up good food, resolves to find a way to attend everyone's meals and take advantage of the hospitality expected by a guest of a family about to eat. When simply running around from house to house proves to be too inefficient, as Anansi is still missing out on certain meals, he devises a plan so that he will never miss the start of a meal. He ties ropes around his waist and gives one end of each rope to a different family and tells them to tug on it when it is time for a meal. His clever plan is undone, however, when all the families pull on their ropes at the same time, squeezing him around the waist from all sides, and thus leaving him with a permanently disfigured tiny waist, just as spiders have in real life. Hospitality is certainly an important concept in West African societies, and Anansi is more than welcome to partake of other families' meals, but his greediness in wanting to attend every meal in order to gorge himself combined with his unwillingness to reciprocate by providing meals for others means that, however smart and clever he may be, he is not demonstrating his willingness to be an integral part of the community. In fact, his comeuppance leads to this stigmatizing and symbolic mark (his narrow waist) that will forever remind others of his lack of concern for communal integrity. In this way, 'Ananse does not teach morals when he is victorious. It is when he fails that the Akan draw ethical conclusions [...] Ananse is the exception that probes and proves the rules'.[6]

Another example can be found in 'Anansi Plays Dead', in which Anansi decides to turn his back on his family and village during a famine in order to better eat on his own. He pretends to visit a doctor and subsequently announces his impending death, asks for specific burial rituals, including being buried near the yam fields and with cooking implements for use in the afterlife, and then feigns his death. When his family complies, he awakes from his grave every night, steals yams, and cooks and eats them before returning to his hiding place by sunrise. Knowing Anansi to have been a smart, resourceful person, his family actually prays to him for guidance in resolving the mystery of the repeated thefts, but, having, of course, no answer, they ultimately decide to leave a trap for the thief instead. The trap consists of a lifelike child made of gum tree sap. When Anansi awakens that night to eat again, he sees the 'child' and greets it. Receiving no answer to his greeting – a very disrespectful act in African societies – he begins striking the child in punishment until all of his limbs are thoroughly stuck. The family then finds him in the morning and judges him harshly for his selfishness and causing harm to his own community. In response, 'he was deeply ashamed, and covered his face with his headcloth. [...] From that day until now, Anansi has not wanted to face people because of their scoffing and jeering, and that is why he is often found hiding in dark corners'.[7] Once again, Anansi may be clever, but in this case he has used that ability to do harm to his own people, and therefore ends up serving as an example of an outcast, of what happens when one does not uphold the integrity required of all members of the community. Note that a variation of the gum doll trap used to catch Anansi can be seen in the famous southern United States' folk tale about Br'er Rabbit being caught by a trap of a lifelike child made out of tar, with the substituting of Br'er Rabbit for Anansi likely due to the syncretism of African-influenced and Native American folk tales, the latter of which often employ the rabbit as a trickster figure.

Anansi, despite his trickster nature, is therefore a fine example of West African communal integrity precisely because he demonstrates two important principles: First, Anansi's usual success through cleverness and resourcefulness, but his occasional use of such skills against his own community shows the danger that even smart, successful people can fall prey to selfish thoughts and actions that go against community integrity. As Barker and Sinclair have remarked, 'Woe to one who would put his trust in Anansi – a sly, selfish, and greedy person.'[8] Second, the fact that when he does fall prey to such selfish temptations, he is sometimes caught and punished, but, more importantly, is always seen as a wrongdoer who illustrates what other members of society might think about doing, but would never actually do. 'The important point is that Ananse, through his actions, subverts and revalidates the ultimate bases of Akan life.'[9] In this manner, Anansi encourages in the community an appreciation for communal integrity and the belief that it should triumph in the end.

Recommended reading

For common collections of Anansi stories, consult Anansi selections in collections such as Peggy Appiah's *Anansi the Spider: Tales from an Ashanti Father* (New York: Random House Children's Books, 1966) and J. Osafoa Dankyi's *Ananse Searches for a Fool and Other Stories* (Accra: Sedco, 1994) along with a wide variety of individual stories presented in illustrated children's books. For a discussion of the importance and transformation of Anansi stories into the Caribbean, see Lieke Van Duin's 'Anansi as Classical Hero', *Journal of Caribbean Literatures* 5 (1) (2007): 33–42; Emily Zobel Marshall's *Anansi's Journey: A Story of Jamaican Cultural Resistance* (Kingston, Jamaica : University of the West Indies Press,

2012), and Monique Blérald's 'Anansi l'araignée en terre guyanaise: Adaptation et évolution d'un personnage mythique', in *Nouvelles Études Francophones* 23 (2) (2008): 98–110. For examples of the first introduction of the Anansi character and story cycle to North American audiences, the two works cited by Haley and McDermott, along with McDermott's 1969 short film *Anansi the Spider* are the best examples, but later works by Verna Norberg Aardema, *Anansi Finds a Fool* (New York: Dial Books for Young Readers, 1992) and *Anansi Does the Impossible!* (New York: Atheneum Books for Young Readers, 1997) are also useful. For further discussions of African philosophical and ethical principles, see Tsenay Serequeberhan's *African Philosophy: The Essential Readings* (New York: Paragon House, 1991) and Lee Brown's *African Philosophy: New and Traditional Perspectives* (New York: Oxford University Press, 2004), or read Thomas Hylland Eriksen's 'The Anansi Position', *Anthropology Today* 29 (6) (2013), which makes a specific application of Anansi stories and African philosophy.

Notes

1 Gail Haley, *A Story, a Story* (New York: Atheneum, 1970) and Gerald McDermott, *Anansi the Spider: A Tale from the Ashanti* (New York: Holt, Rinehart, and Winston, 1972).

2 Kwame Gyekye, *An Essay on African Philosophical Thought* (Philadelphia: Temple University Press, 1987), 133.

3 Christopher Vecsey, 'The Exception Who Proves the Rules: Ananse the Akan Trickster', *Journal of Religion in Africa* 12 (3) (1981): 161–77, 172.

4 Gyekye, *African Philosophical Thought*, 131–2.

5 Harold Courlander, *A Treasury of African Folklore* (New York: Crown Publishers, 1975), 515–17.

6 Vecsey, 'The Exception Who Proves the Rules', 173, 174.

7 Courlander, *A Treasury*, 151.

8 W. Barker and C. Sinclair, *West African Folktales* (Northbrook, IL: Metro, 1972 [1917]), 25.

9 Vecsey, 'The Exception Who Proves the Rules', 163.

23

The Cookes and the Kayes

Assertions of virtue among the 'middling sort' in post-Reformation England

Robert Tittler

The concept of integrity is not, at first glance, a subject that readily lends itself to visual depiction, but in the intensely competitive and only partially literate society of post-Reformation England it became important to devise a visual means of displaying it. After all, this was an era of enormous insecurity in a kingdom whose Tudor dynasty ruled by conquest, whose often newly empowered local governing officials strove for respect and whose society witnessed the most intense era of social mobility and competition in its history. All those circumstances called out for assertions of personal and even institutional integrity so as to earn the respect of others.

The political and social tensions of the age are most familiar to us in the context of the Tudor dynasty itself. In their effort to assert and symbolize the integrity upon which the legitimacy of their rule heavily rested, the Tudor kings and queens from Henry

VIII onwards fully exploited the portrait medium in its literal as well as its metaphoric sense. Henry VIII set the tone for this by employing the inimitable Hans Holbein the younger to forge the imperious and now iconic image that springs to mind at the very mention of that King. Though his immediate successors, Edward VI and Mary Tudor, reigned too briefly to develop much of their own visual imagery, Elizabeth made up for lost time by encouraging and eliciting the elaborate imagery that just as readily springs to mind when we think of her.

As we know, myriad aristocrats and landed gentry emulated the royal fashion by employing portraiture to display their loyalty to the Crown, their claims to social standing and their political influence. 'Noblemen and gentlemen', the late Lawrence Stone famously wrote, 'wanted above all formal family portraits which take their place along with genealogical trees and sumptuous tombs as symbols of the frenzied status-seeking and ancestor worship of the age. What patrons demanded was evidence of the sitter's position and wealth by opulence of dress, ornament and background.'[1] This role for the painted portrait certainly bore implications for the sitter's personal integrity. It did so largely by including symbolic images that reflected essential qualities of mind and character, qualities considered critical in the self-fashioning of contemporary elites. The elite portraiture of the day still forms the core of art historical scholarship and gallery exhibits alike.

But far less familiar is the coincident tendency of those much further down the social scale who also employed portraiture to promulgate their personal virtues. It may have been an exaggeration to claim, as one wag did in 1598, that 'every citizen's wife that wears a taffeta kirtle and a velvet hatt ... must have her picture in the parlour',[2] but the range of portrait patronage and consumption in these years is substantially broader, in both social and geographic terms, than has until recently been assumed. Couples like the Gloucester benefactors John and Joan Cooke, or the minor Yorkshire gentry John and his wife Dorothy Kaye, were very far from the subjects whose portraits we might see in the National Portrait Gallery. Yet, as we will see at greater length later, they were also portrayed in this era.

Portraits commissioned by the sitter, in contrast to some of those commissioned by a third party, reflect what that sitter wished the viewer to think of him or her. Many of these lesser sitters engaged in portraiture not to demonstrate affluence, of which most had but little, or lineage, for which the same could often be said. Instead, such portraits emphasized qualities of character that, taken together, built a strong case for the coveted appearance of personal integrity. These might include symbolic references to such qualities as courage, humility, loyalty, hospitality, steadfastness, charity, piety and service, all of which could be considered components of integrity.

This need to demonstrate virtue applied to the strivers of the day, middling people 'on the make', but it also applied to local institutions, and to their officials. Mayors, schoolmasters, masters of university colleges and even of trade guilds, all sought to promulgate the virtue of integrity, both of their office and of their person, so as to elicit deference and respect from those over whom they ruled. They often did so by commissioning portraits of themselves or of their predecessors in civic guise, showing them as models of charity, humility, benevolence and wise counsel. Whether they were commissioned by striving individuals on their own behalf or by civic officials on behalf of their institutions, we might well think of the consequent paintings as 'portraits of integrity'.

Given the often modest social status of their sitters, it is also the case that such portraits were often commissioned on limited budgets and without ready access to the more refined portrait painters working in London or at court. Portraits commissioned by these aspiring backwoodsmen, minor gentry, religious recusants, borough mayors, schoolmasters and so forth, had most often to rely on local painters typically working in the traditional English vernacular. They were likely to produce images that were quite crude compared to what high-end, especially London-based, painters could do.

In addition, and partly because these local craftsmen lacked the skill to show such a quality as integrity by subtleties of gesture and expression, such patrons often fell back on the depiction within the picture of material objects that could suggest such things as literacy (books), lineage (coats of arms) or either official or personal status (forms of dress). As if these were inadequate to the task, patron-sitters often had inscriptions added to the frame or picture plane describing acts of loyalty, charity or wise rule. Taken together, the inclusion of such a range of elements offered a less subtle, more laconic and therefore more easily read impression of personal character.

Once one looks beyond the familiar, high-end portraiture of the post-Reformation era and into portraits of the middling sort of people and local institutions, examples of such visual strategies abound. Two in particular serve to demonstrate most of these aims and characteristics. First, consider the early-seventeenth-century double portrait of John and Joan Cooke, Mayor and Mayoress of Gloucester, shown in Figure 23.1. This is a posthumous, *civic* portrait, commissioned not by the sitters, who died, respectively, in 1528 and 1543, but by the civic fathers of the city of Gloucester around the sixteen-teens. It dates from a difficult time in the city's

FIGURE 23.1 John and Joan Cooke, oil on panel, 813 x 755 mm. © Gloucester City Museum and Art Gallery.

economic and civic life, and it seems to have been done as one of a series of contemporary paintings of Gloucester benefactors intended to remind that community of the long and laudable history of civic benefaction and public service undertaken by earlier citizens of the city.

John Cooke made his fortune as a brewer and a mercer before turning to a life of civic service in Gloucester. He served twice as sheriff and four times as mayor, and left in his will, among other bequests, funds for a paved causeway and for the foundation of a grammar school attached to the parish church of St. Mary's Crypt, where it may still be seen. His will instructed his wife and executrix Joan to see that the foundation proceeded as planned. She demonstrated her own integrity by faithfully and selflessly carrying out his will, getting the school built, up and running, in the fifteen years remaining to her after John's death.

Crude though it may be as a work of art, the design of the painting itself tells the story. We see John as deceased: his evidently comatose, glassy-eyed appearance suggests no less. He continues to wear his red, fur-lined mayoral robe, but it is *she* who has inherited his freeman's gloves, and the status that they symbolize, and it is *she* who employed that status to carry forth his will as his life mate and executor. We see her, looking very much alive and straight at the viewer, taking his hands and leading him forth towards that end.

As if the carefully constructed tableau didn't speak clearly enough on its own, those who commissioned the painting had an inscription added to celebrate the Cookes' integrity as benefactors and civic officials. Intended as a model for current and future generations, it reads as follows:

> Though death hath rested these life mates/ Their memory survives
> Esteemed myrrors they may be/ For majestrates and wives
> The School of Crist ye Bartholomews/ The Causeway in the West
> May witness wch ye piuous minde/ This worthy man possest.
> This vertuous dame performed ye taske/ Her husband did intend
> And after him in single life/ Lived famous to her end.
> Their bountye & beneficence/ On earth remains allways
> Let present past a(nd) future time/ Still Celebrate ye Praise

This is not, of course, a painting intended by its sitters to stake claims of social standing at nearly a century's remove. Instead, it has been posthumously commissioned by the city fathers of a later generation so as to exemplify for current and future generations the value of civic benefaction and of marital fidelity. It came at a time when the city of Gloucester had come upon hard economic times, and appears to have been part of a civic campaign to remind Gloucestrians of the necessity, as well as the virtue, of such benefactions. It was, indeed, to quote from the inscription itself, 'a mirror... for majestrates and wives', but also for citizens who might thus be encouraged to perform acts of civic benefaction as their predecessors had done.

Of all those portraits which might serve to exemplify the portraiture of *personal* integrity, there can be few more vivid examples than the 'Woodsome Hall Panels' presenting the lives and characters of John and Dorothy Kaye of Woodsome, Yorkshire, now preserved at the Tolson Museum in Huddersfield. These joined wooden panels consist of four tableaux, one on each side of each panel.[3] The first (Figure 23.2) is a crude portrait of John Kaye, who is surrounded here by three poems, twelve miniature human figures hovering in space and bearing inscribed scrolls, and the Kaye family coat of arms topping the whole.

On the reverse side (Figure 23.3) appear sixty-six coats of arms laid out symmetrically in perfect rows all topped by three written texts.

The second panel consists, on its face (Figure 24.4), of Dorothy's equally crude portrait, surrounded by five inscriptions and topped by the arms of the Maleverer family to which she belonged.

On *its* reverse (Figure 23.5), we see a 'Jesse Tree' image of the three generations of the Kaye Family, starting with John's father Arthur at the root, John and his two siblings just above him, and then some (but not all) of John and Dorothy's *fifteen* children.

Both panels were placed, not flat against the wall, which would have obscured one side or the other, but suspended perpendicular *to* the wall so that both sides could readily be seen. As a whole, these panels provide intriguing visual images of John and Dorothy, whose images remain at the centre of two of the panels. But in addition, as we will see, they also include several communicative and symbolic devices that not only offer elements of portraiture, but also elements of autobiography.

FIGURE 23.2 Anon., John Kaye of Woodsome, c. 1567. Oil on panel, 110 x 92 cm. Tolson Museum, Huddersfield, ref. KLMUS 1990/399 (recto). © Kirklees Museums and Galleries.

If there were ever a poster boy for the striving and competitive gentry of rural England, it would be hard to find someone better suited than John Kaye. Throughout his long years Kaye acquired land, fulling mills and stock; renovated and improved two houses and his parish church; built myriad cottages for new tenants; pursued his interests aggressively before the law; eventually held minor office; and generously provided for those of his fifteen children who reached adulthood. But in 1567, the putative date of the panels, nearly all of this lay in the future.

FIGURE 23.3 Anon., Coats of Arms of Kayes' Friends and Kin, c. 1567. Oil on panel, 110 x 92 cm. Tolson Museum, Huddersfield, ref. KLMUS 1990/399A (verso). © Kirklees Museums and Galleries.

Well before that time, and at an unusually early age, John had married Dorothy Maleverer, daughter of a neighbouring clan of minor to middling Yorkshire gentry. As he tells us in verse,

> My wife and I together met
> According to our parents will
> Wedded we were at yeares sixteen
> When neither of us had great skill.[4]

FIGURE 23.4 Anon., Dorothy Kaye, c. 1567. Oil on panel, 110 x 92 cm. Tolson Museum, Huddersfield, ref. KLMUS 1990/398 (Recto). © Kirklees Museums and Galleries.

As John would later recall in an autobiographical poem of 1591, the couple began with but a modest income, and presumably lived in one of his father's properties until he inherited the family seat at Woodsome sometime in the early or mid-1570s. As he tells us,

> Our feoffament was but xxie markes
> A yeare to bring all things to pas
> My father lyvyd such tyme complete,

FIGURE 23.5 Anon., Kaye Family Tree, c. 1567. Oil on panel, 110 x 92 cm. Tolson Museum, Huddersfield, ref. KLMUS 1990/398A (verso). © Kirklees Museums and Galleries.

> Tyll six and fortie years I was
> The graunge & lyngarthes he did purchace
> With nyne oxgangs in Farnlay towne
> That his heires might have moore albowe Rowme[5]

From that time on John worked assiduously and very successfully to build up the estate and extend its holdings. Over time, he did, indeed, place the House of Woodsome on a very secure footing for generations to come. He brought prosperity and local repute to his son and principal heir, Robert (c. 1550–1620); and established the groundwork for future generations of the family. His pride in those achievements reverberate clearly through his financial accounts and other writings, which he kept up nearly to his death in 1594.

Throughout these years, John remained committed to the moral outlook proper to the gentle status to which he so ardently aspired. He also understood the importance of instilling those virtues in successive generations of his 'house' as essential marks of honour. Both the panel inscriptions and other writings, including several autobiographical and philosophical poems, clearly enunciate his own sense of personal integrity. One of those poems reads:

> Foure Poyntes for a gentylman
> A clenly howse, lodging, meate, dryncke, & fyer,
> provyd for the frend, he hath his desyer.
> Than armor & weapon fytt for thy degree
> to defend thy king, thyselfe, & thy countrye.
> Thyrdly in stable a Byard or stede
> that will goo thy Journey & serve the at neede.
> But chiefly a closet or some secrett place
> to observe God in daylie, and call for his grace.
> Who hath these things ready, hys neds must I scan
> to know well the dutye of a right gentilman.[6]

Similar sentiments appear on John's panel itself, in the poem inscribed *as Vita Discriptio*:

> I Lyve at home in husbandry/Wythoute office or fee trulye
> As servyth myne abylitie/I mantayne hospitalitye
> Teaching to thes humanytye/By rules of Chrystyanitie
> In cause of ambiguity/I never shew extremytie
> Where malice ys I pacify/Where just cause is I gratify
> My promes ready to fulfyll/Thus have I lyvid & will do still
> Hooping by lyke to have such gaine/As after death to lyve again

Both the poem and panel serve as revealing artefacts of John's early middle years. They acknowledge the family arms, at the top centre of his portrait panel, which he inherited from his father Arthur, while at the same time recognizing how far he had still to go to fulfil his ambitions. John could not yet strut his stuff before his peers upon the social stage, but he keenly hoped to do so, and he set out in these panels for all to see the moral roadmap on which he relied to bring him there.

The main inscription on Dorothy's portrait panel, placed at the bottom centre and possibly (judging by the style) written in the first person by John for her, has been entitled 'Vita Uxoris Honesta'. As a counterpart to John's panel poem it speaks most eloquently to that 'Life of an Honest Wife' as follows:

> To lyve at home in howswyverye
> To order well my familye
> To see they lyve not Idillye
> To bring upe children veertuslye
> To relyeve poore fowkes willynglye
> This ys my care with modestye
> To leade my lyfe in honesty

Platitudinous as they may strike us today, these and other invocations to proper behaviour generously marble the Kayes' poems and panels. They stake out for all to see the values by which John and Dorothy aspired to live and make their way. Not only were they intended as, in John's words, 'Instruccions meete and necesarye for the Hayres of Woodsome to understand', but also for the friends and neighbours of those 'hayres' to take in. Whereas the written verse in his surviving papers remains private by its very nature, the panel verse brought his maxims to the 'public' attention of anyone who entered Woodsome Hall. Taken together, they articulated a virtual code of manners of the sort that, as Anne Bryson has put it, 'expressed and projected particular visions of authority and legitimacy of the elite, and ... provided a basic language both of solidarity and competition within that elite'.[7]

Among the emphatic virtues thus expressed, hospitality, good husbandry (or, in Dorothy's case, 'housewyvery)', charity to the needy, personal modesty, moderate behaviour, piety and humility, some degree of learning and loyalty (the latter expressed not towards any feudal authority but to crown and country) stand out clearly. They do so by dint of visual imagery as well as by the written word.

These two examples of portraiture, depicting the Cookes of Gloucester and the Kayes of Woodsome, represent a little-known chapter in the history of English painting. But they also give us much to ponder about the meanings and display of integrity among the middling sorts of people in Elizabethan and Jacobean England.

Recommended reading

Anna Bryson's, *From Courtesy to Civility: Changing Codes of Conduct in Early Modern England* (Oxford and New York: Clarendon Press, 1998) offers a lucid discussion of civility as it applied to Early Modern England, while the seminal work on self-fashioning in the same era remains Stephen Greenblatt, *Renaissance Self-Fashioning: From More to Shakespeare* (Chicago: University of Chicago Press, 1980). Kevin Sharpe's, *Selling the Tudor Monarchy: Authority and Image in Sixteenth-Century England* (London and New Haven: Yale University Press, 2009) is the best guide to the ways in which the Tudor monarchy fashioned its own image, while Robert Tittler's *The Face of the City: Civic Portraiture and Civic Identity in Early Modern England* (Manchester: Manchester University Press, 2013) illustrates how local civic leaders used portraiture to build images of respect and authority. His study of 'The "Gloucester Benefactors" after Four Centuries', *The Antiquaries Journal* 95 (2015): 305–24, offers a context for John and Joan Cooke.

Notes

1 Lawrence Stone, *The Crisis of the Aristocracy, 1558-1641* (Oxford: Oxford University Press, 1965), 712.

2 John Lily, *Queen Elizabeth's Entertainments at Mitcham: Poet, Painter and Musician, Attributed to John Lyly*, ed. Leslie Hotson (New Haven: Yale University Press, 1953), 27. I am grateful to Lindsey Cox for tracking down the origin of this reference.

3 Catalogued respectively as Tolson Museum, Huddersfield, ref. KLMUS 1990/399; KLMUS 1990/399A; KLMUS 1990/398; and KLMUS 1990/398A.

4 Yorkshire Archaeological Society, Leeds, MS. 178, 5.
5 Ibid.
6 Ibid., 29.
7 Anna Bryson, *From Courtesy to Civility: Changing Codes of Conduct in Early Modern England* (Oxford and New York: Clarendon Press, 1998), 24.

24

Titus Pomponius Atticus

Writing the life of an uncommonly honourable Roman

Linda McGuire

Cornelius Nepos is not a particularly familiar figure from the Roman world. Little can be said about his life with any certainty except that he lived at the end of the Republic, making him a contemporary of Titus Pomponius Atticus. Of the few writings associated with his name, it is his biographical series that stands out. Entitled *On Famous Men*, it included an estimated 400 biographies of great men from Greek and Roman history. Only one full-length life survives. The earliest biography from the Roman world is Nepos' biography of Atticus.[1]

The *Life of Atticus* has several unusual features, not least of which is Atticus. He was not strictly speaking an eligible subject. In the ancient world, biographies were devoted to those belonging to the senatorial order who contributed to Rome's greatness through political achievement. Atticus was no such man.[2] Instead, Nepos offers his readers a depiction of his character, more specifically a rare portrait of a man of integrity. Yet, for those seeking to make sense of it, that portrait can only be described as challenging.

We begin with a few words about the subject of this life. Titus Pomponius Atticus (110–32 BCE) was born in Rome into the equestrian order, considered less prestigious than the senatorial order. Atticus devoted his life to two activities. One was making money: using inheritances of two and ten million HS (5.2; 14.2), he increased his wealth to become one of the richest men in Rome (13.6). This was done through purchasing income-generating estates like the one in Epirus (modern Albania) and lending money at interest to Greek city states such as Sicyon (Varro, *Rust.* II.2; Cic. *Att.* 1.19.9, 1.20.4; 2.1.10).

His second main occupation was as a scholar in antiquarianism. It was a branch of study concerning the past, particularly religious customs and political institutions, having strong moral overtones. His writings, like the *Liber Annalis*, are barely mentioned in the biography and are no longer extant. Yet, his various activities in this domain have been sufficient to earn Atticus the reputation of an important figure in Roman cultural life. If we know something about him today it is because he was fortunate in his friends and acquaintances. Two of them wrote him into their works. In addition to Nepos' *Life of Atticus,* Atticus features in sixteen books of correspondence that Cicero (106–43 BCE) addressed to him entitled *The Letters to Atticus.*

Biography in the Roman world was political in that it served to pass on to future generations the deeds, and thus values, of great men. What this meant is typified in the later writings of Plutarch (c. 46–120 CE). Plutarch's life of *Cato the Elder,* for instance, devotes five sections to military service, four to tenure of the office of censor, four to writing and oratorical skills, two to various political posts and one to law court cases. His rise through public office culminated in the position of censor, the highest that could be attained in the Republic, and an extraordinary achievement for a new man – the first in his family to become consul.

This is not quite what we find in Nepos. Nepos cannot describe Atticus' political and military feats, as there were none. Instead, the entire biography focuses on developing personal qualities including adherence to ancestral values (*mos maiorum*), sense of duty (*officium*), head of the household (*paterfamilias*), generosity (*liberalitas*) and devotion (*pietas*). The difficulty, however, does not end there, as the resulting portrait appears to offer a conflicting image of Atticus. Moreover, the impression it gives of integrity is not necessarily a positive one. A couple of examples will be studied by way of illustration.

First Nepos addresses the awkwardness of Atticus as a biographical subject. Section six of the *Life of Atticus* outlines Atticus' reasons for not participating in politics. Nepos explains that Atticus' sense of duty and ancestral values did not allow him to hold public office or belong to any political faction. Normally elite men – that is, those belonging to the equestrian or senatorial orders – were expected to participate in public life, with the former taking up lower offices. In earlier times, the idealized past that never existed but was very real to Romans, he could have entered politics, says Nepos. The corrupt times in which he lived, however, would have required him to compromise his values, by indulging in bribery or some other dishonest act, and he was simply unwilling to do this. There is almost the implication that in this respect Atticus surpassed those who followed a traditional career path, like Cato, or even Cicero, elected consul in 63 BCE.

Next Nepos tries to find substitutes to fill this void. Atticus' sense of duty, that saw him forego a life in the political arena, led him to provide assistance to others. Put another way, Nepos evokes the Roman concept of *liberalitas* (generosity). Cicero, in his work entitled *On Duties*, defines it as offering services or money according to one's means (*Off.* 2.52). As a man of considerable resources, Atticus felt it his duty to help as many people as he could in any way he could (11.1). This theme runs throughout the biography forming its backbone. It is noticeable, though, that Nepos only depicts him assisting the rich and powerful in distress.

For instance, Atticus managed the finances of several prominent senators such as Marcus Junius Brutus and Cato the Younger (15.3). Then there are his gifts to consider. He gave 250,000 HS to Cicero when the latter left for exile in 58 BCE (4.4). In 44 BCE when Mark Antony fled Rome before being declared an enemy, Atticus came to the aid of Antony's wife Fulvia several times, including acting as guarantor for a loan (9.4–9.5). A total of 400,000 HS was made available to Brutus when he was forced to flee Italy (8.6).

So along with other traits like honesty (15.1), being a man of his word (15.2), as well as his consistent devotion to his family (17), the image presented to the reader is that of a man of outstanding honour and upright character. This might well have been how Atticus saw himself or even how Nepos perceived him. It will be quickly noticed, however, that all this information can be read in ways that reflect negatively on Atticus. And this might account for the very different perceptions that emerge in writings about him.

Concerning the first point, Atticus rejected an important Roman expectation for someone of his social standing. Nepos tries to make him into a man whose personal dignity was at odds with the current political climate. It is worth pointing out how surprising this comment is. The reasoning offered is rare in surviving Latin sources and a little unexpected considering that his education, under the same tutors as Cicero, prepared him for politics. As someone who lived much of his adult life in Greece and who was well read in its philosophy we might wonder if Atticus was trying to echo sentiments attributed to Socrates (Pl. *Ap.* 19). Indeed, Atticus could have taken inspiration from several Greek philosophers who opted out of politics (Cic. *Off.* 1.69-73). Nepos never offers these justifications for good reason: Romans did not look to the Greeks, but, rather, to figures from their own history to emulate – and these figures did not shy away from political engagement.[3]

Alas, there are no Roman role models in the extant literature to justify Atticus' abstention from a political career. On the contrary, there were plenty to inspire him to take up public office. One such was Cato the Elder (234–149 BCE). Like Atticus, he was born into the equestrian order and acquired his wealth independently. Both men preferred a lifestyle of extreme frugality, somewhat surprising in one as rich as Atticus (Plut. *Cat. Mai.* 3-4; *Att.* 13-14). Cato, too, was concerned with behaving (and seeing others behave) according to traditional Roman values like integrity and honesty. Here the similarities between the two men end. Cato chose public life, which he also considered a duty, where he set the example of self-restraint and virtue. Far from being corrupted by the opportunities for self-enrichment, he became the outspoken scourge of anyone he deemed had acted dishonourably. Moreover, he was known to make disparaging comments about Greek philosophers including Socrates, whom he called a windbag (Plut. *Cat. Mai.* 23). Cato seemed to believe that Greek philosophy was dangerous in that what it argued was contrary to the principles and standards of conduct he considered Roman and to which he had devoted his life.[4]

Does Atticus' non-involvement sit awkwardly beside Cato's energetic participation? Perhaps no Roman dared to compete with the formidable reputation of Cato, who was considered throughout antiquity as severe (Symm. *Ep*.1.4; Plut. *Cat. Mai.* 19). How much of a transgression Atticus committed is likewise difficult to gauge two millennia after he lived. He was certainly not the only elite man to turn his back on public duty in the late Republic. There were equestrians, like Lucius Papirius Paetus, who led similar lifestyles, not known from biographies but stray letters (Cic. *Fam.* 9.15-26). Whatever the reasons, Atticus' stance caused offence. Quintus, the younger brother of Cicero, was furious that Atticus had refused the post of legate he had offered him (6.4; Cic. *Att.* 1.17.7). The appearance of this same justification in the correspondence suggests that Atticus needed regularly to explain his life choices.

Concerning his generous handouts, Nepos depicts them as selfless acts of duty with no ulterior motive (11.3). Yet, various motives suggest themselves. Atticus' actions could equally be interpreted as buying favours from those in power. The men he helped financially appeared to represent his interests in the senate. He expected Cicero to block legislation that might damage his business interests with the Sicyonians (Cic. *Att.* 1.19.9; 1.20.4). At least, Cicero was a friend of long standing who shared his political ideals (6.1). What of Mark Antony and Fulvia, helped at the same time as Brutus when they were on opposing sides of the civil conflict? This neutrality was un-Roman, although Atticus practised it all his life.[5] The reason he went to live in Greece in the first place was to avoid being caught up in the civil disorder caused by Cinna (2.2). It was certainly pragmatic to ingratiate himself with those on both sides of the civil war, but we might doubt if it could be seen as honourable.

Upon regaining power, Mark Antony did repay the kindness shown to Fulvia. He protected Atticus during the proscriptions and arranged a highly favourable marriage for his daughter, Attica, with Marcus Agrippa who was Octavian's most trusted right-hand man (10.4; 12.1-2). Of course, this marriage might have had more to do with her sizeable dowry. It had the consequence of giving Atticus an alliance with the most powerful family in Rome, especially once his grand-daughter, Attica's daughter Vipsania, became betrothed to Tiberius Claudius Nero, who would become the second emperor of Rome. Nepos devotes one entire section to the friendship between Atticus and Octavian, who were in contact daily (20). It was at the urging of Atticus the antiquarian that Octavian undertook to restore the temple of Jupiter Feretrius (20.3). Thus Atticus appeared to wield some influence in the political sphere, without having any official role in it. Moreover, this acquaintance with one of the men responsible for the gruesome death of his friend Cicero (or with two men, if you count Mark Antony), could imply a lack of scruple on Atticus' part.

In the end two distinct pictures of Atticus emerge from this portrayal. In the first he appears to be a man with deeply personal and somewhat old-fashioned values out of step with the world around him and its demands. In the second, he is a rich rogue who used wealth, and his daughter (which was totally acceptable), to purchase access to power. Indeed, these marriage connections hint at ambitions that go beyond protecting financial interests.

Add to this the possibility that Atticus himself might have been behind the circulation of both works in which he featured. Atticus was alive when parts of the biography were written. This is highly unusual. It is easy to get the idea that he commissioned Nepos to write his life, as 19 out of 22 sections were composed before Atticus died, by someone he knew personally (19.1; 13.7). Moreover Atticus had asked him to write other lives in the series, such as the abbreviated *Cato the Elder* that also survives (Nepos, *Cato* 3.5). The *Life of Atticus* remains the only biography from the Roman world written about a living person and an equestrian. Are these innovations, like those attributed to Nepos' earlier lost works? Or did Atticus simply exploit his close association with writers like Nepos? Likewise *The Letters to Atticus* became public after the death of Cicero through the agency of an unknown person. One theory places Atticus in the role of editor and distributor of this work.[6] In the end, not only could Atticus have infiltrated Rome's ruling elite but also seen himself written into Rome's history.

Finally, what can Nepos' biography teach us about integrity? It might be possible to argue that it is not easy to portray this quality. This comment is not directed at the genre of biography, but, rather, suggests that the actions and traits associated with integrity tend to be too open to interpretation. They can easily cause misunderstanding. Of course, one might just suppose Nepos was a second-rate writer who was not up to the task.[7] But Nepos was not alone in facing this difficulty. Cato's actions, too, were variously interpreted by writers both ancient and modern. According to one biographer, his legendary self-restraint and frugality led him to exploit his slaves, selling them off when, too old, they were no longer any use to him. In an extended criticism of this act, Plutarch wonders if greatness or pettiness of spirit was behind treating humans as kitchen tools (5). The significant number of speeches Cato composed, and Cicero read 150 of them, hints that he spent much of his life defending in the law courts his unbending principles (Cic. *Brut.* 65; Nepos, *Cato* 2.4).[8] Perhaps the reader is witnessing the biographer wrestling with a difficulty inherent in the portrayal of integrity.

But Atticus seems to be a particularly challenging subject in this respect. Nepos tells us that Atticus served the interests of *his own* dignity and *his own* sense of duty (6.5; emphasis added). Yet, can one be seen as a person of integrity when one's notions of duty appear different from, even incompatible with, those of the society in which one lives? Several instances of this mismatch are found in the biography. There was the issue of Atticus' neutrality and his willingness to accept criticism rather than to conform to expectations by following the career path he was schooled for. During the Republic the only way to achieve fame – and thus a biography – was through the actions and choices that Atticus avoided. Nepos does not shy away from such problems but neither does he satisfactorily resolve them.

There might be something else we learn from Nepos' depiction – namely, that integrity was an important value to the Romans, even if it is rarely found in their surviving writings, especially at such length. After all, Nepos' unusual biography came to be written largely through a particular set of circumstances. During a difficult moment in their friendship, Cicero wrote to Atticus outlining why he appreciated him (Cic. *Att.* 1.17.5). It is interesting to note that integrity (*integritas*) featured prominently along with uprightness (*probitas*), conscientiousness (*diligens*) and fidelity to obligation (*religio*). He also makes a point of referring to Atticus' non-involvement as an honourable withdrawal from public life (ibid; 1.5). Of course, these comments, made in private correspondence to a close friend, should be taken as they were intended in a spirit of reconciliation and affection.

The very fact that we can still read this work could likewise hint at its importance. Its survival is unlikely to be entirely accidental. At this period, the ancient equivalent of books were hand-copied by those with special training. It was an expensive and arduous undertaking and such gargantuan effort was not wasted on works that had no meaning. In the late Republic a group of scholars, which may well have included Atticus, was busy laying the foundations for a literary culture in Latin. Their choices are reflected in the writings available to read today. The founding of the first public libraries under Octavian is attributed to showing off the new ruler's wealth and culture. Might a work extolling Roman virtues have found its place inside one of them?

To conclude, Titus Pomponius Atticus was not a great man according to the expectations of the Republic but his biographer tried to portray him as an honourable one. This chapter has touched only on a few elements of this intriguing work. The term integrity never appears, but it is present throughout Nepos' portrait of Atticus as a man of traditional values, scrupulous honesty and, above all, principle. Ultimately, this biography results in a confusing portrait that eludes comprehension but provokes debate. It asks important questions about whether integrity poses particular difficulties for those trying to depict it. Here might be another reason behind the enduring popularity of this work. It has been read for centuries due to its simple Latin, perhaps the only simple aspect of it. If nothing else, the *Life of Atticus* suggests that integrity, while it is valued, is far from straightforward.

Recommended reading

First published in 1935, Ronald Syme's *The Roman Revolution* remains an entertaining and highly informative background for this time period. The fullest modern account of Atticus the person can be found in Shackleton Bailey's *Cicero's Letters to Atticus* (1965), 3–59. Rex Stem's 2012 publication, *The Political Biographies of Cornelius Nepos*, provides a good starting point for the controversies surrounding the writings of Nepos, some of which are mentioned in this chapter. An extended discussion on Roman political biography can be found in Tomas Hägg's *The Art of Biography in Antiquity* (2012).

Notes

1 Hägg, *The Art of Biography in Antiquity* (Cambridge: Cambridge University Press, 2012), 189–90 suggests it was a separate work.

2 His apparent inclusion among the biographies of Latin historians is also problematic as the Romans considered government experience necessary to write history, Rawson, *Intellectual Life in the Late Roman Republic* (London: Duckworth, 1985), 91–2.
3 Edwards, *The Politics of Immorality* (Cambridge: Cambridge University Press, 2002), 21.
4 Astin, *Cato the Censor* (Oxford: Clarendon Press, 1978), 177; chapter 8 discusses at length Cato's complex relations with the Greeks.
5 Hägg, *Art of Biography*, 191; Syme, *The Roman Revolution* (Oxford: Oxford University Press, 2002), 62.
6 Shackleton Bailey, *Cicero's Letters to Atticus* (Cambridge: Cambridge University Press, 1965), 59–76 outlines the various theories.
7 Hägg, *Art of Biography*, 188–97; Horsfall, *Cornelius Nepos. A selection, including the lives of Cato and Atticus* (Oxford: Clarendon Press), 8; and Frances Titchener, 'Cornelius Nepos and the Biographical Tradition', Greece & Rome 45 (2003): 90–1.
8 Astin, *Cato Censor*, 264–5 and 102.

25

Henryk Sienkiewicz's *Letters from America*

Creating a speaker with integrity

Anja Burghardt

Sienkiewicz's nineteenth-century documentary, *Letters from America*, gives rise to an image of the reporter who readers take to be trustworthy, and judge to speak with integrity. In what follows, we will examine the textual devices used to create this impression of this particular persona. Although the *Letters* present themselves as non-fiction, there is no line of inference – direct or indirect – between the author (Sienkiewicz) and the narrative voice. Our interest, instead, is in the character of the narrative voice created through the textual devices of the *Letters*. Our study is of the text itself, and how it gives the readers confidence in the reliability and trustworthiness and thus a sense of the integrity of its speaker.

It is perhaps unusual, in thinking about integrity, to stick so resolutely to the text; so I begin with some considerations of what this way of reading means. The second part analyses passages from Sienkiewicz's *Letters,* identifying textual devices that give rise to the image the reader has of the reporter. Located firmly within the nineteenth-century realist tradition, the *Letters* stands at the forefront of what would become the *genre* of 'reportage'; as such, investigating the devices by which it creates a narrative voice we trust – so crucial precisely because of its status as nonfiction – will shed light on the development of the genre of literary documentaries.

The pleasure and appreciation of reading prose fiction depends upon the willing suspension of disbelief. Fictional texts thus have great freedom in deviating from ordinary experience and its norms. The criterion for following the text (and in this sense, for an enjoyable read) is its (internal) plausibility. With factual texts, however, it is different. With factual texts, the claimed ties to reality bring with them certain limits to the freedom of imagination. Indeed, it might be quite a task for the reporter to establish something as plausible, for example, when he tells about a foreign country that is very different from the experience of his readership. One of the peculiar features of the genre of the *Letters from America* (and its comparable versions in other literature, the sketch – *ocherk* – in Russian, the *Reportage* in German or the *reportaż* in Polish literature) is that what is depicted is told in such a way that the readers will vividly imagine the unknown situations, events and locations. We must be able to rely on the narrator not betraying us. Usually we are not aware of this trust in the speaker.[1] In this sense, as with narrators of fictional texts, the integrity of reporters in factual texts is a prerequisite for our willingness to follow them on their 'journeys' in regions we are to imagine. We would stop reading and probably never waste our time again with such texts, if we were to find out that a reporter is not able or willing to inform us about, say, someone's interesting life or an unusual event.

Nowadays this trust in the reporter is often linked to a somewhat serious tone. So if we look at nineteenth-century documentaries, we might at first be astonished about the humour and entertaining style, notable, for instance, in Mark Twain's *A Tramp Abroad* (1880) or – though in quite a different way – in Charles Dickens' *Pictures from Italy* (1846). An entertaining tone is fairly widespread also in other literatures of the nineteenth century. Judging from this kind of depiction the reporter in nineteenth-century literature must manage – at that time usually by means of words alone – to entertain his readers with stories of far-off lands, without losing our confidence that this is, indeed, how it is, or is, indeed, what happened, in that distant land. This balance of entertainment and reliability requires certain writing techniques. Reading these literary texts in order to find out about a foreign place in the world made it necessary for the readers to get an impression of the speaker that would allow them to position him as a person with certain values – and he must do this not by revealing details about himself (his personal history and preferences) or about his daily life, but simply through how he reports on what he sees abroad. To this end, the reporter might, for instance, evaluate, draw comparisons and refer to shared knowledge and experiences. Readers did and do not have to agree with the reporters in every single respect, with their judgements or their political position. But the sense of inhabiting a shared space and having a familiar frame of reference enables the reader to grant or withhold their credulity and confidence in the narrator's report.

Henryk Sienkiewicz's travels over two years (1876–1878) took him through most of the United States, to remote places as well as to main cities. The *Letters* were published in one of the main Polish newspapers and journals during this time, a book publication following in 1879. When Sienkiewicz published his *Letters from America*, the literary reportage (as a genre of documentary) was only in its infancy. The field of factual text genres was not yet fleshed out. At that time in Polish literature we find memoirs, letters, 'chronicles' (*kroniki*), feuilletons, which are not clearly defined in their genre characteristics. Sienkiewicz's *Letters* are now regarded as one of the first examples of what was to become the genre of the reportage, and in this sense they became a paradigm of it. With a view to the issue of integrity, in Sienkiewicz's *Letters* the speaker's image as a reporter is more important than his image as a traveller. To some degree the field of realist (and naturalist) literature as well as newspaper and journal publication in the second half of the nineteenth century safeguards against suspicion of the reporter's reliability anyway. Nevertheless, the urge for authenticity (which is necessary for us to believe him) requires the reporter to give fair accounts of situations as well as of the society in the remote country, and to make moral judgements. In all that he shines through as a person.

The difficulty lies in the fact that the reader usually has nothing by which to judge the 'fairness' of the accounts except the reporter's words. Demonstrating consideration for the reader is one thing that establishes the reporter's integrity; this is done through directly addressing the reader, and by appealing to shared knowledge in reporting unfamiliar things, thus marking out common ground between reporter and reader. The reporter must also establish that he was, in fact, on this foreign journey, which might be done by including explicit and implicit references to places, or through conveying a sense of time passing in the course of the travels. Variations in tone, depending on the content, play an important role in that his sense of appropriateness comes through. Seeing his ability to distance himself, for example, by means of humour and irony, to argue for his position if necessary and to convey his 'sources' give rise to his integrity. And finally in positioning himself against commonly held views, when he holds them unfair, shows his courage and that he cannot deviate from certain principles of justice.

The book version of Sienkiewicz's journey to America is preceded by an introduction in which the reporter introduces himself as 'a child of his times'. This self-description goes along with various quotes of well-known Polish authors (mostly of romanticism), and – as he himself is working for the press – about contemporary authors and journalists (most prominently Bolesław Prus). In the course of this introduction we get the impression of a more or less well-educated person (in addition to references to antiquity, he interjects Latin and French phrases) with a good sense of humour. But at times he appears somewhat silly:

> When our running clock struck one p.m., I was still sitting at the very same place and thinking: to travel or not to travel? – like Hamlet with his: 'to be or not to be'. But if I don't travel, what will I do then? Will I burn the midnight oil with writing? ... But in America I can write as well. What is more, the doctor advised me not to write at night. But since in America the night will come precisely when it is day here, writing in America during the night is writing in Europe at day time, or: to travel to America means to fulfill the commands of one's doctor. (9)[2]

And he concludes that staying in Warsaw is pretty senseless: he might get married, a possibility that he sets aside with a jesting reference to the Biblical Eve and to the Ancient Diotima.

This might not appear an ideal attitude for someone who is to give a serious and faithful report about America. However, once he has set upon his journey, and even more once he has arrived in America, a change of tone becomes prominent. As long as he tells about the familiar realm, then, he has the freedom to mostly entertain his readers. At the same time the entertaining opening is a promise to the readers they he will not bore them.

Another feature that adds to our sense of the narrator's integrity is his candour. In his report of the crossing from Liverpool to New York, he concentrates on his fellow travellers. Various conversations are given (partly in direct quotes), of course, some details about the ship, the meals and his troubles with English, which he admits knowing only very poorly. (Over the two years he will overcome these difficulties.) For the time being, he relies on Polish fellow travellers who are fluent in both languages, or meets with persons who know French so that his lack of English does not appear as a hindrance to the accuracy and quality of his account. The fact that he speaks openly about the languages makes him appear trustworthy.

Also, in laying open his sources of knowledge and his preferences, his integrity and trustworthiness are underlined in various other situations: at the beginning, for instance, he points out that he is not interested in reading about the country, but wants to see how people act, and observe as much of the society as he can (very much in accordance with his time, where empirical knowledge is what is valued highly, and with the genre of documentary, for which first-hand accounts are preferable). Time and again he reports what he is told by others, but for the most part he describes his travels, and narrates impressions of towns, areas and encounters with others.

In his reflections and arguments also, he appears as a responsible person. Sometimes he does not come to a conclusion about what to think of a given phenomenon – for instance, of the many different ethnicities in America who do not seem to build a people (*naród*). That he states his uncertainty openly shows him as someone who is cautious in his judgements.

On the whole, the changes of tone appear as an important source for our trust in him: for here he indicates both his awareness of the readers and his sense of an appropriate way of conveying his experiences, and in this sense displays a genuine desire to communicate and share his experiences with the readers. For instance, his story of a storm has almost slapstick elements:

> I went on deck. The day was dreary, grey and windy. The seagulls flung themselves into the wind, the waves were unrestrained. It was difficult to stand on one's feet. [...] Near the steps I meet the physician with red sideburns, who leans over me and – in order to shout over the storm – screams: 'Comment ça va, monsieur?'
> I feel so awful that I not only don't answer him, but also cannot reach the stair. [...] 'Look at me!', calls the physician, 'I don't hold on to anything, and I can now stroll on deck.'
> 'How?' I groan, 'Do you not fall down?'
> 'Je suis trop vieux marin pou cela!' he answers. And in the same moment I see his legs at that place, where his head has just been, which proves to me that he can not only stroll but also turn somersaults. (51)

A further report of the storm during the night follows. The reporter tells about the (mostly hopeless) attempts to go on deck again, about the monotonous sailors' calls 'Ooo – ho!', the still worsening weather and so on. A similarly vivid account is given for the (not very tranquil) night:

> But the whole night was stormy. At times we had to hold onto something, in order not to fall out of the drawer-like berths. The ship rolled so strongly that from time to time we found ourselves in our beds in a standing position, sometimes on our feet, sometimes – worse – on our heads. I noticed the fur coat, which hung on the wall opposite to my bed, all of a sudden floating directly over me. Our suitcases and shoes flew over the floor, along the walls and banged against the partitions. (53)

What kind of person emerges from these descriptions? The reporter seems to have a good sense of humour – at least in retrospect. More importantly with respect to issues of trustworthiness, the very accuracy in the detailed description, and the vivid depiction of how far usual movements can get out of control on a ship underline the fact that he was an eyewitness to such an incredible storm. The authenticity of his report is stressed by direct quotes of other passengers (or their inability to answer). In addition he stresses that this was an entirely new experience, when he mentions that until that moment he could not believe that waves could be high as houses. The humorous tone is entertaining, but it does not cut against the reporter's trustworthiness.

In contrast to these entertaining moments, the tone is absolutely serious in many passages.

> After about half an hour, the train began to move again. The route, ascending continuously, runs through a region without any woods. For we were approaching the huge plateau, which covers the whole middle part of the United States and which is covered by steppe, or as it is called here, the prairie. [...] Here and there in the moonlight I recognized corn fields, on which the high, black and withered stalks from the last year towered sadly. The further we hurried west, the more desolate the land was. [...] Also from the people, who got on the train, it was noticeable that we had left behind the borders of civilization. Instead of elegantly dressed gentlemen, the train was now filled with bearded characters in worn-out clothes, with filthy bundles and a revolver at their belts. Conversations were loud and vivacious; now and then curses were audible. Thick tobacco smoke rose to the ceiling. The doors were opened by strong hands and slammed again with a crash. (103)

The fairly precise reference to the time and the reference to the moonlight, which stresses that time passes by, underlines that he himself experienced the situations. Citing the name of the landscape (prairie) together with some impressive single details (e. g., single stalks of corn), into which he inscribes the impression he got from the region, have a similar effect. And here in his description of the passengers he maintains the standpoint of an observer, who does not engage with the persons around him. This is stressed in particular by concentrating on the sound of the doors, opened by 'strong hands' (not a particular person), the smoke and so on.

The serious tone prevails also in his report about the further travel, where he notices that astonishingly many people are there, and finally comes to know from another passenger (who speaks French) that they are gold diggers or, rather, simply adventurers.

Since the Sioux are the owners of this land, heavy fights have taken place as he knows from the news, and more are to be expected in future. The following longer narration about the situation of the American Indians in the United States concludes by questioning the notion of civilization and criticizing how the Indians are treated in the United States:

> In short, this brave, though wild, race will be extinguished mercilessly throughout the States. [The Indians] cannot accept the civilization, which presents itself in its worst form to them anyway, and they are not willing to do so, and thus this civilization rubs them out from the earth's surface equally mercilessly and brutally. [...] (104)

Into his account of the Native Americans he intertwines a criticism of the press: instead of informing the gold diggers and trying to calm them as they might, newspaper reports often exaggerate and thus goad on the hatred against the Indians. In addition, their stories often resemble a novel rather than a report. And he concludes with the comment that he is only certain about that which 'he has seen with his own eyes' (*patrzyłem własnymi oczyma*, 106), namely the circumstances that are filled with passions and have given rise to the kind of stories he has just re-told. His comments on the events and his critical evaluation of the press – his own profession – show him as an attentive and careful observer, which makes him appear all the more trustworthy. This is another concrete instance of the reporter arguing for his position where he can and, where he can come to no clear judgement, admitting this and reflecting on competing positions.

A number of devices that give rise to a trustworthy person come together in the reporter's concluding narration about the Sioux after he had met a small group of them at a railway station. Together with the French passenger, who knows 'English, the language of the Sioux and God knows which else' (108), he comes to talk to them, and the main focus of the encounter lies on the conversation. So here we have one more example of direct quotations, which serve as a marker of the documentary status. He contrasts the Native Americans briefly with those one imagines after reading James Fenimore Cooper (among others), a means of suggesting to his readers that they might well share the same images, and more broadly that they have the same cultural background. He thus gives them good reasons to trust his depictions and in a sense also him as a person. In addition he thus invites them to come to more realistic pictures of Native Americans. On the whole, the reporter does not go for sensationalist versions of things. This balanced approach inspires something beyond trust in his accuracy: it is more trust in his integrity in how he sees and experiences the world. Similarly and throughout his reports he reveals an unprejudiced and morally alert character in his selection of what to narrate. When he sometimes makes explicit such choices, he draws the readers' attention to this aspect of his work, which, in turn gives rise to the impression that he does not wish to surreptitiously influence his audience.

When it comes to describing the Native Americans he pays attention mostly to their appearance and dresses; he makes no claims on their character, let alone generalizing comments on 'the Indians'. Contrast these to the persons in the train, a little earlier (cited above): they do not gain shape as persons, but are in some way reduced to a number of persons who create a fairly unpleasant atmosphere on the train. In that this implicit judgement is consistent with what the reporter states explicitly, the suggested sense of him is that of a coherent person. The reporter gives a far more detailed account of the reaction of his fellow travellers, who reproach the reporter and his translator for talking to the Native Americans, before they even re-board the train. As the other passengers continue to speak only of this as the journey progresses, the speaker summarizes this with a remark that in the borderlands the extent of hatred against the Indians is incredible. In the following reflection on 'how this civilization presents itself to the Indians' (110) he shows himself in his argument. His reasons are well grounded. Apart from his unprejudiced role – integrity as a reporter – his personal integrity here comes to the fore in that he maintains both his distanced consideration and positions himself against the general sentiment, which is inflamed, against the many rough and strong hands. The force of his persuasion lies in the fact that his conclusion rests on what he has just seen and experienced. Seeing his serious reflections one might well be willing to agree with him, or otherwise he thereby enables the readers to come to their own conclusions.

Since we come to know the reporter in Sienkiewicz's *Letters* mostly in his own words (and not from descriptions given, for example, by an external speaker), we have to create our own image of him from the way he speaks, what he speaks about and – something that is rather prominent in the *Letters* – his evaluations, implicit as well as explicit. As I have suggested, if we take together these aspects, the reporter gains a fairly clear shape in the course of his reports.

Reading nineteenth-century documentaries like his with all their entertainment and humour might make us rethink current notions of what accounts of 'reality' need. Current notions tend to link sincerity and reliability in documentaries to seriousness and something like neutrality (often presenting itself as objectivity). In contrast, Sienkiewicz's *Letters* as well as other writings of the time suggest that the means of showing a speaker's integrity and thus offering reliable accounts are much broader and manifold.

Recommended reading

A translation of Sienkiewicz's documentaries is available in an edition by Charles Morley, *Portrait of America: Letters of Henry Sienkiewicz* (New York: Columbia University Press, 1959). Readers looking for Sienkiewicz's 'America fiction' can find a selection in Marion Moore Coleman's edition: Henryk Sienkiewicz, *Western Septet: Seven Stories of the American West* (Cheshire: Cherry Hill Books, 1973). An introduction and overview of Polish literature, marvellously written, as one expects from a Nobel Prize winner of literature, is Czesław Miłosz, *The History of Polish Literature* (Berkeley: University of California Press, 1983). The section on Sienkiewicz also includes a short biography. For literary criticism, Jonathan D. Culler, *The Literary in Theory* (Stanford: Stanford University Press, 2007) gives a concise and very rich introduction. An approach on the basis of an author's experience, which at times might be almost as entertaining as his novels, can be read with David Lodge, *The Art of Fiction: Illustrated from Classic to Modern Texts* (London: Secker & Warburg, 1992).

Notes

1 In fictional texts we might be made aware of it in the case of the so-called unreliable narrator, one who turns out to tell us this, that or the other which is not 'true' (in the fictional world), for example because

he keeps contradicting himself or his world view becomes continuously stranger, he is mad and the like. In these cases part of the joy of reading lies in that all of a sudden (or slowly) we come to understand that what is at stake is precisely a very odd attitude towards the world or a very strange mindset. There is not really a parallel to unreliable narrators for documentaries.

2 Henryk Sienkiewicz, *Listy z podróży do Ameryki* [Letters from the Journey to America], ed. Jerzy Jaworowski (Warszawa: Państwowy Instytut Wydawniczy, 1986).

26

Virginia Woolf

'Writing without hate, without bitterness, without fear, without protest, without preaching': Integrity and the woman writer in *A Room of One's Own*

Lorraine Sim

'It was thus that I found myself walking with extreme rapidity across a grass plot. Instantly a man's figure rose to intercept me … he was a Beadle; I was a woman. This was the turf; there was the path. Only the Fellows and Scholars are allowed here; the gravel is the place for me … and though turf is better walking than gravel, no very great harm was done. The only charge I could bring against the Fellows and Scholars of whatever the college might happen to be was that in protection of their turf, which has been rolled for 300 years in succession, they had sent my little fish into hiding.'[1]

This passage from Virginia Woolf's 1929 essay *A Room of One's Own* describes the female narrator's experience of being told by a Beadle at a fictive university in England named 'Oxbridge' that she is not permitted to walk on the grass (4). When she later attempts to enter the university library to undertake research on her assigned topic of 'women and fiction', she is informed that 'ladies are only admitted to the library if accompanied by a Fellow of the College or furnished with a letter of introduction' (7). What is instructive about this passage for an exploration of integrity, is the narrator's observation that the 'only charge' she could make against the 'Fellows' and 'Scholars' is that this act of exclusion and protectionism 'sent [her] little fish into hiding'. That 'fish' was the unformed 'thought' on the topic of women and fiction that had suddenly motivated her to action – to walk rapidly across the grass plot (5). As *A Room of One's Own* makes clear, contrary to the narrator's deliberate understatement, a great deal of harm has been caused by such acts of patriarchal admonishment and exclusion, be the exclusion related to the realm of spaces (lawns and libraries), literature or politics. As the following discussion will elaborate, for Woolf artistic integrity – and quite often personal integrity – is inextricably connected to issues of gender, patriarchy and power.

A Room of One's Own was developed from two lectures that Woolf presented at Newnham College and Girton College, Cambridge, in October 1928.[2] Briefed with the task of presenting a paper on 'women and fiction', *A Room* comprised Woolf's influential feminist critique of patriarchy and the mechanisms by which it had prevented women from developing a literary tradition of their own and, thereby, the opportunity to provide 'a supplement' to the 'lop-sided' history that has comprised the Western literary and intellectual tradition (41). In the essay Woolf argues that in addition to encouragement and education, women require basic material things such as an independent income and a room of their own in order to write. The question of 'women and fiction' quickly morphs into questions about gender inequality and the 'effect [of] poverty on fiction' and creativity (23). According to the narrator, '[t]he lamp in the spine does not light on beef and prunes' – the frugal dinner she shared with students at a fictional women's college that evening (16).[3]

In *A Room of One's Own* Woolf broaches the topic of integrity in relation to the work of art and the writer and this discussion is connected to her broader meditations on sexual difference and patriarchy. As Woolf outlines in the first chapters of the essay, prior to the nineteenth century there was no tradition of women's writing in Britain or Europe because so few women were given the encouragement or means to write. It was from the nineteenth century that women writers started to forge their own literary traditions and began the task of representing the previously unrecorded landscape of women's lives and experience. But for the few women during the seventeenth to the nineteenth centuries who did, and against numerous odds, write, much of that work according to Woolf was compromised by their 'personal grievance[s]' at the institution of patriarchy itself (66). Too often, she suggests, anger, frustration, fear and resentment get in the way of the woman writer's creative voice and vision. This is the fault she finds with the work of the seventeenth-century poet, Lady Winchilsea, whose mind is 'harassed and distracted with hates and grievances' at the position of women in society, grievances which hamper her at times clear capacity to issue words of 'pure poetry' (54). Woolf claims that the novels of Charlotte Brontë suffer for the same reason; 'she will never get her genius expressed whole and entire. Her books will be deformed and twisted ... She will write of herself where she should write of her characters. She is at war with her lot' (63).

Thus, throughout the early chapters of *A Room*, Woolf maintains that the personal grievances borne from the inequalities and injustices of patriarchy presented a significant obstacle to the integrity of the woman writer: it limited her capacity to express 'her genius ... whole and entire' (63) and write with a mind that was 'incandescent' (51) and calm, not frustrated and, understandably, enraged. If T. S. Eliot maintained in his influential essay 'Tradition and the Individual Talent' (1920) that good poetry depends upon 'impersonality' and 'not the turning loose of emotion, but an escape from emotion', Woolf reminds us that this was a much more difficult task for the woman writer who in the past had neither tradition, encouragement, education or practical means to support her efforts.[4] Therefore, in *A Room* Woolf contends that artistic integrity has historically been a more difficult thing for the woman writer to realize because she has had so many more grievances, as well as practical impediments, confronting her writing practice. In that essay and others dealing with the topic of women and writing she claims that only Jane Austen and Emily Brontë managed to write without their work being negatively impacted by their personal frustrations at the system of which they were a part: 'That, perhaps, was the chief miracle about it. Here was a woman [Jane Austen] about the year 1800 writing without hate, without bitterness, without fear, without protest, without preaching' (61). Far from suggesting that women writers should not address the social and political conditions that shape their reality (Woolf's fiction deals with all manner of such issues), or that Woolf concurs with Eliot's particular theory of 'impersonality', she does suggest that the ego or 'I' of the writer is a risk to the integrity of the work.

Later in chapter four, Woolf turns to the idea of integrity and the novel and again introduces the question of sexual difference but in more positive and generative terms. Using Leo Tolstoy's novel *War and Peace* as an example, the narrator wonders what it is that makes some novels 'hold [...] together' and endure and contends it is because they have 'integrity' (65). Here, integrity relates to both the unity of the work of art and its capacity to present life or some aspect of it in a way that seems true and convincing to the reader:

> [I]t has nothing to do with paying one's bills or behaving honourably in an emergency. What one means by integrity, in the case of the novelist, is the conviction that he gives one that this is the truth. Yes, one feels, I should never have thought that this could be so; I have never known people behaving like that. But you have convinced me that so it is, so it happens. (65)

Coinciding with Woolf's broader view of truth and reality as 'various',[5] 'erratic [and] very undependable' (99) – not immutable and objective – here she describes a dynamic relationship between the reader, the novel and 'truth'. Woolf goes on to suggest that integrity might depend on a correspondence between life as it is presented in the novel and as the reader believes it – or more mysteriously, unconsciously knows it – to be. If 'Nature, in her most irrational mood, has traced in invisible ink on the walls of the mind a premonition which these great artists confirm', it is a novel's capacity to make the reader recognize '[b]ut this is what I have always felt and known and desired!' that is the mark of its integrity (65–6). If the novel is both life and not life – bearing a 'correspondence' to it (67) but at the same time a 'looking-glass likeness' containing 'simplifications and distortions innumerable' (64) – Woolf then introduces the question of whether 'her sex' would 'in any way interfere with the integrity of a woman novelist' (66). Returning to the topic of 'personal grievance' discussed above, Woolf then moves on to the more generative and perhaps more fundamental issue of values and the novel (66). If the novel bears a correspondence to real life, the 'values' of the novel are, she suggests, 'to some extent those of real life' (67). And it is the difference in systems of value that are necessarily part and parcel of different gendered experiences that Woolf believes the woman writer must honour in order to maintain her artistic integrity:

> But it is obvious that the values of women differ very often from the values which have been made by the other sex ... Yet it is the masculine values that prevail. Speaking crudely, football and sport are 'important'; the worship of fashion, the buying of clothes 'trivial'. And these values are inevitably transferred from life to fiction. This is an important book, the critic assumes, because it deals with war. This is an insignificant book because it deals with the feelings of women in a drawing-room. A scene in a battle-field is more important than a scene in a shop – everywhere and much more subtly the difference of value persists. (67)

This argument sets up one of the most crucial points in Woolf's discussion of the woman writer and artistic integrity in *A Room of One's Own*. Historically, too often the woman writer 'had altered her values in deference to the opinion of others' (67). Woolf exhorts her readers and any future female writers therein to be courageous and remain true to their values and to their vision of what she terms in the 1924 essay 'Character in Fiction', 'life itself'.[6] Throughout her career Woolf endeavoured to meet this responsibility; that is, to interrogate scales of value – what is deemed 'trivial' and what 'important'. She achieves this in her fiction by, among other things, breaking with established literary conventions, maintaining a fidelity to the experience of ordinary people ('Mrs Brown', the 'old lady in the corner opposite')[7] and through representing the complexity and richness of daily life.[8] Similarly, her essays, which span a broad range of topical issues of the day, are addressed not to the literary critic or specialist but to the 'common reader'. In *A Room of One's Own* Woolf presents the novel and literature more broadly as the space within which the present and future woman writer can undertake a reevaluation of values and make the reader aware of different perspectives and 'truths' that lie currently unilluminated in the walls of the mind. To have achieved this in the nineteenth century required, as she observes, enormous courage and tenacity:

> But how impossible it must have been for them not to budge either to the right or to the left. What genius, what integrity it must have required in face of all that criticism, in the midst of that purely patriarchal society, to hold fast to the thing as they saw it without shrinking. Only Jane Austen did it and Emily Brontë ... Of all the thousand women who wrote novels then, they alone entirely ignored the perpetual admonitions of the eternal pedagogue – write this, think that. (67–8)

Thus, in *A Room* Woolf identifies the many impediments that patriarchy has imposed on the woman writer – impediments that were institutional (education), material (money, space), psychological (lack of encouragement) and emotional (anger, fear). Such obstacles made the ideal of artistic integrity – thinking of 'things in themselves' and 'be[ing] oneself' (100) – harder for a woman writer to realize. In addition to resisting the temptation to use literature as a platform for dogmatism or the expression of personal frustrations, the woman writer must never conciliate her values or her vision of life to the 'perpetual admonitions of the eternal pedagogue', that is, she must not be intimidated and thereby allow her 'little fish to go into hiding'.

In her critique, Woolf repeatedly presents egotism – the 'desire for self-assertion' – as a key impediment to integrity. In chapter six of *A Room*, following her comments on the idea of the 'androgynous mind' (that is, of masculine and feminine elements coexisting in the mind and how their balance might relate to artistic creation), the narrator turns her attention to contemporary novels written by men. She selects a novel by a contemporary writer, 'Mr A', and is soon struck while reading by 'a shadow shaped something like the letter "I"' which seemed to impress itself forcefully upon every page (89–90). This 'I' makes it impossible 'to catch a glimpse of the landscape behind it': 'Whether that was indeed a tree or a woman walking I was not quite sure. Back one was always hailed to the letter "I"' (90). The 'I' that is the author's self-assertion here functions as an 'obstacle' and 'impediment' to the 'fountain of creative energy', just as it had for some of the nineteenth-century women writers Woolf had discussed earlier in the essay (90). Woolf surmises that this tendency to self-assertion in the work of some contemporary male writers is perhaps a response to women's Suffrage: 'He is protesting against the equality of the other sex by asserting his own superiority. He is therefore impeded and inhibited and self-conscious' (91).

This example resonates with many instances in Woolf's fiction and non-fiction in which the assertion of the self and the imposition of the 'I' at the expense of the Other functions as a barrier to integrity and the ethical life more generally: 'Possibly when [Professor von X.] insisted a little too emphatically [in his 'monumental work entitled *The Mental, Moral, and Physical Inferiority of the Female Sex*'] upon the inferiority of women, he was concerned not with their inferiority, but with his own superiority' (31, 28). If, since the time of the Greeks, personal integrity has been understood to depend upon a unity of mind or character, a shoring up of the 'I', Woolf, instead, foregrounds a model of integrity that must remain other-oriented, whether that Other be the novel one is writing or the people with whom one lives in proximity.

In her unfinished memoir *A Sketch of the Past*, Woolf reflects upon her father, the philosopher and literary critic Leslie Stephen, and how his many admirable attributes were often overshadowed in his personal life by his indomitable egotism. While admiring his intelligence and 'integrity', and 'his dignity and sanity in the larger affairs', these, she recalls, were 'so often covered up by his irritations and vanities and egotisms'.[9] Like the character Mr Ramsay in *To the Lighthouse*, who was modelled on Woolf's father, Leslie Stephen's egotism and his need for self-assertion and female sympathy had a very damaging effect on his family relationships. Her father's self-centred and sometimes tyrannical behaviour led Woolf to this conclusion:

> From it all I gathered one obstinate and enduring conception; that nothing is so much to be dreaded as egotism. Nothing so cruelly hurts the person himself; nothing so wounds those who are forced into contact with it.[10]

Woolf explores this idea in her fifth novel, *To the Lighthouse*. In the opening scene of the novel, the young James Ramsay is thrilled at the prospect of travelling out to the lighthouse by sailboat the following morning, only to be dashed by his father's assertion 'it won't be fine' and that the trip must be postponed.[11] The narrator reflects thus:

> What he said was true. It was always true. He was incapable of untruth; never tampered with a fact; never altered a disagreeable word to suit the pleasure or convenience of any mortal being, least of all his own children.[12]

This scene further exemplifies how, for Woolf, egotism can serve as a limiting case for integrity. James never forgets this moment and he never forgives his father for the emotional violence his self-assertion brings to bear on his family.

Throughout her reflections on integrity – be it artistic, intellectual or personal integrity – Woolf believes that it requires a fidelity to one's values and vision of 'life', but cannot be corrupted or shadowed by the effects of egotism and self-assertion. For Woolf, integrity cannot entail the suppression of the Other: it must be realized without the need to send another's 'little fish' – be it their thoughts or their values or their desires – into hiding, or, worse still, into silence.

Recommended reading

A Room of One's Own (1929) is Woolf's most famous and influential critique of patriarchy in which she discusses – among other topics – women and education, women and writing, and artistic integrity. Woolf's unfinished memoir, *A Sketch of the Past* (in *Moments of Being*, 1985), provides fascinating insight into some of the keystones of Woolf's philosophical thought including her theory of 'moments of being' (a version of the modernist epiphany), writing and trauma, the role of the writer/artist in society, and her philosophy of a 'pattern'. The memoir offers a detailed account of her childhood and family life growing up in late Victorian England, and the impact of patriarchal society and culture on Woolf's thought and life. In 'Character in Fiction' (*The Essays of Virginia Woolf*, 1998) Woolf discusses her concept of the modern novel, its distinction from conventional novels of the period ('Edwardian' novels), and the central importance of character to modern fiction. Her account in that essay of character, and the task of faithfully conveying character, offers insight into her ideas about the modern writer, modernist aesthetics, integrity and responsibility.

Notes

1 Virginia Woolf, *A Room of One's Own*, in *A Room of One's Own and Three Guineas*, ed. and Intro. Michèle Barrett (London: Penguin, 1993), 5. All subsequent references to this text will be cited in the essay.
2 See Woolf's note at the start of *A Room*, 3, and Barrett's introduction, xviii–xix.
3 This dinner is contrasted with the lavish lunch that the narrator had at 'Oxbridge' University earlier that day, 9–10.
4 T. S. Eliot, 'Tradition and the Individual Talent', in *The Waste Land, T. S. Eliot*, ed. Michael North (New York: W. W. Norton, 2001), 119. Woolf comments in *A Room* that more deleterious than a lack of encouragement was the fact that nineteenth-century women writers 'had no tradition behind them ... For we think back through our mothers if we are women', 69. This was a significant counterpoint to Eliot's contention in 'Tradition and the Individual Talent' regarding the central importance of the Western literary tradition and the 'historical sense' to the modern poet/writer, a view that failed to recognize that the 'tradition' he described was androcentric, Eurocentric and, as Woolf notes, exclusive; see 'Tradition', 115.
5 Virginia Woolf, 'On Not Knowing Greek' (1925), in *The Essays of Virginia Woolf*, vol. 4, ed. Andrew McNeillie (Orlando: Harcourt, 1994), 46.
6 Virginia Woolf, 'Character in Fiction' (1924), in *The Essays of Virginia Woolf*, vol. 3, ed. Andrew McNeillie (San Diego: Harcourt, 1998), 436.
7 Woolf, 'Character in Fiction', 425.
8 Ibid., 435–6; see Lorraine Sim, *Virginia Woolf: The Patterns of Ordinary Experience* (Farnham: Ashgate, 2010).

9 Virginia Woolf, 'A Sketch of the Past', in *Moments of Being: A Collection of Autobiographical Writing*, ed. Jeanne Schulkind, 2nd ed. (San Diego: Harcourt, 1985), 111, 142.

10 Woolf, *A Sketch*, 146–7.

11 Virginia Woolf, *To the Lighthouse*, ed. Stella McNichol, Intro. Hermione Lee (London: Penguin, 1992), 8.

12 Woolf, *Lighthouse*, 8.

AFTERWORD

The purpose of this portrait gallery was to clarify our thinking about integrity, but it was not to simplify it. On the contrary, by staying close to the 'rough ground', as Wittgenstein called it, integrity appears in this volume in as many guises as there are persons or structures of integrity depicted. Each essay illuminates some dimension to integrity, or casts familiar features of integrity into new light, but none seeks to be the final word or to stand as the archetype. A reader will also discover among these portraits novel forms of failure of integrity – in Confucius' village worthies, in Anscombe's hypocrisy of the false standard – pernicious precisely because of the way they adopt the clothing of integrity without the substance. These are not the forms of hypocrisy most commonly called out, but they might be the more prevalent and damaging to honest discourse.

Certain *motifs* do recur: a love of truth, and honesty about and with oneself, that does not calculate the risks and benefits of truthfulness (Boethius, Gandhi, Sher-Gil); an unwavering attention away from oneself and concerns of pride and petty vanity (Job, Woolf); a willingness to be socially provocative, even fatally so, if necessary (Antigone, the Tolstoyans). It is no surprise to see that personal integrity and integrity of the social world may come into tension with one another; but it is eye-opening to see that this happens in a different way in each of the portraits in which it arises (Arendt, Anansi, 'Albert', Abai, Lambert Strether, Huang Zongxi). Simple cases of 'dirty hands' do not really come up. Even in those cases of conspicuous integrity, where the notion of the 'isolated moral actor' might have seemed most apt, these portraits go beyond the individual and explore integrity as something that is negotiated and challenged within institutions and in society at large. There are as many lives of integrity as there are political and historical contexts in which a life can be lived.

If integrity is an especially elusive concept to articulate, this is in part because it intersects centrally and inescapably with many other virtues and concerns. Inadequate though a definition of courage as 'standing firm in the face of pain and loss' may be, it is at least a start. Temperance is about handling pleasures well, courage is about handling pains well, says Aristotle. But it would be a greater challenge to say what integrity is *about*, even as a first stab. While we can shoehorn the notion into many specific definitions (steadfastness, unity, consistency) fitting at least some of the phenomena, our willingness to grant or withhold a claim to integrity seems to hang to an unusually high degree on our estimation of other virtues and values (consider Lord Guan).

Integrity worth remarking on is not simply sticking to one's own projects and principles, nor 'moral rectitude plus courage under pressure'. Such rectitude cannot be thoughtless (Rāma); and these projects must themselves be good. Indeed, there may be only one such 'project', a commitment to the Good (Boethius, Weil, Gandhi), perhaps in some particular guise or another, as the situation demands (Dahlmann and Waitz, Sher-Gil). At least, it seems we grant or withhold the commendation of 'integrity' according to whether we judge someone to have got the real thing in hand, not according to whether we judge them to have acted according to their own personal conception of the good, however sincerely they believe that conception. Consider the ambiguity of Atticus' integrity, as depicted by Nepos, or the terms on which the Cookes' and Kayes' portraits must be accepted in order to do their intended work. It is where we judge someone to be treating something as having more or less real value than we judge it to have that we say 'fanatic', 'charlatan', 'bloody-minded' (Winstanley, Gandhi, Weil), 'impostor', 'pedant', 'short-sighted' (Atticus, Waitz, Ella Baker).

This means that there is an element of moral luck in integrity. If you have made a mistake about whether your overriding good is, in fact, good, then you turn out to be a madman or a charlatan or a monster, after all. But this also means there is a non-accidental connection between integrity, humility, thoughtfulness, and self-awareness (as the cases of Socrates and Lord Guan, Rāma and Lambert Strether, all in their different ways show) – no claim can be laid to integrity where there is no appropriate caution and self-awareness about the possibilities and dangers of getting it wrong.

The moral philosopher Philippa Foot once remarked that 'moral' is the superlative of 'serious'. Her observation is especially pertinent to this collection. The concept 'integrity' seems most fitting, most apt, when individuals are grappling with what is really – objectively, clearly, strikingly – of serious importance. This is perhaps why it is most easily identified when an individual finds herself in an especially serious predicament. When 'moral' is the superlative of 'serious' it concerns not what is serious for the individual but what is serious for *us* (Winstanley, Bamba, Socrates, *Letters...*, Cookes & Kayes). So when we are confused about whether what we have is an instance of integrity or madness, we may, in fact, be confused about what matters to us – about how we want to live together and what we value in our communities and institutions. We see this – or something like it – in the portrait of Dahlmann and Waitz, or Ella Baker, or Atticus. We get the most extreme cases when communities are in transition or disagreement or upheaval on the question: How should we live? What really matters? Here what someone does can be an invitation to others to *see this as important*. But invitations can be rejected. And even when things are fairly stable, the complexity of human relations offers up ample opportunity for an individual to be serious.

Whatever constancy may have to do with integrity, it is not an obtuse insistence that one's principles must be applied come what may. The world does, and ought to, change and this throws the applicability of principles into constant question. It is all very well to insist on maintaining one's devotion to God, for instance; but what that means under circumstances of oppression, occupation or state-sanctioned injustice remains open to be rediscovered anew in each new complex set of circumstances. Complicity and selling out must at all costs be avoided. Yet doing so in an inconstant world, while staying true to principles and committed to goodness, requires openness and imagination (Antigone, Bamba, Gandhi, Weil).

Such an attitude of attentive flexibility is also required in the face of the world's complexity. For all that integrity demands perfection, it is also clear-eyed about the world and even creative about the possibilities for manifesting integrity in action. Uncompromising insistence on perfection in an imperfect world tends to become insensitive to the harm it causes others. It may lead one to despair of acting altogether, preferring, instead, some form of 'inner exile' – a retreat to one's personal purity in the face of circumstances where no perfect action is possible. But while the false hypocrisy of the ideal standard (Anscombe) is perhaps one we are all tempted by on occasion, it is striking how little the figures depicted here are focused on *purity*. Instead, we see over and over a fierce commitment to applying one's principles in action – even when that action may be imperfect, and come at great personal cost.

Those who get closest to integrity avoid both the cynical abdication of responsibility to act by appeal to a false standard of perfection, and the obtuse application of principles to circumstances without creative regard for what *these* particular circumstances require. Integrity, we might say, demands as much attention to the complex and changing circumstances of the world and the people in it, as it demands commitment to the truth about how that world might be better than it is. The integration integrity aims at, and perhaps sometimes achieves, does justice to the larger truth and to particular persons and situations, without compromising either.

Integrity seems to combine, then, an attentiveness to particular persons and circumstances, and a determination to engage – to act or be in the world in such a way as to manifest some kind of good of utmost significance. Once we notice this, we might then begin also to notice just how frequently *love* emerges in these portraits, in some form or another. The relevance of love to integrity is easy to overlook if our central associations with the latter are consistency, inflexibility, being true to one's self or one's projects. But it would not have surprised Simone Weil or Boethius, who explicitly recognize a deep affinity between attention, love and ethics. Naturally, whatever Baker and Woolf, Bamba, Abai and even Huang Zongxi had, and Rāma or the village worthies lack, is not precisely the same thing. But the former share qualities of unsentimental attention to others, of care and a spirit of generosity. These aspects of care do not appear, in these portraits, as external components, merely riding alongside integrity, responsible perhaps for our inclination to consider these people 'decent persons' in a quite generic way. They seem, rather, to be intimately linked to integrity's simultaneous concern for truth about goodness and honesty about the world, and to sustaining relations of the persons in it.

Sher-Gil, Antigone, Albert, Arendt and the constructed narrator of Sienkiewicz's *Letters from America*, all in their different ways are concerned with others, and their actions expressing integrity are a manifestation of their care. Integrity, in this collection at least, seems in the end to involve an attempt to be honest about the nature of the concrete and social world around us, and to remain true to that in one's action. While keeping the good and love of truth firmly in view, that same love of truth demands that we pay attention to what is right before us – lack of attention is a recurring theme in failures of integrity; its presence is a recurring feature of those who get closest. Attending and describing – what scholars, artists, writers do – is, as Iris Murdoch observed, an act of love and of justice; and it can be a contribution to the communal task of making a world in which we can live with integrity.

Charlotte Alston, Amber Carpenter, Rachael Wiseman

INDEX

academic integrity 1, 207–15, 212, 223
  academic virtues 208, 213
  Hannah Arendt on 219
  in history of scholarship 208–9
  national identity 208–9
  politics 211–12, 221–2
  Waitz and Dahlman as models of 213
action, collective 164, 170, 284
  vita activa 218, 221
Addams, Jane 134–5
Akan society (Ghana) 227–8
'Albert' (banker) 6, 73–81
Ali, Asaf 126
Ānandavardhana (Ānanda) 39
Anansi the Spider 9, 227–34
  tales of 230–3
Anscombe, G. E. M. 6–7, 111–19
  false hypocrisy of the ideal standard 113, 111–19, 281, 283–4
  Oxford moral philosophy 115
  'turning counsels into principles' 113–19
anti-colonialism 8
Antigone 5, 45–52
  Antigone in Ferguson (Missouri) 47
Arendt, Hannah 8, 52 n.7, 217–25
  Eichmann in Jerusalem 219–20
  Hannah Arendt (film) 216–17

The Human Condition 222
The Life of the Mind 223
  on plurality 222–3
Aristophanes 16
Aristotle 282
art
  authenticity in 204
  integrity in 195–206, 235–48
  rasa 202, 206 n.5
asceticism 130, 176, 252
  brahmacharya (vow of asceticism) 122–3
  scholarly 210, 212
attention 59, 107–9, 135, 147, 281, 284
Atticus, Titus Pomponius 9, 249–57
  assisting the powerful 251, 253
  Life of Atticus 9
  public office 251
Austen, Jane 273–4, 276
authenticity 7, 97–8, 203, 261, 264–5
  artistic 196–8, 203–4

Bajaj, Kamalnayan 127
Baker, Ella 6, 63–72
  views on feminism 68
Bamba, Amadou 8, 173–81
  exile 177–8
banking 74–5, 79
basanos (touchstone) 127–8
benevolence 106, 156
Bhagavad Gita 123

Boethius, Manlius Severinus 27–34
  biography 27–8
  The Consolation of Philosophy 28
Brontë, Charlotte 273
Brontë, Emily 273, 276
Brown, John 3
Brown, Michael 47
Bunyan, John 124

Camus, Albert 142
capitalism 93, 135
Cato the Elder 252, 254–5
chastity 113, 123, 130
Chekhov, Anton 133
Christianity 113–14
  Christian anarchism 130
  'severe and practicable' 115
Churchill, Winston 122
Cicero 250–5
civil disobedience 51–2 n.5, 52 n.7
Civil War, English 164–5
cleverness 228; *see also* Anansi the Spider
Coetzee, J. M. 145
colonialism 174, 189
  French 177–8
  primitivism 202
communism 68, 165
  Tolstoyan communities 136
  Winstanley's vision of 165–9
community 9, 48–9, 51–2 n.5, 230
  vs. individualism 228, 229, 233
compassion 42
complacency 76–7
compromise 3, 22, 47, 79, 94, 251
  Abai Kunanbayev 188
  Hannah Arendt 220, 222
  as incompatible with integrity 117–18
  Simone Weil 144, 146–7
  Tolstoyans 133, 136–8
conformity 21
Confucius 101–9, 153; *see also* village worthies
  Analects 107
  Confucianism 84–5, 88, 160 n.8
  importance of norms 106
conscience 7, 59, 97–8, 131–3, 136, 168, 190
consciousness 93–4, 97–8, 205
consistency 1, 16, 22, 124, 171, 282
contemplation *vs.* action 218–19
conversion, religious 209
Cooke, Joan and John 235–48
corruption 33, 76–7, 114–15, 153, 175, 191, 251–2
  integrity as incorruptibility 114, 118, 144, 146, 278
courage 123, 146, 148–9, 153, 156, 208
  definition of 282
  Socrates' 17
Cox, Damian 208
Cromwell, Oliver 167
cynicism 7, 115, 118, 284

Dahlmann, Friedrich 8, 207–15, 211–14
Dalmia, Yashodhara 199–201
deception 104, 107
  expense of community 230
  integrity 228, 281
  self-deception 94–5, 159
definition, as philosophical method 2
democracy 222
desires, integration of 22
devotion 174

dharma 36, 38, 41
Diamond, Cora 93
Diggers, the 8, 163–4
'dirty hands' 281
division of labour 74, 76, 80
Donglin academy 85–6
double-consciousness 93–4, 98
Du Bois, W. E. B. 71 n.7
duty 155, 157, 174, 209, 255
    cost of 28, 251
    'reluctant ruler' 70

eccentricity 22, 122
Eeden, Frederik Van 131–2
ego 223
    egotism 277–8
    and literature 274, 276–7
Eichmann trial 219
Eliot T. S. 142, 273, 279 n.4
empowerment 127–8
English Revolution 163–72
enlightenment 131
ethics 37
    communitarian ethics 228
    ethically superior persons
        (*junzi*) 106
    ethical standards 102, 108
    humanist ethics 228–9
    professional ethics 73–81
evil
    action against 218, 221
    'banality of' 219–20

feminism 69
    in art 199
    in literature 271–80
Foot, Philippa 282
force 142
    physical and moral 134–5
freedom 203
    in art 203
    as defined by relation to the
        earth 166
    illusion of 97

Gandhi, Mohandas 7, 121–30,
    203, 204
    antipolitical 125–6
    autobiography 123–4
    compared to Socrates 25 n.3,
        127, 130 n.12
    empowering others 126–7
    experiments with truth 124
    non-violence 174
    'shrewd and
        manipulative' 122–3
Gauguin, Paul 199
Gaus, Günter 220
gender 48, 272
    and integrity of woman
        novelist 275
generosity 32, 251, 284
German Empire 209
God 34, 143, 174–8, 191
    in Book of Job 52–60, 147
    Puritan conception of 168,
        170
    and true happiness 30, 33
    as truth 124
    Winstanley's conception
        of 170
Golden Rule 74
good, the 5, 32, 33–4, 107,
    147–8
    commitment to 16–17, 282–3
    prudential *vs.* moral 148
    social harmony 228
The Good Place (TV series) 12 n.3
The Great Gatsby 218
grief 39, 40
Guan Yu (Lord Guan) 8, 151–61
Gyekye, Kwame 228

happiness 30, 32
harmony, inner 106
heroism 5–6, 64–5, 83–4, 88,
    113, 158
    moral 83
    vs. servility 90

INDEX

Hirschman, Albert O.
 'voice' and 'exit' 78
history, study of 207–15
Hobbes, Thomas 207
Holmes, John Haynes 121–2
Holocaust, the 219–20
honesty 36, 186–7, 191, 246, 251, 256, 281
 and Tolstoyans 133
Honig, Bonnie 46
honour 180, 213, 245, 252
House of Un-American Activities Committee 68
Huang Zongxi 6, 83–91
 Waiting for the Dawn 86–7
human nature 20–2
humility 148, 157
humour 123, 260–4
Hu Shih 158
hypocrisy 7, 102, 105, 108
 false hypocrisy 113, 281, 283–4

identity 104, 199, 201, 209; *see also* national identity
individualism 228, 229, 233
injustice 32
inspiration, divine 170
institutions 6, 80, 83–91, 88–90, 237, 281
integrity; *see also* academic integrity
 as adherence to principle 42–3, 47–8, 174, 176, 180, 282–3
 in ancient Greece 16, 20–2
 artistic 196–7, 235, 238–40, 240–7, 276
 and attention to others 284–5
 as authenticity 196–7
 in Bible 58–9
 civic 238–47

 as collective project 48, 49, 50
 commonplace 83, 93, 115–16, 118
 and compromise 144, 146–7
 condition of genuine thought 223–4
 constructing the appearance of 259–69, 254
 cost of 28, 47, 78, 85, 88
 definition of 2–3, 4–5, 11, 36, 50, 254, 281–2, 284
 excessively demanding 22, 30–1, 117–18, 138
 in face of adversity 53–61, 77, 167, 178–9, 180
 and the good 148, 282–3
 and good character 189
 heroic 5–6, 83–4, 88, 90, 113–15, 118, 158
 identification with moral standards 108
 as incorruptibility 114, 118, 144, 146, 278
 institutional conditions for 83–4, 88–90, 191, 219
 integrated soul 5
 journalistic 259–69, 267–8
 loss of 146–8
 personified 213–14
 physical and mental 146–7
 political 64–5, 205, 221–2
 in *Rāmāyaṇa* 36, 43
 reconciling opposing norms 186–7, 188, 283
 as rectitude 30–1, 32–3, 38, 52, 146, 153
 as reflection on one's role 77, 78
 relational 30, 96, 98–9, 103, 277
 reward of 58
 and risk 8, 21, 49, 66–8, 104, 156, 274, 281

self-integration 196, 199, 201
tam 52, 54, 55, 57, 60 n.1
and truth 284–5
as unity of character 23–4
within a system *vs.* contra a system 144–6
'of the world itself' 219
for world *vs.* for individual 224, 255
Ismene (Antigone) 47–9

James, Henry 93–100
  The Ambassadors 6, 93–100
  Lambert Strether 93–100
Jesus 118, 170
  in middle-class secular Western thought 113–14
Jewish historians, in German Empire 209
jihad 174–5, 179
  as struggle against ego 175
Job 6, 53–61, 147
justice 124–5
  Simone Weil on 146
just war 112

kāvya (poetry) 34–5, 39
Kaye, Dorothy and John 235–48
Kendirbaeva, Gulnar 192
Kenworthy, John 133–4
King, Martin Luther, Jr. 63, 66
Kohlhaas, Michael 3
Kropotkin, Peter 138
Kulturkampf 209
Kunanbayev, Abai 8, 183–93
  Abai's Way 185
  biography 184–5, 188–90
  Book of Words 184

Lambert Strether 93–100
law 183
  adat 186
  in Kazakh society 185–7

Leslie Stephen 277–8
Levellers, the 8, 163
life
  'facing life as a whole' 134
  living honestly 130
  meaningful 97, 190
  of solitary contemplation 218
literature 39, 274–5
love 5, 21, 31–2, 33, 123, 134, 143, 148, 191, 284
  divine 31, 33
Luther, Martin 5

Mao Zedong 160 n.6
Mark Antony 253
Martin, Heidegger 216
martyrs 5, 83–4, 88–9, 127, 135
Mencius; *see* Mengzi
Mengzi 101–2, 156, 158
moral exemplars 41, 117
morality
  adat 183
  institutional conditions for 219
  moral particularism 94, 98
  and pretence 104
  'severe and practicable' 115
  undermining of 105, 113
  'Woollet' moral categories 6, 96, 98
moral luck 282
Muhammad 175, 179
murder 112, 116, 142
Murdoch, Iris 117, 142, 285
Muridiyya (school of Sufism) 174
mysticism 174
  Tolstoy 131

narcissism 90
nation, idea of 203, 204, 209
National Association for the Advancement of Colored

People (NAACP) 63, 65–6, 68
national identity 208–9
nationalism 204, 205
Native Americans 266–7
Nepos, Cornelius 9, 249
  Life of Atticus 249–50, 254
non-violence 134–5, 174
Nussbaum, Martha 100

oppression 68–9, 175

pacifism 113–14, 119 n.4, 133, 134, 142
  befuddling effect of 112–14
  Simone Weil on 146
Parks, Rosa 56
patience, of Job 54, 59–60
patriarchy 50, 66, 196, 272–3, 276, 277
perfection 3, 27, 53, 57, 283–4
  Rāma's 35–44
Philosophy, Lady (Boethius) 29–31, 32
piety 59
Plato 5, 16, 147
  account of integrity 20–1
  Apology 19, 130 n.12
  Gorgias 15
  Laches 127
  Phaedo 25 n.1
  philosophical psychology 20–1
Platonism 32
Plutarch 250, 254–5
poetry 34–5, 39
Polak, Henry S. L. 126
politics 221–3
  Ghandi's suspicion of 125–6
  opting out of 251–2
  political commitment in scholarship 211, 212
  and religion 175, 180
  serving the common benefit 86–7
Polonius 7
power 70, 122, 147, 167, 222, 272
  Amadou Bamba 175–7, 180
  Atticus, assisting the powerful 251, 253
  divorced from reason 21
  and servility 84, 190
  and truth 125
  pretence, as threat to moral values 104
pride 20, 127
primitivism 202
principles 5, 77, 94, 101–2, 115, 163
  Atticus 252
  Confucianism 160 n.8
  divine 174, 178, 180
  and Rāma 36, 42
  Tolstoyans' 135–6
  'turning Christian counsels into principles' 113–15
Proverbs 55, 56
Prussian School of History 212–13
psychē 16
purity 63, 97, 102, 173
  'retreat to' 283

Rāma 5, 35–44
  character traits of 37–8, 41–2
  rejection of Sītā 40–1
Rāmāyaṇa 5, 35–44
Ranke, Leopold von 208–9, 210
Reformation, the 235
religion 168–9, 171
  and political power 175
reputation 41
resistance to oppression 175–6, 179
'respectability politics' 67

righteousness 153–5, 156
risk; see under integrity
roles, organizational 75–6, 78
*Romance of the Three
    Kingdoms* 7–8, 151–61

sacrifice 126
safety; see integrity, and risk
Satan 54
satyagraha 125
Scholar Fang 84–5, 88
self, the 25, 28, 178, 212, 277
    whole-souled 30
self-control 38
self-deception 95, 159
    'double consciousness' 95
self-knowledge 99
servility 84, 87–8
Sher-Gill, Amrita 8, 195–206
    and nationalism *vs.* colonialism
        in art 204
Shoah 219–20
Sienkiewicz, Henryk 9, 259–69
sin 56
Sītā 37
social transformation 66–7, 170
Socrates 5, 7, 15–25, 252
    compared to Ghandi 127,
        130 n.12
śoka (grief) 39
Sophocles 46
soul 16, 32
Southern Christian Leadership
    Conference (SCLC) 63,
    66
Southern Conference Educational
    Fund (SCEF) 68
spiritual helplessness 168–9
spirituality 142
    and Ghandi 126
    'the measure of human
        beings' 176–7
    and work 137

standards 3, 6–7, 75–6, 79, 102,
    106–8, 111–19, 284
Stoicism 30
Student Nonviolent Coordinating
    Committee (SNCC) 67–8
subjectivity 93
success, worldly 30
suffering 174
    in Sufism 178–9
    as test from God 175
Sufism 174, 178–9
Sybel, Heinrich von 210–11
Sytin, Ivan 135–6

Tagore, Abanindranath 203–4
tam 52, 54, 55, 57, 60 n.1
temperance 282
temptation 21–2
thought
    'for the sake of the world'
        221
    integrity as condition of
        222–3
    plurality of ego as essential
        for 222–3
    thinking for oneself 220, 222,
        224
Tolstoy, Leo 7, 131–40, 274
Tolstoyans 7, 131–40
torture 146–7
transformational agency 73–4,
    76, 78–9, 164
Truman, Harry S. (US President)
    111–12, 117
trust 176, 259–65
truth 130–1
    antithesis of action 222
    candour in journalism 263
    coercion 222
    democratic decision-
        making 222
    Ghandi's view on 125
    literature 274

love of 190
satyagraha 125
'Truth and Politics'
  (Arendt) 221–2
woman writers 276
Tudor dynasty 235–6
tyrants 87

unity 5, 33, 204
  community 9
  of the person 16, 20, 22, 277
  virtuous 28
  work of art 274

Vālmīki 39
values 6, 21–2, 147, 208, 275
  absence of 103–5
  feminist 69
  in institutions 77
  Roman biography 250–1
  woman writers 276
  Woolf's view on 275
  'Woollet' moral values 6,
    96–7
vanity 32, 210, 281
Varma, Ravi 203–4
vegetarianism 130, 137
victim, blamed for own
  suffering 29
village worthies 6, 101–9, 113,
  281
violence 175–6, 179
virtue 32, 89, 107–8
  academic 210–11, 212
  and character 101
  Confucius' view 107–8
  demands of 21–2
  demonstrated in
    portraiture 237
  Ghandi's 123

human virtues 123, 156
'ideal standard' 113
and institutions 89
political 222
Rāma's 36
semblance of 156, 158
'thieves of virtue' 101, 105
thinking for oneself 220–1
virtue ethics 158
von Trotta, Margarethe 216

Waitz, Georg 8, 207–15, 210–14
Wallace, John Bruce 135
weakness of will 16, 21
Weil, Simone 7, 141–9
whistle-blowers 80
White, Walter (NAACP) 56, 63
wickedness 32, 57
Winstanley, Gerrard 8, 163–72
wisdom 59
Wittgenstein, Ludwig 3, 281
women
  in Bible 61 n.13
  depicted in art 196, 202
  erasure of women's voices 63,
    98
  excluded from
    universities 209, 272
  A Room of One's Own
    271–80
  women's spaces 195–6
  Women's Suffrage 277
  women's writing 273, 279 n.4
Woolf, Susan 117–18
Woolf, Virginia 10, 271–80

Xenophon 16, 22, 24

Yongle Emperor 84–5
Yu Jiyuan 160 n.8

www.ingramcontent.com/pod-product-compliance
Lightning Source LLC
Chambersburg PA
CBHW050337230426
43663CB00010B/1890